# Corporate
# Legends
# and Lore

# Corporate Legends and Lore

The Power of Storytelling
as a Management Tool

## Peg C. Neuhauser

**McGraw-Hill, Inc.**

New York   San Francisco   Washington, D.C.   Auckland   Bogotá
Caracas   Lisbon   London   Madrid   Mexico City   Milan
Montreal   New Delhi   San Juan   Singapore
Sydney   Tokyo   Toronto

**Library of Congress Cataloging-in-Publication Data**

Neuhauser, Peg C., date.
   Corporate legends and lore : the power of storytelling as a
management tool / Peg C. Neuhauser.
      p.     cm.
   Includes index.
   ISBN 0-07-046326-3
   1. Communication in management.   2. Communication in
organizations.   3. Corporate culture.   I. Title.
HD30.3.N48     1993
658.4'5—dc20                                93-14759
                                                  CIP

1 2 3 4 5 6 7 8 9 0   DOC/DOC   9 9 8 7 6 5 4 3

ISBN 0-07-046326-3

*The sponsoring editor for this book was James H. Bessent, Jr. and the
production supervisor was Pamela A. Pelton. It was set in Baskerville by
North Market Street Graphics.*

*Printed and bound by R. R. Donnelley & Sons Company.*

*Citations and excerpts on pages 33, 55, 205, and 207 are reprinted by
permission of Warner Books/New York, from* Lincoln on Leadership,
*Copyright © 1992 by Donald T. Phillips.*

*Citations and excerpts on pages 91, 116–118, and 131 come from*
Customers for Life *by Carl Sewell. Copyright © 1990 by Carl Sewell. Used
by permission of Doubleday, a division of Bantam Doubleday Dell
Publishing Group, Inc.*

This book is printed on recycled, acid-free paper containing a
minimum of 50 percent recycled de-inked fiber.

*To my Aunt Mimi:*
*The first storyteller I knew*
*and still the best I ever met.*
*Thank you for the gift.*

# Contents

Preface    xiii
Acknowledgments    xv

## Part 1.  The Purpose of Storytelling in Organizations                                          1

### 1. Getting the Message . . . The Power of Stories                                              3

One Company's Favorite Stories    3
Stories Stick Like Glue . . . Remembering and Believing    4
Stories Make Information Easier to Remember    4
Stories Make Information More Believable    6
Productive or Destructive Stories—What Makes
  the Difference?    7
Storytelling in Your Organization . . . The 90 Percent
  Factor    9

### 2. Is It a Positive or Negative Story?                                                         11

Defining Positive and Negative in Storytelling    11
  Outcome or Message: Definition of Positive
    and Negative Stories    12
  Is the *Outcome* of the Story Positive or Negative?    12
The Age-Old History of Storytelling    13
Are Your Stories Positive or Negative?    14

**3. Six Types of Positive Stories in Organizations**                16

    1. Hero Stories     16
    2. Survivor Stories     19
    3. Steam Valve Stories . . . Letting Off Steam     20
    4. "Aren't We Great" Stories     22
    5. "We Know the Ropes around Here" Stories     23
    6. "Kick in the Pants" Stories     24
    What about the Stories in Your Organization?     26


**4. Retelling Your Organization's Stories**                27

    The "Spin" You Put on a Story     27
    Reshaping Your Stories by Changing the "Spin"     28
    The Two Main Purposes of a Story     28
        Grounding Stories: Key Values in Action     29
        Instructive Stories: How We Do Things around Here     31
    The Art of Telling the Story . . . Creating Pictures in the Mind     32
    The Skill of Telling a Story     34
        Plot     34
        Characters     34
        Action     35
        Timing     35
        Fluency     35
    How Skillful Are You at Story Listening?     36


**Part 2. Leading with Stories**                39

**5. Your Corporate Heritage: Sacred Bundle Stories**                41

    What Is in Your Organization's Sacred Bundle?     42
    Questions about Your Organization's Sacred Bundle     43
    The Difference between Your History and Heritage     44
    Examples of Organizations' Sacred Bundle Stories     45
        Physical Objects in the Sacred Bundle     45
        People in the Sacred Bundle     46
        Crisis Stories in the Sacred Bundle     47
        Collection of Stories in the Sacred Bundle     47


**6. The Leader as Storyteller**                49

    Leaders: Protectors of the Sacred Bundle Stories     49
    Leaders: Teachers and Guides through Stories     50
    Leaders: Keepers of the Tribal Campfires     52
    Conversations around the Tribal Campfires     53

How Leaders Get the Stories Started in Organizations    54
Questions to Consider for Getting the Stories Started    55

7. **Inspiring Stories or Corporate Propaganda?**                              **57**

Stories Have to Match Behavior That Has Been Seen    58
Optimism That Is Out of Touch with Reality    59
Leadership Isolation . . . Are You Talking Only to Yourselves?    60
Consistent Toleration of Poor Performance    61
Listening to the "Yes, Buts . . ." in Your Organization    63

**Part 3.  Connecting the Individual
and the Organization**                                                          **65**

8. **What Is Your Autobiography of Stories?**                                   **67**

Bringing Your Personal Stories to Work with You    68
What Are the Stories in Your Personal Sacred Bundle?    70
How Do Your Personal Stories Relate to Your Work?    71
Examples of Personal Sacred Bundle Stories    72

9. **Who Are the Heroes in Your Organization?**                                 **76**

An Organizational Hero Story    76
The Organizational "Antihero" Story    78
The Characteristics of a Hero    78
Teams Can Be Heroes, Too    80
Who Are the Heroes in Your Organization?    82

10. **Storytelling and the New Employee**                                       **84**

Storytelling as Training . . . Who and What
  Do They Believe?    85
Improving the Orientation Process    86
What Did They Learn *before* Their First Day of Work?    87
Stories That Work and Those That Don't in a New-Hire
  Situation    93

11. **Storytelling and Relationships inside
the Organization**                                                              **94**

Folklore as the Internal Cultural Road Map    94
What Is the Folklore Road Map of Your Organization?    97

What Does the Folklore Road Map Tell You about Employee
Relationships?  98

## 12. Protecting Employee Morale                                    100

The Pivotal Role of Trust in Organizational Culture    102
Building a Folklore of "Trust" Stories    103
Watch Out for the Ripple Effect of Stories    104
Forgiving and Forgetting . . . How Do People Repair
Past Damage?    107
Repairing Damaged Relationships    107
Forgiving and Forgetting . . . Grieving and Healing    109
How Does Your Organization Grieve and Heal?    114

## 13. Storytelling and Relationships with Your Customers    116

How Important Are Your Customers . . . How Many Stories
Do You Tell about Them?    118
Listening to the Customers' Stories    121
What Are You Learning from the Stories Customers
Tell You?    122
Diagnostic Questions to Understand and Use Customers'
Stories    124
Customer Stories Are Essential in Continuous Quality
Improvement Work    125
Using Stories to Sell Your Ideas and Products
to Your Customers    126
Mini-Negotiations . . . Everyone Is Selling Something
in Organizations    127
Stories as Verbal Persuasion    129
Success Can Make You Stop Listening to Your
Customers' Stories    130
Questions to Ask about Your Organization's Customer Stories    132

# Part 4. Storytelling as a Tool
# for Managing Change                                            135

## 14. The Folklore of Organizations Built for Change        137

The Role of Storytelling in Cultures Built for Change    137
The New Story Line . . . Adaptive Cultures Built
for Change    139
Four Key Topics in Change Stories    139
Risk Taking and Innovation . . . Do the Company Stories
Emphasize These Values?    141

Change Stories Include Controversy    142

Stories about Cultural Norms and Rules That Support
Change    144

Cultures Built for Change Hire People Who Are Attracted to
Change . . . The New Storytellers    145

Stories Focusing on Change as Improvement    146

Is Your Organization Adaptive? Listen to the Stories It Tells    147


**15. The Role of Storytelling in Creating
an Adaptive Organization                                          149**

Telling Stories That Build the "Habit" of Expecting Change    150

Being Your Own Futurist . . . Stories about Change    151

Getting Employees Involved in Telling Stories about Change    152

The "Hit the Ball and Drag Charlie" Syndrome    153

Creating a Shared Vision of the Future through Storytelling    154

The Vision Cannot Be Private Property    156

Changing an Old Vision Requires a New Story Line    157

Listen to Current Stories before Trying to Change
the Culture    158

Questions to Ask When Listening to Current Stories    158

Old Stories That Tell the "New" Message    160

Find the Current Stories That Are Supportive
of the Change    161

Include the Informal Leaders as Storytellers    163

Persuading Reluctant Informal Leaders to Participate
in the Storytelling    164

Stories about Informal Leaders Who Refuse to Participate    165

How Long Does It Take to Create a New Story Line?    167


**16. Using Stories to Communicate Effectively
during a Change                                                   169**

Using Storytelling to Communicate Effectively *before*
the Change Arrives    169

Stories Help Employees Understand the Changes    171

Telling the Truth in the Change Process    172
  Withholding Information for Too Long    173
  Not Keeping Promises Made during the Change    174
  Bad News Is Not Good News . . . Don't Try to Pretend It Is    176
  The Role of Storytelling in Telling the Truth    176

Face-to-Face Storytelling during the Change    177

The Role of Gossip in the Communication of Change    179

Using Stories to Talk about Sensitive Topics    180

**17. Using Storytelling to Manage Resistance to Change      184**

Storytelling Used to Encourage Both Stability and Change      184
The Status Quo Is Not All Bad      186
Reducing Resistance by Getting People Involved in the Change      187
Getting the Resisters Involved to Create a Shared Story      189
Understanding People's Past Stories about Change
  in This Organization      190
Going Back to the Original Story      191
Demystifying the Old Story      192
Letting Go of the Old . . . Finishing the Story      193
Creating New Rituals and Ceremonies after the Change      195

**18. Using Storytelling for Creativity and Innovation      198**

The Barometer Story      198
How Does Storytelling Contribute to Creativity?      199
  Logic-based Thinking versus Visual-based Thinking      199
Using Analogies and Metaphors to Trigger Creativity      201
  Real-Life Analogies      202
  Symbolic Analogies      203
When Analogies Stop Being Creative and Become Lying      204
Using Humor in Stories      204
Constructive Use of Self-Talk: Stories You Tell to Yourself      205
Creative Leadership as Catalyst and Storyteller      206

**Conclusion      209**

**Addendum.  Building Your Own Collection of Great Stories      211**

Retelling Classic Leadership Stories      211
Stories Told by Well-Known Leaders      212
Stories Told about Well-Known Leaders      214
Stories That Are Metaphors Applicable to the Workplace      217
Ministories in the Form of One-Liners      218

References      221
Bibliography      231
Index      233

# Preface

Five years ago, I wrote *Tribal Warfare in Organizations*. In that book, I asked the readers to follow me on an anthropological tour of their organizations and take a look at the tribal behavior all around them. Much of the conflict and confusion that occurs in the workplace is a result of tribal miscommunications or disagreements. My goal at the time was to show people ways to build bridges between the tribes and help them work together more productively. As I wrote in the book and have repeated over and over again in speeches since that time, tribal loyalties are a valuable part of human behavior and should be protected and cared for in organizations. We do not need to eliminate the tribes; we need to build better bridges between them.

As I listened to employees, managers, and leaders talk about life among the tribes, it gradually dawned on me that some of the most important tribal traditions were not being cared for and protected in many organizations. These questions kept going through my mind as I watched and listened:

"Where are your tribal campfires?"

"Where are your stories being told?"

"Who is passing on your legends and lore to the next generation?"

Storytelling has been used for thousands of years as a way of connecting the past, present, and future of a community's life. Without stories, it has always been difficult for people to know who they are or where they fit into a complex world around them. It seems, however, that modern organizations have forgotten this old truth. In fact, in many organizations, time spent sitting around telling old stories is viewed as "wasting time."

Because of this disturbing discovery, I decided to investigate the state of corporate storytelling in more depth. I started asking people in organizations to try to remember stories that they had heard recently about their organization. Many people had a hard time remembering any recent stories and had to be coached by their colleagues to come up with just one example of a story. When I then asked their opinions about whether the stories carried a positive or negative message about the organization, I was astonished to find that over 90 percent of the people in *every* organization voted that the stories they were remembering were negative. Actually, there was one group that voted 60 percent negative and 40 percent positive. I was so excited. I went on and on flapping my arms and talking about what wonderful things this must mean about their culture. I should have paid more attention to the uncomfortable looks I was getting from the audience during my ravings because, at the next break, nine separate people came up to me privately to confess that they had lied in their voting! They were really thinking of a negative story, but had voted positive just to be polite. I was so disheartened at this point that I never tried the experiment again. This event, however, was also the beginning of my determination to write *Corporate Legends and Lore.*

→ Storytelling is the single most powerful form of human communication. It is the primary tool that human beings use to pass on their cultures. We can use it to inspire, teach, comfort, and entertain. Or we can use it to destroy, stir up hate, and demoralize. Jesus Christ and Adolf Hitler were both great storytellers. It is in our hands to decide how we will use this powerful tool. Charles Dickens is reported to have said that good storytelling should make you laugh, make you cry, and make you worry. Although this book is not intended to make anyone cry, it certainly is my goal to make you laugh and make you worry. I hope you find this book entertaining and fun to read. I also hope it causes you to think about what kind of storyteller you want to be in your organization in the future.

*Peg C. Neuhauser*

# Acknowledgments

During the writing of this book, I have come back over and over again to the stories told to me by my clients in organizations all over the United States. These are the people who have been the inspiration for this book. As most of them have heard me say, I see myself as a "professional listener." I love hearing their stories. Recently, a woman approached me after a seminar I had just finished conducting and said, "You know, what I enjoyed most about this seminar was watching you enjoying us." I can't remember ever hearing a comment from a client that I appreciated more.

Special thanks go to a few of these clients who have taken the time to share their stories, their laughter, and their wisdom with me during the writing of this book. Dan Sisto, president of the Hospital Association of New York State, is an inspiring leader who tells his stories with passion and humor. He is a joy to know. Many of my clients at AARP have contributed substantially to this book. I am particularly grateful to Kirk Stromberg, Karen Gravenstine, and Emily Smith for sharing with me their creativity and commitment to the AARP vision. To the many people at Advanced Micro Devices, Inc.—who have told me their stories and even *drawn pictures* of them for me on their famous office white-boards—your energy and spirit is reflected in many places in this book. Special thanks to Rich Previte and Steve Zelencik who introduced me to all those characters at AMD. And last of all, my thanks to Bill Arnold, president of Centennial Medical Center in Nashville. There are so many stories about him floating around the organization, I think he probably qualifies as a legend in his own time. People often call just to fill me in on one of the latest "Bill" stories. It is people like him who keep us all going. I wish every one of these people the very best. It has been an honor to work with all of them.

I would also like to thank my editor at McGraw-Hill, Jim Bessent, for his patience, his ideas, and his belief in the book. The invisible hand of a talented editor is a major contribution to the quality of any book. And last of all, I would like to thank my husband, Scott Bridgeman, for his endless reading and rereading of the manuscript, for keeping the business going on an even keel while I was writing, and for having the patience to put up with months of seven-day workweeks as this book was being created. It is a trial to live with someone who writes and travels for a living. I couldn't have done it without you. Thank you.

*Peg C. Neuhauser*

*God made man because he loved stories.*
ELIE WIESEL

# PART 1

# The Purpose of Storytelling in Organizations

# 1
# Getting the Message . . . The Power of Stories

## One Company's Favorite Stories

### A Corporate Story by Warren Buffett

> The role that Charlie and I play in the success of our operating units can be illustrated by a story about George Mira, the one-time quarterback of the University of Miami, and his coach, Andy Gustafson. Playing Florida and near its goal line, Mira dropped back to pass. He spotted an open receiver but found his right shoulder in the unshakable grasp of a Florida linebacker. The right-handed Mira thereupon switched the ball to his other hand and threw the only left-handed pass of his life—for a touchdown. As the crowd erupted, Gustafson calmly turned to a reporter and declared: "Now that's what I call coaching."

That story by Warren Buffett, chairman of the board, appears on the first page of the letter to the shareholders in the 1991 annual report for Berkshire Hathaway Inc.[1] Their annual reports are filled with similar stories about their "managerial stars and triumphs," how his wife and Charlie Munger (vice chairman of the board) would handle the company if he died tomorrow, and descriptions of what Buffett calls his "Mistakes Du Jour."[2]

You may not know what Berkshire Hathaway Inc. is or know the line of business of the company, but after hearing these stories, you could probably give a general description of the culture of this company . . . what it's like to work in their offices, what it takes to be a hero around there, some of the rules of the game for handling decisions and taking risks. And you would probably be reasonably accurate in your assessment.

Stories are the single most powerful form of human communication. This has been true all over the world for thousands of years and is still just as true today in our organizations, communities, and families. If you want someone to *remember* information and *believe* it, your best strategy in almost every case is to give them the information in the form of a story. Warren Buffett knows the power of stories and uses them masterfully in his writing and speaking. Listen to how he ends his letter in one of their annual reports.

> Nicholas Kenner nailed me—again—at last year's meeting, pointing out that I had said in the 1990 annual report that he was 11 in May 1990 when actually he was 9. So, asked Nicholas rather caustically: "If you can't get that straight, how do I know the numbers in the back (financials) are correct?" I'm still searching for a snappy response. Nicholas will be at this year's meeting—he spurned my offer of a trip to Disney World on that day—so join us to watch a continuation of this lopsided battle of wits.[3]

In case you are thinking that these are just folksy stories from some small-time company, these are the stories of a company whose stock went from $38 per share in the early 1970s to over $12,000 per share in 1993 and increased its net worth during recession year 1991 by 39.6 percent.

## Stories Stick Like Glue . . . Remembering and Believing

A well-told story has the ability to stick with people long after facts and figures have faded. It is also true that the story will be repeated with far greater frequency than any statistical report. And it has the best chance of convincing its audience of the truth of its values or ideas. What makes a story so powerful as a method of communicating information or ideas? According to social scientists, there are two main reasons:

- Stories make information easier to remember.
- Stories make information more believable.[4]

## Stories Make Information Easier to Remember

Although no one knows the reasons for sure, one of the theories for why stories are remembered so well is that you are using your "whole brain" to take in the information. Your brain is constantly processing information using facts, figures, emotions, and visual imagery. Stories allow a person to feel and see the information as well as factually understand it. The assumption is that because you "hear" the information factually, visually, and emotionally, it is more likely to be imprinted on your brain in a way that it sticks with you longer with very little effort on your part. Ned Herrmann, developer of thinking models for learning and creativity, describes this as the brain's capacity for "hard processing" (logical/rational thinking) and "soft processing" (emotional/visual thinking).[5] According to Herrmann, any key learning points should be delivered through media that covers this range of thinking talents of the human brain.[6] Stories are one of the best communication tools for covering this range of thinking.

This theory was put to the test a number of years ago in a situation where several organizations were converting from an old financial computer system to a new multifacility system. This change requires the relearning and *remembering* of thousands of facts, figures, and reporting procedures. The teaching method used was a one-week, eight-hours-a-day course for the business office and accounting people. During this course, the instructor factually explained all the input documents, reports, and procedures that these people were to use on the new system. Each person was given a notebook that included examples of each document that they would need to know. The notebook was about 2 inches thick. People were expected to remember all this information to be able to do their jobs accurately on the new system. At a minimum, they were at least supposed to remember where to go to look up the information they needed in the 2-inch-thick notebook. Needless to say, this training method was not working very well.

It was not a surprise to anyone that the people attending these classes had a hard time remembering all this information. Frustration, confusion, and mistakes were rampant during the start-up of the new system. The instructors decided to make some changes and see if they could improve the situation. They could not eliminate the one-week course format because of time constraints. It was not possible to eliminate any of the information that the people had to learn. It was all essential for running the system. So, what they decided to change were the materials and the teaching approach.

The instructors created a sample organization and a group of customers who would be buying all kinds of services and products from this business. They created a series of stories about the customers' experiences with the mock company. In the class, the participants processed these customers through their entire experience in that company. They filled out input documents, watched the information they had entered show up on reports, and tracked down mistakes that were purposely slipped in on them. They watched the story of these customers' experiences unfold before them as the week progressed.

The change in the retention of all this factual information soared. The brain-dead, glazed-over looks by the second day of the seminar diminished. The frustration levels and number of mistakes dropped significantly during the system start-up phase. That experience was a convincing demonstration that even when you are trying to get people to remember factual information, a story is the best method to use.

## Stories Make Information More Believable

There was an experiment done to study the effectiveness of an advertisement for a winery. The people chosen for this study were quantitatively trained MBA subjects.[7] They were given a policy statement that would be used in the advertising to explain the company's commitment to the excellent wine-making techniques that were used in the Chablis region of France. The subjects were then divided into three groups and each group was given a different type of supplemental information. One group received a story about the founder of the company and his father, who was a wine maker from Europe. The story ended with the statement "As Joe tasted his first vintage wine he thought, 'My father would have been proud of this wine.' " A second group received a table of statistics and no story. The third group received both the story and the statistics. All of the supplemental data was positive and supported the feasibility of the policy statement.

After the three groups read the materials, all the subjects were asked a series of questions to determine whether they believed the company's policy statement and the advertising that went with it. Of the three groups, the people who received *only* the story were more likely to predict that the company would follow its policy and that the advertising was truthful. Even with MBA-trained subjects, a story was more persuasive than statistics.[8] I was describing this research during a seminar when a participant spoke up and said, "They wouldn't have gotten those results if the subjects had been CPAs!" That may be true, but I have found that finance people like a good story as much as anyone, as long as you keep it short.

Another way of looking at the believability factor is to picture this situation. A new employee is hired in your organization and goes to an elaborate orientation program during the first week. After the orientation is over, that employee goes to the work area for the first time. Two of the long-time veterans of the department see this new person walk in the door and take it upon themselves to pull the new employee off to the side to tell the stories about how "we *really* do things around here!" If the stories this new employee hears from the organization's veterans do not match the formal information, which set of information do you think that person will believe? I have asked that question to more than one hundred audiences and without exception people have answered that the stories would be believed. Stories carry tremendous power in terms of their believability factor. Even if the information was inaccurate, it would still have an impact that dry facts cannot. As with any communication tool, this is a power that can be used for either productive or destructive ends. It all depends on the message and the intent of the teller.

## Productive or Destructive Stories—What Makes the Difference?

The message and intentions of the teller of a story are the key factors in determining whether a story has a productive or destructive effect. When someone is extremely unhappy in an organization, that person is more likely to see events and other employees in a cynical light. Cynicism is what turns a story in a destructive direction. *Cynicism* is defined in the *New Webster's Dictionary* as "disbelief in the goodness of human motives and a tendency to displays of this disbelief by sneers and sarcasm."

A cynical approach to storytelling usually includes themes such as "Don't believe a thing they tell you" or "Nothing ever works out here the way they say it will." There is usually an additional theme in their stories that sends the message, "If you believe what anyone else tells you around here, then you are a fool!" If the new employee returning from orientation runs into this type of organizational veteran, the version of the stories they will hear will have a tendency to leave the new person wondering why they ever took this job at all.

A cynical approach to a story usually makes it very clear that the listener should not hope for any improvements in the future. In other words, they are not just condemning the past behaviors and practices in the organization. They are also writing off the future as hopeless. There is often a large element of "victim" mindset in cynical storytellers. They see themselves as having been harmed in the past and powerless to stop this sort of thing from happening again in the future. "Victims" thinkers are usually angry and frightened, and that is what they communicate in their stories.

Contrast this to storytelling based not on cynicism, but on realism, or even optimism. If that new employee runs into a realist veteran after the orientation, the approach that the realist might take could sound something like this: "Keep in mind that the orientation information isn't the whole story around here. I will help you sort out who and what you can trust and what you need to be careful of. There is plenty of both. The key is to know the difference and to have your own strategies for how to get things done and to get along with people here." This is not a wild-eyed optimist's view of the organization, but it is not cynical either. The intent of the teller and the messages that this person will impart are likely to be useful to the new employee and not leave that person worried about having taken the wrong job.

There are, of course, work environments that are truly dangerous. The leaders and people who work there really do victimize other people who work there. The mission of the organization may even be destructive or evil in intent. In this case, cynicism is a very sane and useful response to the environment. Everyone is in danger and the best advice is probably to get out. In my experience, this scenario is fairly rare. Most organizations are similar to most individuals. They are partially good and partially bad. They do great things sometimes, and they make mistakes or are incompetent at other times. Often it appears that the biggest flaw in many organizations is that many people in them, including at times the leaders, can be oblivious to the effects their actions are having on other people in the organization. They do not intend harm, but they also do not put out enough effort to make sure that harm does not occur. This can be a very frustrating situation to work in, but it is not a setting that *requires* a cynical mindset to survive.

I am reminded of a colleague who worked in a large corporation that had the usual amount of trustable and untrustable people and situations. It was a highly political setting, and she was known for her skill in forging relationships and getting things done. She was trusted by most of her colleagues and seemed well liked around the company. She told me a story of the time that an employee who was leaving the company came to her to say good-bye.

The person who was leaving was frustrated with the politics of the organization and glad to be getting out. In her good-bye to my colleague, she said, "I will always remember you. You were the one person in this place that when I walked into your office and asked you a question, you told me the truth!" She meant the realistic truth, instead of the company party line. My colleague laughed and responded, "Yes, I decided a long time ago just to pretend that telling the blunt truth was the standard rule of the game around here. As long as I do it with enough humor, I can usually get away with it." This is the attitude of an organizational realist who also liked risk taking and humor. There were a few people around the company who did not like her—but many more who did. Her career in that competitive corporate environment was quite successful. And her impact on the place was probably positive, even if that impact may have been on a small scale and never changed the basic culture of the organization.

Most people are not pure versions of cynic, realist, or optimist. Most of us are capable of being any of the three, depending on the situation or mood.

If you want to focus more of your energy on the productive side of communications with other people, the key is to learn to edit your own storytelling and listening based on these factors. Learn to beware of cynicism, whether you are the teller or listener. Unless the situation is one that truly calls for a cynical "get me out of here" response, try to find a more balanced, realistic version of the story to tell. "There are two sides to every story" is an old saying that is usually true. If you form the habit of thinking in realistic terms, you are much less likely to cast yourself (or to *be* cast) in the role of victim in the organization's stories.

Some of the best research on stress-resistant people indicates that one of their skills is to focus their attention and energy on what they *can* control and do something about, and forget about the things that are beyond their own control.[9] This may be the key factor in being able to be a realist or an optimist in most settings. In any case, when people fall into a pattern of storytelling that is cynical about the organization, it is important to realize that a powerful communication tool is being used for destructive ends for the teller, listener, and the organization as a whole. The only positive value cynical stories have is that they serve the purpose of allowing the teller to vent feelings. If venting is the goal, going out to the company parking lot to kick tires, scream, curse, and leap around in the air is a much more productive communication tool to use for this purpose. Just be sure no one else is in the parking lot when you do it.

## Storytelling in Your Organization . . . The 90 Percent Factor

How is this powerful communication tool being used in your organization? Do people understand that the ripple effect of just one story can be massive? Is anyone managing this powerful tool or is it a loose cannon in your organization that is used in a haphazard way? Over one hundred audiences of managers and employees from different companies were asked to think of a story that they had heard or told in the past few weeks about their organization. When asked to vote on whether the story they had in mind was positive, negative, or neutral in the message that it carried about the company, *over 90 percent of every audience voted negative.*

If this informal survey of storytelling in organizations is an accurate reflection of what is really going on out there in companies, this is a very dangerous situation. Any culture that tells over 90 percent negative stories to itself about itself is being destroyed from the inside out. The history books are filled with examples of once-powerful cultures that have disintegrated and died from internal rot, not external attack. Is the 90 percent negative storytelling report by these organizations a clue that the same kind of internal self-destruction may be happening in your organization?

Stories are a manageable communication tool that can help produce the best results for accomplishing your mission, protecting the morale of your employees, and satisfying your customers. This book is filled with stories and suggestions about how any company can use storytelling to understand its strengths and weaknesses.

# 2

# Is It a Positive or Negative Story?

Before you start reading this chapter, think of a recent story that you have heard or told about your organization. It can be a big story or a little one. You can use any story that pops into your mind from the past week or two at work. Now read this chapter, and use your story as a "case study" for applying this information.

## Defining Positive and Negative in Storytelling

What was the definition of a positive story and a negative story that caused all those people to choose to vote negative in the experiment described at the end of Chapter 1? To truly know whether the 90 percent negative vote is a dangerous indicator for an organization, it is important to know what kinds of stories the people are calling negative. As people were asked to tell the stories they were thinking of in this experiment, it became clear that most people in the audiences were using a very different definition for positive and negative storytelling than will be used in this book.

Most people decided which way to vote based on the *style* and *topic* of the storytelling. In other words, if the story was upbeat and cheerful in tone and had themes of "everyone is wonderful" and "everything is going well," then it was voted a positive story. The definition of positive or negative storytelling used in this book is based on the *outcome* or *message* behind the story. When you use this definition, a story might have a critical tone or be about a problem situation, but still qualify as a positive story. The key issue is not to determine how pleasant the story is, but to measure what impact the story has on the people who hear it.

## Outcome or Message: Definition of Positive and Negative Stories

*Positive Story*

The people who heard the story walked away better off for having heard it (learned something, felt proud, lowered tension, etc.).

Or the organization was better off because this story was told.

*Negative Story*

The people who heard this story walked away worse off for having heard the story.

Or the organization was damaged in some way by the telling and repeating of the story.

## Is the *Outcome* of the Story Positive or Negative?

Here is an example of a story that usually earned a negative vote. The setting is probably one of the most extreme "bad news" work environments that exists this side of military warfare . . . a hospital emergency room. It is a place that is often filled with pain, death, and sorrow. And it all happens at crisis-level speed. You regularly hear comments such as "We had to move him into Room Four, because we were getting gunshot wounds and stabbings and auto accidents at the same time. There must have been sixty patients in the ER."[1] Listen to this example of one of the milder stories that you might hear from emergency room professionals.

> "Before 9:00 there was only a trickle of patients. Now there's a river of people in here needing help, people with colds, urinary infections, and chest pains. The waiting room, which looks like a bomb shelter, is packed."[2] . . . An eighteen-year-old, who was shot in the stomach, is brought into the ER and no one really expects him to make it. While the surgery team works on the boy, the other rooms are filled with a woman being treated for a stab wound from a barroom brawl, a boy who was thrown from a motorcycle, and a man with an arm and both legs broken in a car accident. By the time the medical team finishes with the boy with the gunshot wound, he has lost a kidney, part of his liver, and a section of his colon. He needed forty pints of blood, but he was going to live. When the surgeon is asked if the boy will make it, he responds, "Sure as hell he'll live."[3]

This story is not upbeat or cheery, nor is it told with a tone of "Isn't everything wonderful here?" In fact, in many of the ER stories the patients die. If you use the style or topic definition of a positive or negative story, this is definitely a negative story. Look, however, at the underlying *message* of this story and the reasons that emergency department (ED) professionals tell these types of stories. Notice that the unspoken message of this story is that these people were skilled enough and smart enough to handle the problem successfully. These health care professionals can take anything you can throw at them. When emergency department people tell these kinds of stories, they are describing skill, courage, and their pride in the care they provide their patients. You will, however, never hear a group of ED professionals sitting around telling "Isn't everything wonderful" stories. They are a tough, irreverent group of people whose stories are filled with descriptions of trauma and constant crisis.

The preceding story was taken from a book written about the Denver General emergency department. It is written as a pictorial and text biography of life in that particular emergency department. The reading is hard to take for a typical non-health care layperson and the photographs are numbing. But the people for whom this book was written cherish it. The emergency department doctor who loaned me his copy for the writing of this book made it clear that his willingness to share this book was an honored gift. It arrived in my office wrapped in a package that would have protected Waterford crystal. There is no doubt that the outcome of reading and owning this book was positive for these professionals. By the way, the name of the book was taken from the nickname that the employees use for their emergency department: *The Knife and Gun Club.*

If you use the definition that focuses on the outcome of the story, not the style or topic of the story, many stories that have positive outcomes or messages are not happy Pollyanna stories in their telling. This is especially true in some industries or professions that have a tough, "we can take the heat" culture. The sample about the hospital emergency department is a classic example of this type of culture. The pride and professionalism of a great emergency department team is based on the stance that they can take anything thrown at them. For the people in the emergency department who tell and hear these stories, the outcome is very likely to be a mixture of increased pride, camaraderie, and probably even some instruction on how to handle similar situations in the future. For the hospital as a whole, the story may well represent a good example of the organization's standards for excellent performance, including the contrast of some of the characters in the story whose performance was not so excellent.

# The Age-Old History of Storytelling

Stories have been used by every culture ever studied for thousands of years as the primary communication tool for transmitting cultural values and rules for behavior. Stories are used to teach the young, reward the people who live up to the values and rules of society, and punish those who violate those values and rules. Without storytelling, any culture—whether it is a traditional tribe or a large corporation—would have a very difficult time protecting and passing on the best of its culture. Tribal chiefs and elders have never handed out statistical reports or lists of facts to teach their followers what is right and wrong in their world. They are master storytellers. In fact, in many traditional tribes a person's skill as a storyteller is one of the reasons that individual is chosen to be the chief or shaman (priest) for the tribe. Skillful storytelling has always been one of the important factors in making someone a respected elder of the tribe.

If you understand the role of storytelling in the development, protection, and change of any culture, then it becomes clear that the primary purpose of storytelling is to produce a specific outcome—learning, reward, punishment, comfort, etc. The style and tone of the story is important in making sure that the story is interesting instead of boring. It is also important for the storyteller to be skilled enough to make the message of the story clear to the listeners. But the real question that defines whether it is a positive or negative story hasn't changed for thousands of years: Is the story good for the group and the individuals who hear it, or is it not?

## Are Your Stories Positive or Negative?

Now go back to the story you were asked to recall at the beginning of this chapter. Using the Outcome Definition, decide for yourself. Is your story positive or negative in its impact in your organization?

- Does anyone learn anything useful from the story? Or does it reinforce an old learning that is important to remember?

- Do people feel proud of themselves or others in the organization as a result of hearing the story?

- Did the story help the teller and listeners to let off steam and reduce their tension or stress level?

- Did you identify a problem or barrier that needs to be addressed for the good of the organization or people in it?

- Did you identify a possible solution to a problem?

- Did the story reinforce in a believable way the values of the organization?

- Did the story point out inappropriate behavior in a way that increases the likelihood that the teller and listeners will behave within the "rules" of the culture?

- Did the story shake people up and get people to start thinking about "cleaning up their act"?

If you answered "yes" to some of these questions, then your story may well be a positive story for the culture of your organization and the people who "live" there, even if the tone might not have lived up to the Pollyanna criteria of storytelling.

# 3
# Six Types of Positive Stories in Organizations

There are many different ways to tell a positive story. The six categories described in this chapter represent the most common types of stories that are told with messages intended to have positive outcomes. As you read about each type, again try to think of an example of a story from your own organization that would fit in that category.

Most organizations have storytelling habits that cause them to tell more of some categories of stories than of others. These preferences are one aspect of the culture of your company . . . which type of stories are encouraged and which ones are taboo. For instance, there are many not-for-profit organizational cultures in which "Aren't we great" stories are taboo. They're not tolerated. If you are an individual within that culture and insist on telling stories about what a great job you did, you are likely to be ostracized by the group. Here, for example, is a statement about a colleague I once heard from an employee of a not-for-profit organization, who said in a disgusted tone: "He is just trying to make a name for himself, so he can get ahead in his career!" Contrast this to a for-profit sales environment where this comment would meet with blank stares. Most salespeople's reactions would be "So, what's wrong with that?"

## 1. Hero Stories

Who are the heroes in your organization? What makes a story a "hero story"? According to Joseph Campbell, an expert on the history of myths and stories, a hero story is one where "the main character has done something beyond the normal range of achievement and experience. A hero is someone who has given one's life to something bigger than oneself."[1] Martin Luther King, Jr., Don Quixote, Christ, and John Lennon are some of the heroes from our society at large that Campbell uses as examples.[2]

One of the key elements that transforms a person and a story into heroic dimensions was captured in the movie *Star Wars* by the term "the Force." As Bill Moyers points out in an interview with Campbell, the voice of Ben Kenobi is heard saying to Luke Skywalker in the climactic fight scene of *Star Wars*,

> Turn off your computer, turn off your display and do it yourself, follow your feelings, trust your feelings.

When Skywalker follows that advice and succeeds, audiences invariably burst into applause.[3] According to Campbell, audiences understand implicitly that what they have just witnessed is the essence of a hero: the ability to live from the heart and to be human.

Heroes are often pitted against insurmountable odds or "evil characters" with whom they must do battle. This brings to mind two organizations that were filled with stories about two of their most unpopular characters. In one organization, the person was nicknamed "Hitler," in the other, "Darth Vader" after the *Star Wars* villain. (His expensive, foreign car was regularly referred to as Death Star.) Both of these people were seen as dangerous, cruel people with tremendous positional power in the organization. They were known as people who could and would hurt anyone who got in their way or who simply annoyed them. And, in fact, some of the most dramatic hero stories were about the people in the organization who had had the guts to take these antiheroes on in battle.

Even if the heroes of these stories did not always "win" those battles, their adventures were told and retold as a part of the valued folklore of the company. The key to a hero story is to be human, to act from the heart, and to reach beyond normal achievements and experience, even if that person does not always survive every battle. Hero stories are among the most important types of stories in organizations and have many special uses for leadership, fostering positive change, and protecting morale. These uses of the hero story will be covered in depth in later sections of this book.

### Examples of Hero Stories in the Workplace

*A Leader's Story.*   Bill Arnold, president of Centennial Medical Center in Nashville, Tennessee and coauthor of the book *Reinventing Leadership,* is a leader who is passionately committed to the management philosophy of continuous improvement and employee involvement. He is also known for "living from the heart." He frequently refers to himself as a "servant leader." Many people in leadership roles say these things about themselves, but in Bill's case there are many stories that float around the organization to back up his claims.

Bill's office, for example, has become a symbol of his approach and is the topic of many stories. When he moved into the office, he got rid of the fancy furniture and replaced it with one long conference table. He had the door of the office removed and hung by ropes in the hall to let the staff know that he was serious about his open door policy. He calls his office his "classroom" and tapes flipchart paper filled with notes from previous meetings all over the walls.

One of the stories that illustrates Bill's relationships with the people around him at work is symbolized by a photograph hanging on the wall in his office. It is a picture of the construction workers who are involved in a building project on the hospital grounds. It is signed by all the construction workers "To Bill Arnold: In appreciation for your support and dedication to quality." The workers requested that this photo be taken in the middle of the project and given to Bill in appreciation for his interest in them and their work. The developer on the construction project points out that this is very unusual behavior for a group of construction workers.[4]

Red Hyde, the supervisor of the hospital building project, explains what inspired the gift. "One morning back in December when it was freezing cold, Bill walked by the building site on his way into work and stopped to watch for a few minutes. We were hanging structural steel and it was cold work." According to Hyde, Bill watched for awhile and then turned to ask him if the guys had coffee or hot chocolate out here to help keep them warm. Hyde explained that they had to wait until the food truck stopped at this site to get coffee. There was nothing available for the crew on site.

Hyde goes on to say, "A couple days later a coffee and hot chocolate machine was delivered to the site, and it was set up for the men to use free of charge. There were 200 guys out there in that cold, and let me tell you they drank a lot of coffee!"

The next week at a construction crew meeting, Hyde suggested to the group that they should do something nice for Bill in response to his gift to them. The group agreed and suggested that they buy him a present for Christmas. They thought of all kinds of gifts, and then someone suggested that a signed picture of the crew would make an appropriate gift. Red Hyde describes the morning that 200 people got together outside in the cold to pose for the photograph. Then they rushed around getting the picture developed, framed, and ready to give Bill by Christmas.

Red and I have both known Bill Arnold for quite a while. When he finished telling me this story, we agreed that the photograph was the perfect gift for Bill. There was nothing they could have given him that he would have appreciated more. Relationships and respect for the people he works with are at the heart of his leadership approach, and the picture in his office is a reminder of this story to anyone who visits him there.

*An Employee's Story.*   Hero stories are not just about the CEOs of organizations. Anyone can be a hero. Stewart J. Leonard, Jr., president of Stew Leonard's food store, legendary for its customer service, loves to tell this story about one of his employees.[5]

Leonard unwrapped one of their tuna sandwiches, and a package of mayonnaise rolled out. Stew thought the sandwich had enough mayo already, so he called the deli manager and told him to get rid of the extra mayo. It's expensive. So the next week, he opened a sandwich and the mayo popped out again. He called the deli manager again and was told that he needed to talk to Mary because she is the one who makes the sandwiches. He called Mary who responded to his question, "Sorry Stew, the customers want the extra mayo, so I'm packing it again."

Stew Leonard uses this as a hero story about an employee who knows what is important and will stand up to the boss when she knows she is right.

*Whistle-Blower's Story.*   Stories about whistle-blowers are a controversial form of hero story. Whether or not a specific individual considers this a hero story depends on one's vested interests in the story. For many people in the United States, the women in the Navy who blew the whistle on the aviators who were sexually harassing them are heroes. Depending on your point of view, Anita Hill or Clarence Thomas was the subject of a hero story during the Senate hearings on his nomination as Supreme Court Justice. In the early 1970s John Dean was a whistle-blowing hero to many people because of the role he played in opening up the Watergate investigations. The movie *JFK* was produced to feature Jim Garrison's hero story as the whistle-blower on the alleged Kennedy assassination cover-up. On the other hand, some people consider Oliver North a hero for his role in participating in the Iran Contra affair a few years ago.

Whistle-blowing heroes do not inspire the universal admiration that other types of heroes usually do, but they almost always have a strong following of people who believe in them and respect what they are trying to do. For those followers, the stories about those people are hero stories.

## 2. Survivor Stories

These are the "everything went wrong . . . and we fixed it" stories. They are often seen as negative because they are usually told in a "wailing and moaning" tone, but in many cases if you look at the impact of the story on the people who tell it and hear it, you discover that it is actually a positive story. The underlying theme of the story is "We survived against all odds." The emergency room story in Chapter 2 is a dramatic example of a survivor story.

**Example of a Survivor Story.**   Listen to this survivor story and decide whether it is negative or positive. A copy machine repairman told this story about his old company where he had been responsible for repairing x-ray equipment. The story is about a day in which the repairman had planned to take off the entire afternoon, so he went in early at 6:00 a.m. to work on the x-ray equipment that was on his schedule that day.

> I didn't finish until about 9:30 that evening, and on my way home my beeper went off again. There was another machine down that needed to be fixed right away. I finished that job at about 4:30 in the morning and went home to get some sleep, because I had to show up for work again by 9:00. So much for my afternoon off!

This is a simple story and clearly a survivor story, but is it negative or positive? It is hard to tell at this point because you have not heard enough to know what this person's message was when he told it. Maybe he was telling it to demonstrate to the listener what a screwed-up company he works for, or how the jerks who operate the equipment don't know what they are doing and break it all the time. In both of these cases, the message of the story would be negative. It is unlikely there would be any positive outcome from telling the story. It would be a cynical story, which is the most common form of negative storytelling in organizations.

Here, now, is the context of the story. The part that is missing is the reason the technician told the story. He started by saying,

> I used to work on x-ray machines, and I wish I still did. I really liked the work.

Then he went on to tell about his 24-hour work stint that blew his day off. This may sound like an unusual way to explain why you liked a job, but it obviously made sense to him. And from the head-nodding of the listeners, it apparently made sense to them. Fixing x-ray equipment was an important and complicated job. He had been proud of his work in a way that fixing copy machines just could not quite match. The positive messages that accompany survivor stories frequently involve a theme of pride about the person's skill and endurance.

## 3. Steam Valve Stories . . .
## Letting Off Steam

Steam valve stories are often positive for the people who tell and hear them—in two ways. One is that these stories help people reduce stress and tension. The second effect can be to build a feeling of camaraderie and team loyalty among the group. Often these stories take the form of "sick humor" and would not be the type of story anyone would want repeated outside the company. It would sound disrespectful or rude outside the context of the group telling the story. The key ingredients of steam valve stories seem to be humor, high drama, and an irreverent tone.

**Example of a Steam Valve Story.** In a brokerage firm, a seminar was being conducted for all the office personnel in the firm who had to work on a regular basis with the retail brokers. Every person who attended the seminar had an ample supply of "The time the broker drove me nuts!" stories. The purpose of the seminar was, of course, to encourage all these people to improve their communications with the brokers, since they are the sales force producing most of the revenue for the company. So it would have seemed that all these "Drive me nuts!" stories would have been inappropriate at that seminar. In fact, they were the basis for some of the best learning that occurred.

Their favorite exercise in the seminar was when they acted out scenes of difficult situations with brokers. Participants were allowed to perform two versions. In the first, they acted out all the things they had always wanted to say or do when talking to the brokers. Then, in an instant replay, they were to do the best job possible communicating with the broker, using the skills they had learned in the seminar. The "worst" versions were hilarious. *Saturday Night Live* had nothing on these groups. The tension release and team spirit within the group was clear to everyone. The contrast of the "worst" and "best" versions of the same scenes also made an excellent learning tool. It was easy to see in these stories that the use of good communication skills really would make a difference in the outcome of many of these situations.

One particular example was a scenario acted out by a compliance manager who was calling a broker to cancel a $1000 commission that the broker had recently made. The trade had been a violation of one of the SEC rules and the compliance department's job was to monitor these regulations and make sure the brokers stayed in compliance. This often meant taking money away from the brokers that they thought they had earned, a situation certain to produce fireworks on the phone. During the worst-case version the compliance officer handled the conversation in an aggressive, hard-nosed manner that communicated the message that the broker was viewed as both a hardened criminal and an incompetent idiot. This version clearly represented all the things this compliance officer had always wanted to say to that particular broker in real life. The audience burst into appreciative applause and laughter as she finished this version of her skit.

Many people in the room were sick and tired of being screamed at on the phone by salespeople, and they took great pleasure in hearing one of them "put in their place" for once. It took a few minutes of listening to "me, too" stories before the group could calm down enough to listen to the best-case version of the same scenario. In that case, the compliance person was just as tough about the SEC violation, but handled it in a more sympathetic tone. She also went on to suggest a method by which they might be able to correct the problem and save the broker part of his commission. The reaction of the person playing the broker was upset, but there was no yelling. The broker was still upset about the commission, but was not furious with the compliance person and in fact ended up thanking her at the end of the conversation for offering to help by telling him how to correct the situation.

When trying to persuade people to change their communication behavior, one of the keys is to give people a chance to let off steam. In this seminar, we used stories as a tool for them to let off steam by having them make up the best "we got 'em" stories they can think of and entertain themselves in the most hilarious and irreverent fashion possible. It is very important to make sure that you end on a positive outcome theme of looking at best-case communication approaches as well. If you leave a group venting and revved up in a "we'll show 'em" mood, the outcome or results of that storytelling would probably be negative. But letting people dump their negative feelings and get some support for those feelings before they are asked to look at the constructive side of the issue is often the key to their willingness to try a new approach.

## 4. "Aren't We Great" Stories

These stories are similar to survivor stories. The difference is that these stories do not beat around the bush or use a subtle approach. They come right out and tell you, "Listen to how great we are!" They are filled with pride, enthusiasm, and sometimes even exaggeration. But if you're on the listening end, be careful about pointing out the exaggerations to the group telling the stories. They will likely ignore you or get angry. Besides, the exaggerations are a clear sign that the story has attained mythical proportions. No one knows (or cares) anymore whether it is true in all its details. The theme or point behind the story is true, so who cares whether the details are correct or not.

During a speech to a large audience a few years ago, I used IBM as an example of a company that has created many wonderful mythological stories about itself. All the Tom Watson stories and services stories were classics. I made the unfortunate mistake of pointing out to this audience that some of those stories were probably not even true in the factual sense of the word. A voice erupted from the back of the audience yelling "Yes they are. All those stories are true!" This is how I discovered that one member of my audience worked for IBM and did not like my example. Everyone in the audience was quite amused to watch me dance my way out of that one by trying to explain that it did not matter anymore whether the stories were factually true or not. The message behind the story was true. They had become corporate myth and are loved in the company. The loyal IBMer was not impressed and continued to mutter that all the stories were true.

**Example of an "Aren't We Great" Story.**   David Armstrong tells this story about his manufacturing company's cafeteria. When you walk into the Armstrong cafeteria, at first everything looks normal. There are the usual tables, vending machines, microwaves, candy machines, etc. Then you notice the difference. All the vending machines are unlocked and there is no cash register. The cafeteria is run on the honor system. The employees put their money for all the food and drinks that they buy in an open coin box. The system is working just fine for Armstrong International.[6] The moral of the story, as Armstrong describes it, is that people are capable of self-management and that people are worth believing in.[7] This is a story of pride and success for a whole company of people. Who knows, maybe occasionally the coin box comes up a little short, but the point is that it does not matter to these people. The story is still *true* in the message it carries about that company.

# 5. "We Know the Ropes around Here" Stories

These are the stories that tell about individuals or teams of people in the organization who are famous for getting extraordinary feats accomplished. These stories describe main characters with unusually high levels of technical job skills combined with a high degree of organizational political savvy. When most people in organizations use the phrase "know the ropes around here," they are referring to a person's ability to get ideas or changes through the bureaucracy and personalities of the company. If you walked into most companies and said to any long-term employee, "Who knows the ropes around here?" that person would be likely to understand what you mean with very little clarification and be able to give you a list of names of people that fit the description. If you asked 10 different people in that same company the same question, you would probably get about the same lists of names from all of them. You would end up listening to the same stories over and over as examples of why these people belong on the list of people "who know the ropes around here."

This is actually a variation on the hero story. Knowing how to be politically savvy is a highly valued skill in North American business and industry and is viewed as one of the key ingredients for individual career or team successes. Because of this, I included it as a separate category.

**Example of an "I Know the Ropes around Here" Story.**   In a large, successful high-tech manufacturing company, there is a person who represents a classic example of a main character in this type of story. He has been with the company for over a decade and is seen as having been very successful, both in terms of his individual career progress and as the leader of the team of people who work with him. He is famous for getting seemingly impossible things done and is featured in many of the corporate stories. He is now in a senior management position and holds a great deal of power in the organization. But if you ask him how he gets things done around the company, he never mentions his position or the power that goes with it.

Instead, he responds with a question. He asks, "What is the *Power* Org Chart for getting this particular project through the system?" He quickly points out that when he refers to the Power Org Chart, he does not mean the official organizational chart that shows everyone's job title and reporting relationships. He means the informal knowledge of who you need to persuade and in what order you have to approach these people if you are going to be successful with your project. This includes the time line for how long it is likely to take to work through this chain of contacts and persuasions. He cautions that many of his efforts have taken as long as two years to get up and running.

He went on to describe an example of a recent accomplishment that he and a team of people were just finishing. It involved getting a new internal electronic communication system in place to link the entire company together for more effective product ordering and tracking. He laughed as he described the times during his travels through that particular Power Org Chart when he was yelled at by key people in the company and told he did not know what he was talking about. Those were the times that he just had to back off and wait to try another day. In his opinion, if you have lots of patience and good timing, you can eventually get most good ideas through the system.

## 6. "Kick in the Pants" Stories

These stories are often seen as negative by the people in organizations, or by society at large for that matter. They are the stories that tell about dangers, mistakes, or shortsightedness. The theme or message of these stories is that the company or individuals in the story are headed for trouble if they do not change their ways. The intended outcome of these stories is to wake people up and get them to think about their current behavior and to get them to change that behavior before it is too late. Newspapers are filled these days with stories about environmental disasters and dangers. These are classic "kick in the pants" stories. They read very negatively and in fact can leave the reader upset or depressed, and that is exactly the intent of a "kick in the pants" story. If they do not upset you, there is no hope that you will change or push for others to change.

The ultimate outcome of a "kick in the pants" story usually takes some time to tell if it accomplishes its mission. You have to wait to see if people do change their behavior as a result of these stories. If all you manage to do is upset people, but no one changes anything to improve the situation, then the final vote on whether these stories are negative or positive is unclear at best. At the time the stories are told, the intended outcome is positive. And yet, people will often count these stories as negative because of their upsetting tone when they are first delivered.

**Example of a "Kick in the Pants" Story in Organizations.** You could give this story the subtitle, "An Arrogance Story." These types of "kick in the pants" stories are common in business and are often the result of arrogance or overconfidence of successful companies and individuals. Joel Barker, who made the well-known video program on paradigms called *Discovering the Future: The Business of Paradigms,* eloquently tells a series of stories about companies that allowed themselves to be caught in what he calls "paradigm paralysis."[8] They became so confident of their old ways of doing things (their old paradigms) that they refused to see changes on the horizon that meant disaster for these old ways.

One of the most graphic examples was the story of Swiss watch manufacturers whose inventors created the technology for the quartz watch. When these inventors presented the new technology to the leaders of their companies, the new idea was rejected because it did not conform with the watchmakers' old paradigm of what a watch should be. They were so confident that this new type of watch would not sell, they did not even patent the idea to protect it on the international market. They let their inventors display the idea at the international watchmakers conference, and Seiko of Japan and Texas Instruments of the United States saw it and recognized the potential. Within a few years, the Swiss watch manufacturer had gone from controlling more than 80 percent of the profits of the market to less than 10 percent. This is clearly a story that they did not listen to when they should have. Joel Barker and others tell the story now hoping that other companies will listen and hear the message in this "kick in the pants" story.

## What about the Stories in Your Organization?

Here are some questions to ask yourself about stories you hear and tell in your organization.

- Which of the six story types does your organization use the most? Which types are neglected or even avoided by the people in your organization?
- What is at least one example of each type of story that you have heard or told in your organization?
- Who are the heroes in your organization and what are the stories people tell about them?
- What kinds of traumas have people "survived"? What tough experiences make them proud of the fact that they made it through?
- How do people let off steam in your organization? What are the funny or entertaining stories they tell about these times?
- What do people brag about that would qualify as "Aren't we great" stories?
- Who knows the ropes around the organization? What behavior or experiences qualifies them for that label?
- What are some of the controversial "kick in the pants" stories where someone inside the company got people to sit up and take notice of something that needed attention?
- What are several stories you have heard in your organization that had a negative effect on the people who heard them? These could be some type of cynical or "ain't it awful" story. See if you can retell the story and put a positive spin on it. Turn it into one of the six types of productive stories. Use the same facts and plot, but try to find a way to tell the story so that it has a positive effect on the people who hear it.

# 4

# Retelling Your Organization's Stories

## The "Spin" You Put on a Story

*The Storyteller's Rule of Thumb:* Any topic or series of events can be told as a positive story or a negative story. It all depends on the telling.

As with any rule of thumb, there are probably exceptions to this one, but in the vast majority of cases this rule holds true. One of the arts of excellent storytelling is the ability to control the "spin" that you put on the story in the telling. You can approach the story with a message and attitude that is hopeful, comforting, instructive, or inspiring. Or you can approach the same series of events and spin it in the opposite direction with the message "See, nothing ever goes right" or "Most people are jerks, aren't they?" Every story told so far in this book could have been framed in either of those directions.

Think of the Warren Buffett story at the beginning of the book. The same set of events in the operating units could easily have been told with a message of all the mistakes the units have made because they did not listen to Buffett. The only reference to mistakes in Berkshire Hathaway's annual reports is the section called "Mistakes of the First 25 Years" and regular updates called "Mistakes Du Jour."[1] But these stories are about the mistakes Buffett and top management made over the years. Buffett explains that he tells these stories "in the hope that public confession may deter further bumblings." The result of this type of storytelling is the rare experience of reading an annual report that is funny, entertaining, and memorable.

The Denver emergency department story is, of course, another classic example of a story that could be given either a positive or negative spin. There are probably few jobs in existence where the people witness as much suffering and pain. The purpose of their work is to be prepared for and to respond rapidly to human crises of life-threatening proportions. The professionals who work in that field often focus on the storytelling messages such as "We can handle anything," "We're a great team," "We survived," or "We're the best." If they did not do this, most of them would burn out in a matter of months. Even their tough, eccentric style is a part of their spin on the stories they tell. Their sense of humor may sound strange or even offensive to people outside their profession, but among themselves it is a source of entertainment, tension release, and camaraderie.

## Reshaping Your Stories by Changing the "Spin"

Think of a few of the stories that you have heard recently in your organization. What spin was put on these stories? What was the general attitude or message? If it was negative, what can be done to respin it the next time you repeat the story? As you think about reshaping a story, keep the following questions in mind. They will help you focus on what you are trying to accomplish with your story and get you started in the right direction.

1. What do you want the listeners to *feel* after they hear your story?
2. What do you want the listeners to *remember* from your story?
3. What do you want the listeners to *believe* as a result of hearing your story?

Answering these three questions is the starting point for shaping a story in a positive direction. If the measure of a positive story is in the outcome or effect of the story, then you had better know clearly what outcome you want.

## The Two Main Purposes of a Story

According to social scientists, two of the main purposes of stories in organizations are:

1. *Grounding*—To clarify key values
2. *Instruction*—To demonstrate "the way to do things around here"[2]

## Grounding Stories:
## Key Values in Action

A key value is a standard of excellence that a company is constantly striving to achieve. Many of Jan Carlzon's stories in *Moments of Truth* are examples of grounding or key values stories. Carlzon wrote this book as president and CEO of Scandinavian Airline System, and in it he describes the methods used to turn SAS from $20 million in losses one year to a company earning $54 million the following year. According to Carlzon, *Moments of Truth* was the customer service tool used to engineer this remarkable transformation. Every time a customer comes into contact with the company is a "moment of truth." How the employee handles that moment will either enhance or damage the reputation of SAS. The key value for SAS is to be "the best airline in the world for the frequent business traveler."[3]

On the first page of his book Carlzon offers a story that is "grounded" in this key value. He tells about a business traveler who was about to board one of their planes when he discovered that he had left his airline ticket on the bureau in his hotel room. The traveler was resigning himself to missing his plane when the SAS ticket agent said to him, "Don't worry, Mr. Peterson. If you just tell me your room number at the hotel and your destination, I'll take care of the rest." She issued a temporary ticket to get him to the next destination. Then the ticket agent called the hotel where they checked the room and found the ticket. Next she sent an SAS limo to pick up the lost ticket and bring it back to her. It arrived before the flight took off. Imagine that passenger's surprise when the flight attendant walked up to him on the plane and said calmly, "Mr. Peterson? Here's your ticket."[4]

Carlzon goes on to talk about how proud he is of that story. He explains that it reflects what they have been about to achieve in the six years since he became president.[5] The story is a symbol of the company's key value in action. Success and pride is captured in the telling of one simple story.

When it comes to values storytelling, the important issue for your organization to consider is to identify the important values that you want to emphasize in your setting. No two organizations are exactly the same when it comes to key values that are close to the heart. There are common categories of values, but every organization tends to define these categories in different ways. Here are some of the common categories of important values in organizations today:

*Customer Service.* The key issue in storytelling about customer service is that the stories must cast the customer in the starring role. The most powerful customer service stories are the ones that help the listener see the situation through the eyes of the customer. In Carlzon's story, anyone who has ever flown on an airplane can imagine the surprise of the passenger when the flight attendant handed him the lost ticket.

*Innovation.*    These stories usually cast employees in starring roles as the courageous risk takers or creators of some new product or service. The 3M story of creating the Post-It Notes is a classic example of an innovation story. Innovation is highly valued at 3M and the company has many stories about their research engineers to back up this value.

*Continuous Improvement.*    Total quality management or continuous quality improvement (CQI) is a newer theme in American business and industry that emphasizes system and process improvements on an ongoing, incremental basis. The starring role in CQI stories is reserved for the quality improvement teams that work over time to gradually improve specific processes in the organization. Individual starring roles are downplayed or blended into the larger story about the group accomplishments.

*Employee Involvement.*    This concept is also known as "empowerment" in today's corporate jargon, but the value itself has been around for a long time under such other names as "participative management" and "teamwork." This is a key concept within the total quality management environment. Stories that emphasize this value cast frontline employees in the starring roles and will often have a heavy emphasis on cross-functional teamwork accomplishments.

Risk taking, integrity, honesty, fun, and humor are some of the other values that many organizations claim as important to them. If these values are real and not just empty claims, there will be numerous stories that describe successes and failures in the efforts of people within the company to live up to these ideals. It is not necessary that every story told in the company represent a success involving a key value. These are ideals and cannot always be accomplished. It is a never-ending process and there is no such thing as perfection. It is appropriate that the stories that people tell about the key values in the organization reflect that reality.

Which of these key values are important in your organization? What are the famous stories from the past about the important values? These stories represent your company's version of these values in action. The stories will give you the specific definition of what that value means in your setting. Customer service is defined differently in different companies when it comes to the details of the service behavior that is expected of employees.

How often do these old stories get repeated? Does your company make a conscious effort to continually create new stories on these same topics? If employees or customers are going to take an organization's key values statements and claims seriously, there must be an ongoing stream of new and old stories based on facts to back up that claim.

Does the mission statement message on the brass plaque on the wall match the stories that are being told in the organization? Brass plaques on the wall with fancy mission statements are nothing but dead words and a waste of brass unless there is a whole collection of true stories to back up the mission claims. Chances are the stories are there. The question is, does anyone tell them and repeat them regularly? These are your hero stories and "Aren't we great" stories in action.

## Instructive Stories: How We Do Things around Here

Another primary purpose of stories is to teach listeners the rules and methods of the organization. There is no comparison between the learning that takes place if you hand a person a policy and procedure manual to read in contrast to telling that person a series of stories that illustrate both right and wrong examples of "how things are done around here." Because well-told stories have the characteristics of being memorable and believable, they have much greater teaching value than any factual listing of information.

If you are writing something like a policies and procedures manual, it would increase the usefulness of the document to include stories that illustrate the points being made. Whenever you start a sentence with the words "For example . . . ," you are about to tell a story. If it is a one-sentence example, it may only be a ministory or partial story, but it will still have the effect of triggering a picture in the reader's mind. That picture represents a powerful teaching tool. Use it whenever you get the opportunity.

An example of an instructive story is told by the personnel manager of a company that had a number of overseas divisions. He tells about the time, working at an offshore site, when he and the plant manager were confronted with an emergency decision and were not able to get in touch with headquarters in the United States for instructions. Finally, they knew they had to go ahead and make a decision on their own, so they asked themselves: "Well, what would the company president do?" The personnel manager told a story that the president had once told him about how he had handled some similar situation. The two managers decided to base their current decision on the guidance offered in that old anecdote. They found out later that top management agreed completely with their decision.[6]

### Other Examples of Instructive Stories

*Action, Not Analysis.* Jack Welch, CEO of General Electric, is known to be a tough boss who is particularly contemptuous of inaction. One of the stories told about him that is instructive to people who work with him focuses on this theme.

According to the story, Welch asked some purchasing people to work on some tasks. After several weeks had passed, he met with the group to review the progress. To his irritation, the only thing they had to report to him was elaborate analyses of the situations and a few half-completed efforts to get some work started with several other departments.

Welch called the meeting to a halt and ordered it reconvened in four hours. The goal of the next meeting was for this group to report on its progress. Four hours later, when the group reconvened, Welch got his progress report. The group had accomplished more in those few hours than it had in the several weeks prior to the meetings.[7]

*Reducing Costs.*    Stanley Gault, CEO of Goodyear Tire and Rubber Co., has made a lot of changes since becoming CEO in 1991. One of his top priorities was to reduce costs and reduce the debt. Many of the actions that he took started with him. Two examples were selling off the company's limousine fleet and five corporate jets. The story that people like best, however, involves light bulbs.

As a symbolic gesture, Gault went all over his office and removed 25 light bulbs from wall sconces, lamps, and chandeliers. This left him to work in a "clublike dimness." Gault calculated that eliminating the light bulbs in his office saved the company $230 a year. After he got rid of his light bulbs, lights were turned out in the halls and offices all over the company.[8]

*Speed and Determination.*    Domino's Pizza has many stories about its reputation for 30-minute-delivery times and its ability to keep the stores running no matter what. Shutting down a store is a major taboo at Domino's.

There is one story in the company about the time that one of the franchises nearly ran out of dough and would have been forced to shut down. They called the distribution vice president, who chartered a plane to fly in dough to keep them operating. One other time when they did have to shut down a store, the entire crew in the store wore black arm bands for quite some time afterward.[9]

## The Art of Telling the Story . . . Creating Pictures in the Mind

There is an art to storytelling. It is the art of using words to create pictures in the minds of your listeners. These pictures combine with the facts being described to create a powerful message that remains in listeners' minds for a long time. Religious leaders have often used these pictures in the mind skillfully to explain concepts and spiritual values that would be very difficult for most listeners to grasp in any other way.

For example, the parables that are used in the New Testament are effective because they trigger mental pictures. Anyone who even casually learned about *The Bible* probably knows the story of the prodigal son, which has a very complex lesson about forgiveness and grace. But the story creates a mental picture that makes this information easier to grasp. The Old Testament is basically one long story. Martin Luther King, Jr. used stories' mental pictures to let people know that he had "a dream." When he spoke you could actually see his dream. People can still conjure up the image of his dream today, even though he has been dead for years.

> *The key to the art of storytelling is the capacity to trigger dramatic and memorable pictures in the minds of the listeners.*

As with any art form, it takes a combination of preparation, skill, and practice to produce a great story. It also takes "heart." One of the first pieces of advice you will find in most books written on the art and skill of storytelling is to be sure that you love the story. The story must be one which the teller cares about and wants to share.[10] Here is an example of a much-loved story that was told repeatedly by one of the United States' most famous and talented storytellers, Abraham Lincoln. He told this as an instructive story to encourage people who worked with him to be innovative and take initiative without waiting for orders.[11]

**Lincoln's Story.** It seems there was this colonel who proposed to his men that he would do all the swearing for the regiment. They agreed, and for months everyone controlled their profanity and let the colonel do all the swearing for the group. The driver of the mule team, John Todd, had a very difficult time controlling his temper as he maneuvered his mule team over rough roads. Finally one day, the mud holes being particularly bad, John couldn't stand it anymore, and he burst forth into a volley of profanity. The colonel heard about his offense and confronted John saying, "Didn't you promise to let me do all the swearing for the regiment?" According to Lincoln, John replied, "Yes, I did colonel, but the fact was the swearing had to be done then or not at all, and you weren't there to do it."[12]

Lincoln loved that story. He repeated it many times during his lifetime. Listeners loved it, too, and it has survived, along with many other Lincoln stories, to become a part of our national heritage.

**Good Reading on the Art of Storytelling.** There are many good sources of reading about the art of storytelling written by professional storytellers and other experts in the field. Here are a few that you might find interesting.

*The Power of Myth,* Joseph Campbell, Doubleday, 1988.

*Myths to Live By,* Joseph Campbell, Bantam, 1972.

*Once Upon a Time: A Storytelling Handbook,* Lucille and Bren Breneman, Nelson-Hall, 1990.

*The "Tale-Teller" Tells All,* Ellen Phillips, Cricket Papers, 1990.

*Zapp!,* William C. Byham, DDI, 1988.

*The Goal,* Eliyahu M. Goldratt and Jeff Cox, North River Press, 1984.

*Managing By Storying Around,* David Armstrong, Doubleday, 1992.

*Spinning Tales, Weaving Hope,* New Society Publishers, 1992.

The National Association for the Preservation and Perpetuation of Storytelling (NAPPS) sponsors a number of publications and storytelling festivals nationwide. NAPPS is the single best source on the art of story-telling. P.O. Box 309, Jonesborough, TN 37659. (Phone: 615-753-2171.)

## The Skill of Telling a Story

There are many skills that contribute to the telling of a great story. Everyone has had the experience of listening to a story that is boring or confusing. Even if the message or intended outcome is clear, the story can still fall flat in the telling. So what is the difference between a compelling story and a flop?

### Plot

It is important to have one central plot in your story. This helps avoid the confusion that can occur if there are several subplots or side stories. If your main plot is strong enough, it does not need secondary plots for the story to make sense. You can edit out everything but the one main story. When it comes to plots, keep it simple, especially for verbal storytelling.[13]

### Characters

Characters in your story need to be interesting and fun. Think of the colonel and John Todd in Lincoln's story. More than likely, you started smil-ing to yourself as soon as you began to entertain the prospect of a colonel who is going to do all the swearing for his regiment. That is a colorful char-acter. It helps to visualize your characters clearly in your mind as you are preparing your story.[14] What do they look like? How do they sound? What are their mannerisms and their motives? Practice using different words and phrases that capture the images in your mind. Say the words out loud, and keep experimenting until you find the ones that communicate the right picture.

According to people who worked closely with Winston Churchill, he used to pace around in his office talking to himself, trying out words and phrases to see which ones worked best for his speeches. (*Biography A&E.*) Lucille and Bren Breneman, professional storytellers and authors of the book *Once Upon a Time: A Storytelling Handbook,* defines this skill as "nowness"[15]— the capacity to relive the story to the extent that the events being talked about come alive for the listeners as they hear the story. When you visualize the characters and events in your story and use imagery so that your listeners can "see" with you, they become physically and mentally involved in the story. One of Lincoln's most famous phrases is a stunning, clear visual image: "A house divided against itself cannot stand." With just seven words, he described an entire era of history in the United States.

## Action

People like action . . . lots of it. It holds their attention throughout the telling of the story.[16] Suspense, not knowing what is going to happen next, is a particularly powerful form of action. Take a lesson from movies and television shows and keep your stories moving with fast-paced action. Identify the important images or moments in your story and place extra emphasis on them with actions. For example, at the key point in Lincoln's story, when the colonel confronts John about his swearing, Lincoln switched to specific quotes for a conversation between the two of them about the problem. He does not just tell you *about* the conversation; he lets you listen in on the action.

## Timing

Keep your stories short. Most stories from folklore run from five to seven minutes.[17] In business settings, it is usually wise to keep them even shorter. One to two minutes is long enough in most cases. If you stick to one main plot and no more than two or three characters, it will be easier to keep your story short.

## Fluency

Fluency takes practice. Just because you are good at telling some stories does not necessarily mean that a new story will come out fluently the first time you tell it. Practice telling it to yourself several times first, if you have the opportunity. Tell it out loud to yourself to hear the tone and style of the way you tell it. Memorize the sequence of events in the story and work on the language you will use at key points in your story. This is also useful for jokes, which are actually just another form of storytelling.[18] Do not memorize every word of the story or it will lose its spontaneity.

Some stories in organizations, of course, do not lend themselves to practice. They are not stories that you have prepared for telling to an audience, but are the spontaneous repetition of events that just happened to you. When you tell these kinds of stories, notice the listeners' reactions at different points. Watch where they pay close attention, where they laugh, and what causes them to appear confused. Try to identify what worked and what didn't, so you can use this knowledge to gradually improve on the spontaneity of your stories. Remember, stick to one plot and only a few characters. Focus on action and keep it short. The most important element, however, in the art and skill of storytelling is to have fun telling your tale. In most cases, if you are having fun telling the story, the listeners will enjoy hearing it.

## How Skillful Are You at Story Listening?

This chapter has focused on the role of the storyteller, but there is another, equally important, role when it comes to stories in organizations, even if you are the CEO or chairman of the board. Are you a good listener to other people's stories? One of the reasons listening is very important is that most people who are good storytellers took their first steps in learning how to tell stories by listening to other people and picking up skills from them. Many people did this as children, if they were surrounded by grandparents and other relatives who were talented storytellers. If you think back to some of your favorite teachers in school, you will discover that many of them were good storytellers and could make their subjects come alive for the students.

Another important reason to work on being a story listener is because listening to the stories people tell teaches you a great deal about the environment around you. This is one of the reasons "management by wandering around," a phrase made famous by Tom Peters, is so effective for leaders.[19] They hear stories as they wander. In fact, if leaders try to wander, but instead communicate to the people they see, "don't tell me anything real . . . let's all just be polite," then the wandering is probably useless at best. Because the messages that stories carry in organizations are so powerful, it is dangerous to be cut off from this important communication channel.

In research done in a manufacturing plant, a cross section of people were asked to list all the significant problems in the organization.[20] The researchers found that only 4 percent of the problems listed were known to top managers. They also discovered that virtually every problem listed by top management was known to at least some of the rank-and-file employees.[21] Richard Whiteley, author of *The Customer-Driven Company,* calls this phenomenon "The Iceberg of Ignorance."[22] The top managers were not listening to the customers or employees, and they knew very few of the problems that the company was facing. This is a dangerous form of isolation. Whether you are talking about the leaders of companies or a personal friendship, storytelling is a two-way street that requires telling and listening to forge strong relationships with lasting results.

# PART 2

## Leading with Stories

# 5

# Your Corporate Heritage: Sacred Bundle Stories

Here's a story from *Leadership as an Art,* by Max DePree, chairman of the board and CEO of Herman Miller Inc.:

> Dr. Carl Frost, a good friend and adviser to our company, tells a story of his experience in Nigeria during the late sixties.
> Electricity had just been brought into the village where he and his family were living. Each family got a single light in its hut. A real sign of progress. The trouble was that at night, though they had nothing to read and many of them did not know how to read, the families would sit in their huts in awe of this wonderful symbol of technology.
> The light bulb watching began to replace the customary nighttime gatherings by the tribal fire, where the tribal storytellers, the elders, would pass along the history of the tribes. The tribe was losing its history in the light of a few electric bulbs.[1]

According to Max DePree this story illustrates what can happen to a group if it loses its "tribal storytellers." According to him, the penalty for failing to listen is that the group will lose its history and the key values that bind them together. Without the continuity of storytelling and the messages they contain from the leadership of the group, the people of any tribe or corporation will "forget who they are."[2]

## What Is in Your Organization's Sacred Bundle?

Organizational consultant, Ray Sells, tells about the time that he was taking a tour of the Chicago Museum of History and came across an exhibit about the Plains Indians of North America. One of the items in that exhibit caught his attention. It was described as a "sacred bundle." This was a bundle of hides containing items that look like a collection of odds and ends. According to Ray, the items could easily have been mistaken for debris. There was a feather, some rocks, an old peace pipe, an eagle's claw, and a few worn pouches. The description that accompanied the exhibit explained that this bundle contained the historical and sacred mementos of this particular tribe. It was entrusted to one of the elders of the tribe, and that person was expected to protect the sacred bundle with his life, if necessary. To lose the sacred bundle would threaten the tribal identity for the entire group.

In addition to protecting the sacred bundle, it was also his responsibility to bring the sacred bundle to the tribal campfires where he would take the items out one at a time and tell the stories that were associated with each one. He was teaching the new members and reminding the old members about the tribal history and "sacred" events that symbolized the values and characteristics of this tribe. For the members to know who they were as a tribe, those people would have to understand what was in the sacred bundle, and what those items symbolized for the group. The sacred bundle is the symbol that represents the heart and soul of the tribe.

In modern societies, we like to think of ourselves as more "advanced" than these traditional tribal settings. In fact, you will often see the word "primitive" used to describe these cultures. When it comes to storytelling, we may need to change that assumption about which group is more advanced in its understanding of how a culture survives and thrives. We often are not aware of the sacred bundles in our organizations. In a physical form, we sometimes do not even have one. The closest thing that we may have to a sacred bundle, in most cases, is a collection of key stories about the company's past that represent its most important values or characteristics. But in many organizations, many people see these stories about its history and key events as relatively useless information. This type of storytelling is often described to me as the "company ego trip."

Many newer employees, including people in leadership positions, know very little of the anecdotal history of the organization. There is rarely any organized method for teaching these newcomers the stories that represent the sacred bundle of this "tribe" they are entering. If they do learn this kind of information, it is usually by accident or in an offhand, casual way. If you ask employees hired within the past year in many companies about the history of the company and the key stories from the past that represent the "heart and soul" of the organization, you will often find that the answers you receive are spotty at best. Some people may know, but others haven't a clue. No one ever told them these stories. As Max DePree points out, this is a "group of people that is beginning to forget who they are."[3]

Try to picture a traditional tribe where the newcomers, the children in their case, did not know what was in the sacred bundle or did not know the important stories from the past. Who would be held responsible for this dangerous oversight in tribal education? You certainly would not blame the children themselves. No one would look at this situation and conclude that the children were unmotivated, not good team players, or just don't care about the tribe and its welfare. The leadership of the tribe, not the children, would be held responsible for this situation. It is the responsibility of the chief, shaman, and elders to be the tribal storytellers and to ensure that everyone in the group understands that the stories and the sacred bundle represent the essence of the tribe's identity.

It is the same situation in an organization. If it is the responsibility of the leadership to pass on the identity of the company, then it makes no sense to conclude, as so often is the case, that the fault lies with the employees when it doesn't get passed on. They are frequently labeled unmotivated, poor team players, or unconcerned about the organization. But look around for the rituals that are the organization's equivalent of the tribal campfires and ceremonies for storytelling. How is an employee supposed to learn what is in the sacred bundle of this organization? If the leadership does not take responsibility for ensuring that these things happen, then it will be left to random chance. When the tribal campfires and sacred bundle storytelling are missing, one of the most basic roles of leadership that has been understood for thousands of years has been ignored or forgotten.

## Questions about Your Organization's Sacred Bundle

- *What is in your organization's sacred bundle?* Think of the five or ten pivotal events in the life of the organization. These might be times of major change, a new CEO, a merger, a significant change in the product mix, etc. What are the stories associated with these major events? What went right and where did the problems occur? Who were the heroes during these times? What do these stories tell you about the strengths and the weaknesses of your organization? The term *sacred bundle,* as it is used here, refers primarily to the "best" of what your organization has been able to accomplish and the characteristics that have contributed to these successes. When people tell stories about characteristics or accomplishments that they are proud of, they are usually describing what is in their sacred bundle.

- *Who are your organization's chief, shamans, and elders?* The elders are the people who have been in the group for many years and hold opinions that are focused on what is best for the tribe as a whole.[4] Shamans are the holy people who have some special knowledge to help the tribe prosper.[5] They are the keepers of the values.

- *What are your "corporate campfires"?* What are the rituals and cere-monies in your organization that are used for storytelling and to pass on your company's heritage? These could be events that represent major rites of passage in the organization, such as orientation of new hires, retirements, or promotions. They could be celebrations of important anniversaries such as the founding, major changes, or key successes.

- *What key values or characteristics of your organization are highlighted in the stories?* If you boiled each story down to a phrase or two that explained the point of the story, what would that phrase be? You could even describe it as the moral of the story.

## The Difference between Your History and Heritage

People often ask what difference the past makes. It is the present and the future that matter to the success of an organization. In fact, they say most organizations dwell on the past too much. They rest on their old, outdated laurels too long or waste time reminiscing about the old days when things were much easier, happier, or better in some way. Or they use the past as a defense with the phrase "That's the way we've always done it." No doubt about it: all of these statements are true. The past can get in the way of the present or the future in the lives of individuals and organizations. The solu-tion, however, is not necessarily to throw away the past completely.

Think of the *history* of your organization as all the events that have occurred in the past. If you were to write the "autobiography" of your orga-nization, it would probably contain a chronological description of a series of events from the founding of the company up to the present. Once you had listed all your chronological dates and events, you could then go back through the whole list and think of key stories about some of the most sig-nificant events from your organization's history. These would be the anec-dotal descriptions of who did what to make these important events happen. Many times they are hero stories about the founders or other individuals who put forth extraordinary efforts to accomplish some feat for the com-pany. Other times they are stories about teams of people and their accom-plishments. For example, the folklore around the development of the

Macintosh computer at Apple is a classic sacred bundle story about a team of people and their extraordinary accomplishment.

These stories represent the organization's *heritage*. Heritage is your symbolic history that links you to the most important elements of your past. Heritage does not and should not remain only in the past. Those stories from your past should link you to the current key values and characteristics of your group and should also provide you with the pathway to your future.

Listen to this example of a sacred bundle story that represents part of the heritage of one organization. This is a very successful medical center that was founded one hundred years ago. They tell this story in a tone of voice that has a quality of "once upon a time . . ." You can tell the story has been told over and over again by generations of employees. They tell the story in elaborate, long versions, but this is its essence:

> Shortly after it was founded in the late 1800s, the town was hit with an infectious epidemic and the hospital was overrun with patients. There were not enough beds and they did not want to mix the infectious patients with the other patients. It had all the makings of a disaster for the young hospital. Their solution: They went out in front of the hospital and pitched tents all over the lawn. They put the infectious patients on the lawn and cared for them there. In this way they stretched to meet the needs of the town for health care services during that crisis.

This story means a number of things to people in that hospital about the care they provide in the community. It also symbolizes one of the more unusual characteristics about this particular hospital's style of solving problems. They are basically a "tribe" of characters who are creative, have a great sense of humor, and will figure out a way to turn potential disaster into success. Is this story anything more than just dead history from the past? The answer to that question is found by asking two questions. What is that hospital doing now in its current handling of events that is today's equivalent of "pitching tents in the front yard"? And what will that organization be doing in five years that is the future version of pitching tents in the front yard? Sacred bundle stories represent the organization's heritage and provide the pathway from the past through the present and into the future. (See Figure 5-1.)

## Examples of Organization's Sacred Bundle Stories

### Physical Objects in the Sacred Bundle

Sometimes companies actually do have physical items that represent part of the sacred bundle of the organization. Ross Perot, founder of successful electronics company EDS, tells about the money that he and his wife

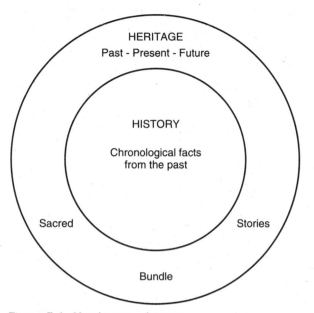

**Figure 5-1.** Your history or heritage.

scraped together to start the company back in the early 1960s. He still has the original $1200 check that launched the company.

Or consider another company that has a barroom napkin encased in glass that hangs on the wall in the president's office. That napkin is a relic from a discussion that occurred in a bar years ago, where the basic marketing plan for the fledgling company was mapped out on that napkin. When visitors come to the headquarters, one of the stops on the tour is the president's office to see the now-famous napkin.

Another example is Maytag. They have a plant in Newton, Iowa and there is a museum in the town that contains models of every innovation Maytag has introduced over the years.

## People in the Sacred Bundle

A high-spirited, successful microchip manufacturer on the West Coast has a different type of physical object as a sacred bundle item. There is a person in their sacred bundle. One of the top people in their sales and marketing department is a person who has earned both the respect and friendship of many of the people in the company, especially the sales force that works for him. When they talk about him, they describe him over and over again as "a regular guy." They go on to tell stories illustrating that, despite the success and power he has attained over the years, he is still just a "regular guy." They tell stories—about his honesty, how he treats people, and how he talks about himself—to show that he is still a regular guy. I asked him in passing one time what he had done for the weekend. He told me that he spent the weekend doing odd jobs for his wife, like cleaning the swimming pool. That was not the answer that I expected from one of the Silicon Valley's high flyers.

In a speech to that company's sales force a few weeks later, I identified one of the characteristics this company valued and respected as "the regular guy" syndrome. When I went on to point out that one of their main symbols for this characteristic was personified by their vice president, they laughed and nodded. I then said to the group, "I guess this means if your tribe breaks camp and moves on, you'll have to stuff Rick in the sacred bundle and drag him to the next campsite." The crowd of 600 salespeople burst into spontaneous applause. They agreed. . . . They knew that this man belonged in their company's sacred bundle.

### Crisis Stories in the Sacred Bundle

National Leisure Group is a successful young company established in the early 1980s that offers discounted travel services, a highly competitive business. One of the things that NLG prides itself on is being "nice to its customers." One of the stories that they tell to illustrate how far they will go to accomplish this mission concerns their handling of the Eastern Airline strike in 1989.

"NLG's competitors refunded customers' money and shrugged off complaints. But NLG did more. It rebooked customers on other carriers and ate the difference in fares. The company lost $375,000."[6] According to the founders, Joel Benard-Cutler and David Failkow, they may have lost money during that crisis, but they gained a fortune in customer loyalty. They wanted their staff and customers to know that they were serious about their commitment to service.

### Collection of Stories in the Sacred Bundle

Any company that has been successful at developing a credible set of core values and is well known for certain characteristics has a large sacred bundle and many different stories that go with it. In mature companies, these stories are woven together into a pattern that is familiar to everyone who deals with them. A classic example of a company with a famous reputation is Wal-Mart, founded by Sam Walton. Almost anyone who has read about the company and Walton or visited one of the stores could give you a general description of the values and key characteristics of their operating approach. In fact, Sam Walton and his approach is often written about in an almost reverent tone.

His son Rob Walton claims that Walton would no doubt chuckle over being thought of as a management guru. He says, "We snickered at writers who viewed Dad as a grand strategist." A friend and colleague, George Billingsley, could recall many times when Walton was asked to reveal the secret of his success, "Sam would tell a different secret every time."[7] And yet, there was obviously a pattern in all those secrets that produced one of the world's most successful businesses in the last 30 years.

Sam Walton has become a part of the American folklore and our national sacred bundle, at least in the world of business. He may have died in 1992, but we will all be telling Sam Walton stories for years to come. It will reach a point where no one even knows anymore if all the details of the stories are true. And no one will care because, when it comes to sacred bundle stories, the facts are not what matters. What matters is the message and the passing on of the story.

# 6

# The Leader
# as Storyteller

## Leaders: Protectors
## of the Sacred Bundle Stories

The key stories that leaders tell in their organizations carry special significance for its success or failure. Each leader or group of leaders must understand that the roles they play are very much like the roles that have existed for thousands of years with the chiefs, shamans, and elders of the tribes of the world. They are responsible for what writer and philosopher Sam Keen would describe as the mythology of the organization.[1] The term *myth* is often misunderstood to mean a "lie" or a "mistake." A myth is often considered to mean the opposite of fact.[2] In the anthropological meaning of the word, a myth refers to a set of interlocking stories and rituals that give a pivotal sense of meaning to the group.[3] The purpose of an organization's mythology is to answer the same questions that myths have answered in cultures everywhere:

- Where did we come from?
- What is the purpose of my life?
- With whom do I belong?
- What are my duties and obligations?
- What is taboo?
- Who are the enemies?[4]

Peter Senge, author of the book *The Fifth Discipline,* describes these mythological stories as "purpose stories."[5] He describes three different companies that he researched when writing his book that represented very different industries: a traditional service business, a manufacturer, and a high-tech company. All three of these successful companies had one thing in common.[6] Their leadership each had an inspiring sense of purpose and a story to tell that explained the vision for the company. As described in Part 1 of this book, most stories have the purpose of either emphasizing a value or instructing the listeners on appropriate behavior, but these stories are the most extreme examples of both of these purposes in action.

Senge describes these stories as "*the* story—the overarching explanation of why they do what they do, how their organizations need to evolve, and how that evolution is part of something larger."[7] He points out that an important aspect of these stories is that they are both personal and universal.[8] It gives the group a personal mission, but at the same time puts their accomplishments in a larger context. When the leaders in an organization have this sense of mission, you have the type of leadership that is described by Robert Greenleaf in his book *Servant Leadership.*[9]

When the leadership concentrates on the telling and retelling of the sacred bundle stories, they are acting as a guide for the organization. They are showing the pathway to the future and they are the ones who are responsible for taking the first steps down that path to continue the exploration of where to go from here. These purpose stories are not manufactured in a boardroom in their complete and final form and then announced to the world, polished and ready for mass marketing. These stories evolve over time as they are being told, and as Senge points out, they are "a result of being told."[10] The development of the sacred bundle stories involves as much *listening* on the part of the leaders as it does talking.

## Leaders: Teachers and Guides through Stories

One of the most fascinating illustrations of this type of leadership is described in a book written by William Byham, called *Zapp!* Using a fantasy setting complete with dragons and suits of armor, he graphically demonstrates the difference in what happens to people when they are "zapped" with bolts of energizing lightning compared to their reactions when they are "sapped" by having the control and pride in their work drained away. The supervisor, Joe Mode, learns from experimenting over time that listening to the people in the organization is one of the keys to zapping. He also learns that listening alone is not enough. He must listen and respond to what people are saying. He must respond by offering help and guidance that keeps everyone on the right path. But he has to do this without grabbing away control and trying to fight all the dragons himself.[11]

*Zapp!* is a mythic story about any organization. Its purpose is to illustrate the key values of empowerment for effective leadership, and it is instructive in how to empower people in a way that produces results. This fable also demonstrates how the company's story evolves over time. Joe Mode made many mistakes and learned how to lead effectively by experimentation and dialogue with one of the "normal" employees, Ralph. After reading this story, the image of zapping and sapping is vividly imprinted in the reader's mind. You can almost see the lightning bolts flying back and forth between people in your organization as they empower or drain each other of energy and enthusiasm. This story is an eloquent teacher for people learning how to be leaders in the old traditions of the tribal shamans and elders. The leader becomes a teacher, listener, and guide and eventually becomes a teller of the sacred bundle stories.

One leader, who is an example of someone who understands this form of leadership, is the president of a major nonprofit association. His job is extremely stressful with constant financial headaches, legislative ordeals, and never-ending turf battles between constituencies. This is an organization with its share of dragons to slay every day. Looking on from the outside, it is a job that by all rights should burn a person out in a matter of months. The president has been in this position for years and shows no signs of walking away from it any time soon. An occasional vacation seems to be all he needs to keep going. When asked how he does it, he just smiles and responds that he knows he is doing what he is supposed to be doing at this point in his life. And he will keep doing it as long as he is needed there.

As Senge described it, this person knows *the* story at both a personal and universal level. He speaks with passion about the mission of the organization and tells many stories about its trials and successes. The themes of his sacred bundle stories are about protecting the quality of services to the people they serve, and the constant encouragement to his staff to take risks, never give up, and accomplish miracles whenever possible. He sees himself and the whole organization as servant-leaders for the people who rely on them. At the universal level, he links the work of this organization and his part in it to his spiritual beliefs. He is doing "what he is supposed to be doing with his life." Unless you specifically asked him, he never directly mentions any of these things, but when you listen to him talk and tell stories about the organization, you know there is something special about this leader. After a conversation with him, you walk away knowing that you have just been zapped.

## Leaders: Keepers
## of the Tribal Campfires

Tribal campfires is the metaphor used in this book to describe the places
and the times where the storytelling takes place. Some of these times and
places need to be formalized and repeated as rituals on a regular basis.
These are the times that the leaders bring out the sacred bundle and tell
the stories that are the past, present, and future versions of the organization's living heritage. In most traditional tribal settings, the campfires are a
nightly ritual. There are also a number of major events during the year that
mark important celebrations.

One example of a yearly celebration that represents a tribal campfire
event is the awards and recognition day that takes place in a large nonprofit
association. Teams of people and individuals are recognized for outstanding achievements and the executive director gives a speech that focuses on
the direction for the association, emphasizing the key values of the organization. An example of an award that was given was for a group of volunteers
whose mission is to visit nursing homes and fight for the improvement of
the quality of care in that setting.

The stories told by this team at the awards ceremony moved many people
in the audience to tears. They ended their description of their work by chal-
lenging everyone in the audience to go out and visit some of these places
and to do their part in helping to improve these services for older people.
Although this event is not required attendance, to accommodate all the
employees and volunteers that want to come, they have to hold the presentation in a large ballroom at a nearby hotel and repeat the ceremony three
times during the course of one day to give everyone an opportunity to
attend. If you visit their offices the day after the ceremony, no one has to tell
you that these people have just been reminded about their sacred bundle.
The stories are still being repeated from the day before, and the enthusiasm
and pride is obvious. For example, one of the recipients of an award
ordered a pizza for lunch for everyone in the department as a thank-you for
all the efforts of the whole team. The lunchtime talk was filled with laughing, stories from the day before, and expressions of mutual appreciation all
around the table. This lunch was another version of a tribal campfire for
that one department.

Another organization has recently started a monthly meeting that they
call the Managers' Forum. It was a spin-off from a management training
series for the group. They had enjoyed being together in the seminar
and getting to know each other better. The seminar series had given
them an opportunity to throw around ideas and brainstorm in a less pres-
sured situation than the usual day-to-day work setting. As a result of this,
they created their Managers' Forum. One of the noticeable differences in

this group is that they really did behave as a team. Often managers who head up different departments are *supposed* to be a team but, in reality, whenever they are together as a group, you can feel the tension. They behave as adversaries who are there to defend their own department's turf. In this case, they were much more blunt about the turf issues between the various departments, and they were unusually creative in their ideas for working out the best solutions they could at that point in time. They also behaved as though they actually enjoyed each other's company. They joked and laughed continually when they were together in these settings. When asked why they were so different from many management teams, they responded, "Our leadership." They described their senior management team as people who were obsessed with quality service and teamwork values. Those leaders expected teamwork and quality from this group and gave them the support they needed to pull it off.

## Conversations around the Tribal Campfires

David Bohm, a physicist, describes the importance of human conversation in the development of new ideas.[12] He describes two different types of conversation—discussion and dialogue—and points out that both types are necessary for any group of people to continue to generate ideas and grow. He defines *discussion* as the type of conversation where a subject is analyzed, points of view are exchanged, and the goal is to reach a conclusion. In most cases, the goal is also to have one's views win out and be accepted by the group. On the other hand, he describes *dialogue* as the free flow of ideas between people. The goal of dialogue is to "go beyond any one individual's understanding."[13] In a dialogue there is an emphasis on "a pool of common meaning" that is constantly developing or changing.

Both forms of conversation have value in an organization. And yet, when people in most organizations are asked to identify the opportunities for dialogue in their company, they come up blank. Sometimes they laugh and mention the gripe sessions in the cafeteria over lunch as the only free flow of ideas between people that they can remember at work. The lunchtime rituals are certainly a possible setting for some type of tribal campfire and the dialogue that goes with it. What these employees are usually recalling, however, is a familiar version of negative storytelling . . . the "Ain't it awful" syndrome. In most cases, this does not produce new ideas, inspiration, or even comfort for the participants. Most lunchtime conversations would simply qualify as a classic example of a sap of the energy of the people who were listening. One the other hand, the Managers' Forum described earlier is a good example of a setting where both discussion and dialogue occur and produce creative and productive results for the group.

## How Leaders Get the Stories Started in Organizations

Not all people in leadership roles are talented storytellers. Warren Bennis, author of a number of books on leadership, makes it clear that there is no single personality style that is required for a person to be an effective leader. He is particularly adamant that personal charisma is not a necessary ingredient of leadership. He describes some successful leaders who are not great orators.[14] Some of these people are not, and never will be, articulate enough to tell a story well. There is, however, no doubt that stories are being told in those successful companies. How do they do it?

Research by social scientists indicates that the key elements that cause stories to "become symbols and provide social integration" in an organization are as follows:

1. Top executives consistently point to general ideas or frameworks. They talk repeatedly about the key values and goals of the organization.
2. Members of the organization take this "material" and fashion their own stories as well as pass along the the stories they hear from each other and from the leaders.[15]

The key here seems to be that the leaders do not have to do all the storytelling themselves. In fact, if the leaders are not storytellers at all but continually talk about or emphasize the key values and goals of the organization, then other people apparently pick up on those themes and start their own stories. To go one step further, consultant Ray Sells states "the stories are *already out there* before the leader even arrives." If the leaders will listen to the stories that people in the organization are already telling, they will find the ones that highlight the themes and values they want to emphasize. The key is to encourage people to retell those key stories, make up new ones, and keep people focused on these important values and goals.

- *Find the stories about key values that are already present in the organization and retell them often.*
- *Make up new stories and keep people focused on the key values.*

Too often people in leadership positions spend entirely too much time and effort trying to figure out how to "do it all themselves." When it comes to storytelling, that will never work. Even if you have the talent to deliver a story as skillfully as Abraham Lincoln, that talent will never replace the need for you to be a skilled listener. Lincoln was famous, in fact, for having what was probably the most extreme open-door policy of any president in the history of the United States. He was either out of his office meeting people where they lived and worked, or he had a steady stream of people lined up outside his office waiting to talk with him at the White House. And he did not just talk with and listen to other leaders or powerful people. He listened to ordinary citizens regularly. He called these conversations his "public opinion baths."[16] He describes them in this way. These conversations "may not be pleasant in all particulars, but the effect, as a whole, is renovating and invigorating."[17]

## Questions to Consider for Getting the Stories Started

- What are the general ideas, key values, or goals about which you want people in your organization to tell stories?

- When and where can you repeatedly bring up these themes so that everyone knows they are on your mind all the time?

- What stories are they already telling that have those themes? Make sure that the frontline people are telling these stories, not just the managers and leaders who surround you.

- How much time do you spend listening to other people in your organization, at all levels, tell their stories? Keep in mind the old saying "God gave you one mouth and two ears for a reason!" The two-to-one ratio applies to leaders at least as much as it does to everyone else.

- When and where could you repeat stories you have heard that represent the themes you want to encourage? Or, how could you get other people to repeat those stories, if you are not comfortable doing it yourself?

Whether you are the manager or supervisor of a work team or the CEO of a large organization, the most important question to keep asking yourself on a regular basis is the following:

*What are the two or three key ideas or themes about this business that the people who work in this organization associate with me?*

When people see you at work or even just hear your name mentioned, those two or three key themes should pop into their head. In behavioral psychology, this is called a *conditioned response*. The subjects have been "conditioned" to connect two objects together in their minds because they have experienced them together over and over again. It becomes a habit. When you think of one of the objects, you also think of the other one. As a leader, the people in your organization need to be conditioned to connect you and your key themes.

A new leader in a large organization was discussing how to keep the department focused on its real mission of customer service and not get bogged down in interpersonal frictions, as it had been known to do in the past. My advice was to turn himself into a conditioned response. Talk about the clients, their needs, and the mission of customer service *constantly*. Worry about it, celebrate and reward it, ask questions about it, tell stories about it, and let everyone in the department know that he is obsessed with this mission. Within a relatively short period of time, whenever anyone in the department sees him or hears his name, that person will automatically think of the customer service mission. And, they will start telling their own stories based on this theme. The stories that all of those employees tell and the creative ideas that they have will be the key to accomplishing the department's mission. That leader, as smart and talented as he is as an individual, can never tell enough stories, think of enough ideas, or perform enough miracles to accomplish that mission alone.

# 7
# Inspiring Stories or Corporate Propaganda?

Every other chapter in this book examines the power of storytelling as a communication tool in organizations. This chapter will look at the limits of that power—when stories do *not* work. When, in fact, are stories capable of doing more harm than good in organizations? The answer to that question is that stories do more harm than good when they are perceived as corporate propaganda, rather than inspiring truthful stories. When a story about the company, especially one that involves its key values or goals, triggers the response from many of the listeners, "Oh, what a bunch of bull!", that is a sure sign of the corporate propaganda syndrome in action.

The first thing that is important to remember when considering the difference between an inspiring story and corporate propaganda is that we are examining *perceptions of the listeners,* not the intentions of the teller. The teller of the story may have intended it to have a positive message, but the listeners did not hear it that way or did not "buy" the message. If the perception of the listener is negative or rejecting of the story, then the story loses its power. At best, it is ignored. At worst, it deepens the cynicism of the listeners even further because they resent being asked to play along with an obvious lie.

If the story was told by one of the powerful leaders of the organization, the public response from the listeners is usually neutral. Their faces are blank, they give minimal verbal responses, and they leave the situation as quickly as possible. Then, later, walking away down the hall, cynical comments and rolling of eyes are exchanged between the people who "know" the truth of the situation.

Two researchers, Joanne Martin and Melanie Powers, tell about an example of this at IBM when the leadership shifted from Tom Watson, Sr. to his son Tom Watson, Jr. When Watson, Jr. took over from his father, he decided that he wanted to encourage more dissent and less conformity than his father had demanded from IBM employees. He expressed this wish numerous times and told many stories including one by the philosopher Kierkegaard about a man on the coast of New Zealand who loved the great flocks of ducks that he saw flying south each year, so he started feeding them on his pond. Eventually, the ducks became tame. They were too fat and lazy to ever bother to fly again. The point of this story is that you can make ducks tame, but you can never make tame ducks wild again. And tame ducks never go anywhere.[1]

Watson's point in telling this story was to illustrate that IBM needed wild ducks. "At IBM we try not to tame them."[2] The employees of IBM were not convinced. Their response to the encouragement from Watson to stick their heads in his office and say "you are wrong" was the following: "You should see the collection of heads that he has in his office!"[3] This type of reaction is not an uncommon response, particularly when a story represents a new idea or way of doing things. People just do not buy it. Why not?

## Stories Have to Match Behavior That Has Been Seen

Stories are a powerful way to illustrate events, values, or emotions, but they will not substitute for the truth. If a story is used to draw attention to something that has happened, it is likely to be an effective communication tool. If, however, you tell a story to illustrate facts, events, or "the way things are done around here," and the story does not match the listeners' experience, the stories are likely to be rejected. Missouri may have a reputation for being the "Show me" state, but when it comes to storytelling in organizations, that motto seems to apply equally well. The stories that are told must be paced to coincide with reality. And it has to be a reality that people can see. They are not likely to simply take your word for it.

An example of this that I have witnessed a number of times takes place in the recruiting of people to be in-house trainers for a program such as customer-service training. If someone is recruited for a trainer's position who does not have a reputation among employees for providing high levels of customer service, there will be a major problem with the effectiveness of the training. Most employees report that they find it moderately nauseating to be forced to sit and listen to another employee "preach" to them about customer service, when they saw that same person being rude to a customer three days before. Credibility in storytelling is crucial. Without it, no one hears or believes the message. Even if that trainer has the best stand-up presentation skills of anyone in the organization, it will not work. When recruiting someone to be an in-house trainer (that is, a kind of storyteller), believability on the topic is more important than any other skill or characteristic of the person.

> *Behavior must match the stories or there is no credibility.*

## Optimism That Is Out of Touch with Reality

Another pitfall that can lead to corporate propaganda is what I often refer to as "pathological optimism." This is a disease that seems to be most likely to attack CEOs and other senior management people. Optimism, in itself, is not the problem. In fact, optimism is an essential ingredient for painting a picture of a hopeful and an inspiring future for any organization. The problem emerges if the impression is created in the listeners' minds that the storyteller has lost touch with the difference between the ideal or future state of affairs and the current reality in the organization.

Sometimes leaders will tell a story that is a dream for the future or an ideal state, but they tell it in a way that makes it sound as though they think it is current reality. An example of this was an organization that had a particularly gifted visionary as a leader. The people in the organization respected him and were excited about his vision of the future. A number of them came to me at one point, however, and said to me, "Will you talk to him and make sure he realizes that the future has not arrived yet!" He was making these people very nervous because he would tell his stories in the present tense, and almost never make reference to how far they still had to go. In talking with this leader one-on-one, it was clear that he was very much in touch with reality. He knew exactly how far there was to go in that organization. He was trying to avoid discouraging people by dwelling on that part of the story and, besides, that part was boring to him. So an occasional "Yes, yes, there is a long way to go" was about the most you could get him to say. One of the unspoken problems that was obvious in listening to the managers talk about their frustration in this situation was that the managers felt mildly insulted. By ignoring the current reality and talking as though the future had arrived already, the leader was not giving them enough credit for all the hard work they were doing to turn the present into the improved future. They liked the idea of the future that they were creating, but they did want some recognition of the blood, sweat, and tears it was taking to get there. As time passed, he learned to communicate the message that he understands both the future dream and the current reality. By giving the current efforts more attention, he actually strengthens the inspiration of his message about the vision for the future.

Creating a tension between the current reality and the ideal future through storytelling is a powerful technique. It creates a picture in people's minds of what is and what could be. It is important, however, to keep in mind that the present is a description of facts and events, and the stories about the future are metaphors, dreams, and plans.

---

- *Pathological optimism confuses and frustrates the listeners.*
- *Dreams inspire the listeners.*

---

## Leadership Isolation . . . Are You Talking Only to Yourselves?

You may tell the most inspiring, hilarious, and meaningful stories in the world, but if only two or three other people are listening, these stories will not have much impact on the organization as a whole. The small group that tells and listens to the stories become the "insiders" and everyone else is left out. The majority of the people in the organization may not even know the stories. Even if they have heard the stories, their reactions are likely to be cynical dismissal.

The biggest danger of this problem occurs in young companies whose original founders are still present in top management. It can happen anywhere, but in these young companies (25 years old or less) the senior management who were the founders often have a special bond with each other. They went through the terrors and the triumphs of starting the company together and no one else is allowed to share that experience with them. The sacred bundle is *their own and nobody else's.*

What happens is that you end up with two tiers of storytelling in the organization. If you heard each of the two sets of stories in isolation, it would be unlikely that you would ever realize that they were coming out of the same company. The tragic thing about this type of corporate propaganda is that the senior management group almost never knows it exists. They think everyone else is listening, too, and is as inspired as they are. They are puzzled by the drop-off in productivity and the bad attitudes of some of the employees, but they never make the connection. The beer drinking and storytelling that happens at the local bar after work for the core group is never seen as having anything to do with the rest of the employees. The irony is that this is exactly the point. They are having their own small tribal campfire . . . they just forgot to invite the rest of the tribe.

One company that had this problem was about twenty years old and still had several of the founders in their senior management ranks. Several additional, long-time employees had been allowed into the insiders group. They had an elaborate and inspiring collection of stories that dated from the founding all the way up to current events. They got together informally on a regular basis at a bar near work to drink beer, reminisce, and talk about the company's past, present, and future.

The key founder was revered by the group and his talents were talked about with almost godlike descriptions. Most employees in the company knew the people in this group, the stories that they told, and that they met regularly to enjoy each other's company. This was probably the single most angry group of employees that I have witnessed in my years as a consultant. Their stories about the company were about unfair benefits, disrespectful treatment, turf battles, and penny-pinching at their expense. They had their own collection of folklore, but it did not even remotely resemble the founders' stories. For all practical purposes, this was two different companies within the same walls.

Sacred bundle stories are created for *inclusive* purposes. They are intended to tie the group together with a common heritage and highlight the key values and characteristics of the group that need to be preserved into the future. When the leadership storytelling becomes the folklore of the insider's group, they are no longer sacred bundle stories. In fact, they have the danger of producing the opposite effect of genuine sacred bundle stories. They are likely to alienate and insult the noninsiders in the company.

---

- *Inclusive, shared storytelling inspires and motivates.*
- *"Insiders" storytelling alienates and insults employees.*

---

## Consistent Toleration of Poor Performance

Even if the leaders' behavior matches their stories, there can still be a problem if the organization is perceived to tolerate mediocre or poor performance from other people who work there. The type of cynicism that this problem triggers is different from what occurs if the leaders are seen as not practicing what they preach. The employees will continue to believe that leaders really mean what they say and are genuine in the commitment to the key values embodied in their stories. Their cynicism will be focused on their opinions that the leadership is ineffective or even cowardly when it comes to being tough about upholding those standards throughout the organization as a whole.

One of the most common complaints from employees about their leadership is that they do not get rid of the people who are not performing up to standards. I have heard hundreds of comments such as this one: "If they put up with the people who are doing a mediocre or lousy job, then what difference does it make that I am doing an excellent job?" The employees tell me that not only are the poor performers not terminated, but they are perceived as getting the same salary or wage increases and even promotion opportunities. Sometimes the employees believe that their leaders are out of touch and do not know who is doing a good job and who isn't. But more often, they express the opinion that the leaders know who the poor performers are, but they just don't have "the guts to step to the plate and do something about it." In either case, the credibility of the stories about key values and characteristics throughout the organization is severely damaged. The credibility of the leaders' personal beliefs may remain intact, but at the organizationwide level, it appears not to make much difference.

An example of this is an organization that was making a serious attempt to examine and change its internal culture. An intensive employee attitude survey was conducted as a part of their efforts. In the results they received, they were quick to notice that two responses were directly contradictory. In response to a question about standards and expected quality of work, the employees indicated that the organization had extremely high expectations, especially in the area of customer service. On the other hand, there was a question about whether the organization tolerated poor performance. In this case, the employees gave one of the highest and most consistent responses—that the organization regularly tolerated poor performance and did nothing about it. A common opinion of the leadership in that organization was that they were well-meaning, committed people, who were ineffective at getting the organization to follow in their footsteps.

There is a tough side to values-driven leadership. Within defined parameters, people in the organization must buy in to the values, standards, and direction of the company or they should not be allowed to stay in that organization. There is plenty of room for dissent and ongoing argument about whether the values, standards, or direction should change, particularly when it is your high performers who are dissenting. But to tolerate mediocre or poor performance on a widespread basis is disastrous to the mission of the organization. Employees cannot be duped on this one. They know in painstaking detail who is performing up to standard and who is not. And they know how the leadership is handling these situations.

In the organization that had conducted the employee attitude survey, I was asked to do an assessment of communication issues in one department.

One of the comments made consistently by every frontline employee in the department was that there was one person who was not pulling his weight. The others were having to pick up on his work and do it for him. They gave example after example of this problem. The department carried a very heavy workload on a regular basis, so from the point of view of these frontline employees they were being asked to carry this workload with one less employee than was allocated for the department.

Several of the best performers in the department indicated that they were considering quitting if the situation did not change soon. I gave the leaders of the department who had asked me to do the assessment my findings in a written report. When I handed it to them and sat down to go over it with them, they were "shocked" when we got to the part about the opinions about that one employee. I assumed from their reaction that they were unaware of the problem. They responded, "No, we know about the problem, it is just a shock to see it written down in black and white." When I pushed them on the issue and asked if they agreed that the employee's performance was a problem, they indicated that they did. When I continued to ask why it was allowed to continue, they said that one of the other vice presidents was really the one who needed to take action and he did not seem to be willing to do so. Later, when I asked him about the problem, he ignored my question and changed the subject.

> *If leaders tolerate poor performance, the credibility of values embedded in their stories is damaged.*

## Listening to the "Yes, Buts . . ." in Your Organization

I repeatedly tell people in organizations that one of my favorite expressions in the English language is the phrase "Yes, but . . ." I explain that, in my experience, some of the most insightful and useful comments to the organization often follow that phrase. If you create an environment where people are afraid or not allowed to use that phrase, you limit dramatically the amount of useful information that you will hear coming out of the organization. One of the key pieces of useful information that you will lose access to is an ongoing reading of the credibility of the stories that you tell as a leader. If employees at all levels are allowed to tell you their "Yes, buts . . . ," they will keep you posted when they see inconsistencies in the behaviors in the organization and the stories you tell. In other words, they will tell you when your words sound like corporate propaganda instead of inspiring, sacred bundle stories.

The problem is that you have to convince them that the risk of telling you, or your representatives, is not too high. People are not fools when it comes to pointless risk taking. They have to know they will not be punished, and they have to see that their comments make a difference at least some of the time. One company had a term for this sort of communication. They called these "Yes, but . . ." comments *CSGs*. This was an abbreviation for Career Shortening Gestures. The only perceived effect of making these comments was to shorten, or at least damage, one's career in the organization. Besides, speaking up never seemed to change anything anyway, so why bother?

The bottom line about the difference between inspiring storytelling and corporate propaganda may well have nothing at all to do with the storytelling itself. The most important element may be your capacity to listen. Listen . . . intensely, aggressively, and with an intent to respond and act on what you hear. You will not always agree with what you hear or respond in exactly the way that employees are requesting, but you can always respond and act. Storytelling is either a two-way street in organizations or it is an empty gesture that probably does more harm than good.

# PART 3
# Connecting the Individual and the Organization

# 8

# What Is Your Autobiography of Stories?

Storytelling is fundamental to the human search for meaning, whether we tell tales of the creation of the earth or of our early choices.[1]

**A Grandfather Sacred Bundle Story.** My autobiography has many "heroes," and one of them was my paternal grandfather. By the time I knew him, he was a crotchety old man who was not known for spending a great amount of time with any of the grandchildren. When we got on his nerves, he would turn off his hearing aids and act like we weren't there. Occasionally, he could be persuaded to play Chinese checkers with me, but it was always clear that he would never "let" me win. He was willing to coach me and explain how to improve at the game, but I knew that I would only win based on my real skill.

One night when I was sixteen years old and staying at my grandparents' house because my parents were out of town, my grandfather told me a story that was to carry me through some hard times in my life twenty years later. We were sitting on his front porch in rocking chairs and, for some reason, he started talking about when he was young and had just started his business. He was a Swiss Mennonite who had left the farm with an eighth-grade education and not much money. He started his own business, a milk processing plant.

He had been in business several years and had been doing fairly well, when he made a disastrous decision by taking a risk in purchasing a large shipment of milk. He bought too high and the price dropped out from under him right after his purchase. He said to me, "I was sitting in my office when I got word about the price drop, and I knew that I had bankrupted myself." And then he said something that I found very difficult to imagine from this old man. He said, "I put my head down on my desk and cried." I sat silently in my rocking chair staring at him, this man that I knew only as a successful, powerful businessman. Then he turned, looked at me and said, "When I finished crying, I got up and started all over again."

Twenty years later, I was the owner of a small business that I had started myself and loved beyond all logic. I had hit a point in my business where, because of my own marketing mistakes, my business had tanked and there was the very real possibility that it might not survive this self-imposed downturn. I have never been more terrified or disappointed in myself than I was at that point. I remember each morning dragging into work, sitting at my desk, and feeling waves of nausea as I tried to face the day. I was sure that I couldn't do what it would take to rebuild the business. Then I would remember my grandfather and could hear him say "When I finished crying, I got up and started all over again." And I would start to work. Within an hour or two, my enthusiasm for the work would kick in and the fears would fade for the day. By the end of that calendar year, I had regained all my losses and finished with a record-breaking year.

## Bringing Your Personal Stories to Work with You

The stories of your own life are a personal treasure. They are your personal sacred bundle. Those sacred bundle stories represent the best of who you are, as well as the wisdom that you have accumulated over the years of your life. Many of the stories in your autobiographical sacred bundle have meaning that can be brought into the work setting. Those stories can be applied to the work setting, just as they can in your personal life. Storytelling is one place where the distinction between a person's personal life and professional life blurs. Or at least this distinction is blurred.

One of the messages that most people have heard at some point in their working history is to leave their personal lives at the door when they arrive at work. There is usually an unspoken assumption that it is better for people to keep their personal lives separate from their work lives. This message tells employees at all levels in the organization to try not to let their personal lives interfere with their work. If that is impossible, then use the company's Employee Assistance Program (EAP) to get confidential help, but still try to keep your problems out of the work setting.

The use of the term *professional behavior* is often defined as behavior that is different from your personal behavior. Professional behavior is more detached and rational than might be necessary in a personal setting. I hear almost weekly in my work the advice given to one person by another: "Don't take it personally." Over the years I have come to the conclusion that this is one of the most absurd statements of modern organizational life. If all the events, relationships, and communication that a person experiences at work are not personal, then what is? Life is personal and work is a part of life. In fact, a case can easily be made that if an individual does not take their work personally, that person is living in a numb, passionless state of mind that could never produce excellent performance in any arena.

To be fair, often when someone is accused of taking things at work too personally, what is being described is a situation where the person is carrying grudges for too long and letting these angry feeling interfere with the quality of work for everyone in the work unit. That is a reasonable concern. What is questionable is whether the advice "Don't take things so personally" is really the best solution. Helping people learn how to "forgive, forget, and move on" might be a more appropriate strategy.

One of the problems with this "keep the personal out of work" message that so many people have heard throughout their work lives is that the organization limits its access to the personal heritages of the people who work in that organization. People learn to edit out the stories or references to their personal experiences where they learned many of their values and beliefs. When you lose access to people's personal stories, you lose portions of their wisdom, passion, and even heroism.

A classic example of this kind of loss was told to me by a CEO of an organization who had just given a speech to a large audience of managers. He was trying to inspire them to get revved up and go out and fight for what they believed in through lobbying efforts with the legislature. They were up against powerful odds, but his point was that they needed to fight on anyway. Never give up or give in. This CEO is strongly committed to his organization and the industry in general and gave what was, I am sure, an excellent speech. A few hours later, he and I were discussing the power of personal stories when they are tied to organization issues.

Our point was that these stories add to any discussion of work issues by making the point more clearly and passionately than a dry, factual explanation ever could. We agreed that sometimes a personal story is even more effective than a work story, because it seems to touch the listeners at a personal level. He stopped, thought for a minute and laughed. He then went on to tell me that he just realized that during his entire speech earlier that morning, he had been thinking of a story about his mother, but he had not told it to the group.

The story that he was remembering was about a day when he was in junior high and was walking home from school. Just as he was nearing his house, the neighborhood bully walked up to him and demanded his cap.

The bully was much bigger and stronger than him and he knew if he refused, the kid would "beat him to a pulp." So he gave him the hat. A few minutes later when he walked in the front door of the house, his mother was standing there and said to him, "What was that I just saw from the window?" She went on to inform him that if he started backing off from bullies that way now, he'd be doing it for the rest of his life.

A few days later, he was on his way home after school and again the bully approached him and demanded some other valuable article from him. This time he said no, fought for all he was worth, and sure enough he got beaten to a pulp! But the bully never bothered him again. He learned something that day that he had never forgotten. Anyone who knew him thirty years later could easily see that he would take on a fight for what he believed in even if the odds of winning were not impressive. And, by the way, he has an incredible track record for winning against all odds. In fact, he has such a reputation for this that he confided once that one of his biggest worries is that everyone now expects him to pull off these improbable victories year after year. Then he just laughed and shrugged his shoulders.

It was obvious that his story could have been used in his speech. He acknowledged that it probably would have added to the impact of his message if he had told the story. It just never occurred to him to tell it.

## What Are the Stories in Your Personal Sacred Bundle?

In a book called *Your Mythic Journey, Finding Meaning in Your Life Through Writing and Storytelling,* author Sam Keen recommends that a person write a personal autobiography.[2] In your autobiography you can identify the key stories and people from your past. Who are the mythological characters from your life who taught you your views about life and work, as well as your views about yourself? According to Keen, once you identify the myths that you carry with you, as an adult you can decide whether to say "yes" or "no" to these stories and their meaning in your life (Keen, Moyers' interview). In other words, you can decide whether you want to leave them in your sacred bundle that you carry into the future or take them out and leave them behind because they are no longer useful to you.

Retelling or reshaping the historical stories and myths that affect your life is a gradual process, but it can be done. Even though cultures and individual personalities are very stable entities and do not change easily or quickly, all one has to do is look at history to know that they do change. People add new stories and myths to their sacred bundles all the time and will continue to do so until they die. The question is, what do you want new myths to be?

The following questions will help you identify some of the contents of your sacred bundle:[3]

- What are 10 scenes from your past which were important pivotal events for you? Describe these scenes in detail, including the circumstances and characters that were present.

- How has your view of these scenes changed over the years? How do these scenes still affect you in your present life?

- Make an outline of your autobiography with chapter titles and section headings within each chapter. What would be the title of your autobiography?

- Draw a "life map."[4] This can be a diagram, chart, or time line. Plot on the drawing your current position in the life map. Where are you going and where have you come from?

- When you look over your 10 scenes, outline of the autobiography, or the life map, what are the phrases or themes that jump out at you as the key messages that you have learned to date in your lifetime?

- Which of these messages do you want to keep in your sacred bundle in the future? Which ones do you want to take out and leave behind?

- What are some new stories and myths that you can create in your life to add to or change some of the items in your sacred bundle?

## How Do Your Personal Stories Relate to Your Work?

When you think of the key stories from your past and the key people who are a part of these stories, it is likely that many of these affect how you work. They affect your view of work, how important it is to you, how you define success, how you define your limits, where you feel enthusiasm and commitment in your work. Peter Drucker is famous for asking client companies the deceptively simple question, "What line of business are you in?" The answer to that question will determine the vision, the scope, the thinking of people in the company and their ability to pick up on new trends and ideas and develop them for their own organization. For an individual, a similar question might be, "What is the purpose of your work?"

The answer to that question is not necessarily limited to the job description that accompanies any particular position. The answer is broader than that. What are the three or four key things that you want to accomplish as a working person? Or what do you want to be remembered for in your professional life? Which stories from your past represent or symbolize these key characteristics the best? They may be about your grandparents, parents, teachers, ministers, friends, or your children. Who taught you the meaning of work and what are the stories that you can tell about those people and events from your past? There is no doubt that there is a collection of key stories in your autobiography. The only question is whether you have consciously identified what is in that collection. If you have not identified these stories, it is unlikely that you will be able to think of them and tell them at the appropriate moments at work.

It is difficult to find personal stories in the literature on business management and leadership. There are many stories to be found, but most of them are work-specific stories and make no reference to people's past or their personal lives. We have all learned the message "Leave your personal life at the door." Consider the questionable wisdom of this statement carefully. Maybe it is worth at least the modest revision to say "Bring four or five of the 'best' stories from your past to work with you and use them to teach, inspire, and comfort each other in the workplace."

## Examples of Personal Sacred Bundle Stories

**A Family Story.**   One example is a CEO who tells an unusual number of personal stories about his family. One of the most dramatic is a story about the time years ago when he saved his son, who was on the brink of crib death. The baby was taking an afternoon nap. The father was out in the yard and just happened to come back in the house at a crucial moment to check on him. His son was lying in his crib with his skin turning a deadly blue. The CEO resuscitated him and rushed him to a hospital. The baby was on a respirator for a long period, but eventually recovered, developing nearly normal levels of functioning.

This CEO is well known for placing a very high priority on family life. He is unusually understanding of family demands on employees' and managers' time. He remembers detailed events and stories that other people have told him about their families and encourages people to talk with him about that part of their lives. He brings his two sons to work with him frequently so they can see what he does and where he does it. This characteristic is one of his most defining traits for the people who know and work with him.

**Family Sacred Bundle Story as Advertising.**   One family's sacred bundle story ended up being used by a company in an unusual way. They made a television advertisement out of it. It is a very short story made to fit within a 30-second time slot for a commercial, and yet it still carries enough impact to convey a message that is clear and dramatic. Following is the copy from that advertisement. As the television viewers hear these words, they see a scene of a professional woman in a white uniform working with patients in a hospital setting. It is obvious that this scene is taking place 30 or 40 years ago.

> She was a physical therapist working with car accident victims in a hospital in Sweden 40 years ago, yet Margit Engelau continues to save lives the world over. The reason? She instilled her horror of accidents in her husband who happened to run a car company called Volvo. You may never have heard of Margit Engelau, but maybe you've seen the monument they built to her.

At that point a picture of a new Volvo sedan appears and the commercial ends. This is a clear example of tying together the personal and the organizational heritage.

**The Hometown Boy Myth.**   During Ross Perot's attempt at a political life, he did a masterful job of creating a set of personal sacred bundle stories that have been used to build his public image as a down-to-earth, get-things-done type of person. Much of the folklore about Ross Perot involves his small-town Texas upbringing and the characteristics that he carried with him from that background into his professional life. There is a great deal of controversy about which parts of his childhood stories are true and which are exaggerated. For example, there is his famous newspaper route that he started, opening up new territories in the poorer parts of town that were considered dangerous at the time.

This story is used to demonstrate his ingenuity and willingness to go into risky situations. He claims that he rode on horseback through some of the dangerous sections of town. Others claim that he never rode on horseback, but instead used his bicycle.[5] Political environments may make these detailed distinctions important. But from a storytelling point of view, the factual accuracy of every last detail of a story is irrelevant. In fact, stories that become larger than life and take on mythic proportions almost always contain exaggerations. The purpose of a mythic story is to send a message or to highlight an important characteristic or value. They are repeated over and over during many years, and somewhere along the way they are usually exaggerated to make the point even more clearly than the original events.

Many of the stories these days about Ross Perot are mythic stories. The basic characteristic or message is true, but the facts and details may be exaggerated. Who knows? It does not matter. What matters is the message. Now, to be fair, it may have mattered whether Ross Perot is telling the truth or not, when he was under serious consideration as a political candidate. We want to know if he lies or not. But as a personal sacred bundle story that captures an important characteristic about his personality and his life, detailed factual accuracy is not very important. The *message* is what must be true for the sacred bundle story to be meaningful.

**Career Success Story.**   Former Beatle John Lennon was one of the most successful and influential songwriters of the 1960s and 1970s. Lennon was raised by one of his aunts. After his success, fame, and wealth was a long-established fact, he gave his aunt a gold plaque, and it was engraved with the words she had repeated over and over again to him as he was growing up: "You'll never make a living playing that guitar."[6]

**Another Grandfather Story.**   Some of the stories that people have in their sacred bundle are more lighthearted or funny, but they still carry a clear message about an important characteristic of the person who is doing the telling. One example of this type of lighthearted story is told repeatedly in my family and is about a well-known characteristic of my grandfather that has been passed on to many of us in the family.

The story is about his trips to visit the Grand Canyon. He first went there back in the 1930s with my grandmother. When they arrived, it was foggy and you couldn't see the view at all. My grandfather was not known for his patience, and the stories vary on how long he waited for the fog to lift. Some versions claim he waited till the next morning, but others say he only lasted a few hours. At any rate, the fog did not clear and he lost patience. He was leaving. He and my grandmother got back on the train and proceeded on to California to continue their trip. From that day on, whenever he got on the subject, my grandfather would tell anyone within earshot that the Grand Canyon was "an overrated tourist trap." He had been there, and he had seen it himself!

We tried to show him pictures, but he just waved them aside and explained that those pictures were a part of the trap. "They show you those pictures, and then it doesn't look like that when you get there." We all gave up. Many years later, after my grandmother had died and he had remarried, my stepgrandmother was able to persuade him to go back again for another visit to the Grand Canyon on a trip west. This time the weather was clear and the views were spectacular. He loved beautiful scenery, so he was very impressed. After taking in the views for some time, my grandfather walked into the gift shop to buy my parents a postcard. Keep in mind that what he wrote on this card was not a joke, because my grandfather had no sense of humor that anyone ever discovered. He wrote these words: "Dear Nancy and Paul, The Grand Canyon has changed a lot. Love Amos."

This story is told so often in my family that it even has a name. It is called the "Grand Canyon Story." If you say those words to anyone in the family, they know exactly to whom and what you are referring, and we all laugh.

I often tell people who are going to be working with me that they should know this story out of self-defense. It forewarns them that one of my family traits can make working with me an exciting adventure or a total pain in the neck, depending on the circumstances. This trait is an instinctive belief in myself, my points of view, and unabashed willingness to tell you my point of view whether you ask for it or not. If you work with me, you work with a person who carries the family heritage of what is probably a pathological level of belief in oneself. A number of times when I have adamantly expressed an eccentric and determined opinion about some overly ambitious task we have taken on, a colleague has groaned, laughed, and said to me, "The Grand Canyon has changed a lot . . . right?"

# 9

# Who Are the Heroes in Your Organization?

Telling the stories about an individual feat or team accomplishment is a connector between the individuals and the organization as a whole. These stories take abstract concepts such as values or cultural characteristics and turn them into concrete events that are easy to understand and people who are memorable. The stories are particularly important if they highlight a valued organizational characteristic such as innovation, customer service, or continuous improvement accomplishments. Art Fry's story about inventing the Post-It Note at 3M is a classic example of a hero story that has become a part of the larger national folklore on innovation inside large organizations.

## An Organizational Hero Story

I heard Fry tell his story at a conference on innovation a few years ago, and he started by talking about singing in the choir at church and being annoyed by the way the slips of paper he used to mark the hymns kept falling out of his book. He said that he sat there thinking about how it would be helpful to have something to use for these markers that would not fall out, but would also not tear the page when you pulled them off. At that moment, he remembered some glue that had been sent around for the engineers to examine at work.

There is a tradition at 3M of passing around failures among its design engineers, in case any of the information learned from that particular failure might be useful on another project. The glue Fry remembered had not been sticky enough for its intended use. The connection Fry made between the slips of paper in his hymnal and the failed glue was the beginning of the creation of the now-famous Post-It Notes. He went on to tell many stories about the process he went through to get from the original idea to the completed design. He ran into many barriers. Marketing did not like the notes because in their market research, no one indicated that they wanted or would use little notes that did not stick very well to anything.

Manufacturing frustrated him because they told him it would take months to have the production equipment ready for operation. He told about going home that night and making a prototype of the production equipment that night in his basement. He also tells about people passing contraband materials to him over cubicle walls, because he was having a hard time getting supplies to work on a project that no one in the company was enthusiastic about except him.

The key elements to this particular story are illustrated by the setting in which I heard it told. Art Fry was speaking to a group of CEOs there to learn how to lead their organizations toward a more innovative corporate culture. Fry was explaining to them that it was not a neat, orderly process to live with high levels of innovation in your organization. It is also significant that one of the senior vice presidents from 3M was sitting in the audience listening to Fry tell about swiping things from the supply room and other undercover behaviors.

Later when the senior vice president got up to speak, he told the group of CEOs that if they wanted innovation, they had better be prepared for lots of headaches. He said that many times when he was driving home from work at the end of a day with a splitting headache, it was one of those blasted innovators at work that had given it to him. His point was that one of the key elements of the 3M culture that allowed it to be one of the most innovative companies in the world was its tolerance for the constant annoyances of living around innovators.

The reason that the setting for this story is so important is because it illustrates that the Art Fry story is one that is endorsed by the organization. The characteristics emphasized in this story are traits that represent the lifeblood of 3M as a company. This was not a story about "how I got back at the company." Fry's behavior in his stories was demanding, difficult, and even sneaky at times, but the senior vice president sat there listening to his stories and laughing with the rest of the audience. "Laughing all the way to the bank" is probably an old expression that would fit nicely here. The Post-It Notes became one of the most successful products 3M has ever produced.

## The Organizational "Antihero" Story

Contrast this to some of the "hero" stories which send the message that the organization is incompetent or overrun with silly rules, the leaders are fools, and "I found a way to get around them." There is a joke going around corporations these days that is a typical example of this type of story. It is about a person who changes divisions in a company. He files his first expense report in the new division following the old division's guidelines. He has his expense report kicked back to him by the vice president of the new division because he included the purchase of a Stetson hat on his recent trip to Texas. The vice president informed him that this was not considered a legitimate expense in this division and told him to get it off his expense report. A few days later the vice president found the revised expense report back on his desk with a note attached: "I have revised my expense report per your instructions and removed the Stetson. The cost of the hat is still in there . . . see if you can find it."

As anyone who has ever filled out an expense report can tell you about stories like the preceding, they are entertaining and certainly have some truth in them. But it is questionable if these are positive stories for the organization as a whole. Usually when these types of hero stories are common in an organization, it is an indication that the systems in the organization do not work well and nothing is being done to improve them. At least, nothing is being done that the employees who tell these stories can see. Under these circumstances, people will use their individual and collective IQ to get around the systems. Correcting this problem is at the heart of the continuous improvement efforts that are being started in many North American companies.

Total quality management or continuous improvement is focused on constantly improving the systems, and using employee involvement to accomplish this goal. It remains to be seen at this point how successful organizations will be at implementing this approach. But without dramatically improved systems, in most organizations many of the hero stories will actually be focused on a form of "antihero." These are the people who beat the system either for their own personal benefit or to protect their department's turf. If, instead, they are given an opportunity to tell stories about how they used the systems in the organization to accomplish impressive feats individually or in teams, then those stories are likely to become a part of the ever-expanding sacred bundle.

## The Characteristics of a Hero

The concept of the "hero" has been present in cultures for thousands of years. There are some common definitions of what makes a hero in all cultures. Joseph Campbell, author of the book *Hero of a Thousand Faces,* is widely considered to be the world's leading authority on cultural myths, particularly hero myths. He defines the hero as a person who "takes off on a series of adventures beyond the ordinary, either to recover what has been lost or to discover some life-giving elixir."[1]

The purpose of the hero adventure must have some "moral objective" that does not involve personal gain.[2] The objectives usually involve either saving a people or supporting an idea.[3] The key to the hero story, according to Campbell, is that the hero is not a spectator sitting on the sidelines watching other people's achievements, but an active participant in making events happen.[4]

One of the defining characteristics of a hero story is personal sacrifice. In fact, in many hero stories, the hero is killed. Martin Luther King, Jr. is an example of a twentieth-century hero in the United States. He was killed, but his accomplishments lived on beyond the end of his life. The biblical story of Christ is another example of a hero story about a person who was killed, but whose ideas lived on. History is filled with hero stories. The adventure and the accomplishments define the hero, not the comfort of that person's life or even survival.

It may come as no surprise, based on the descriptions of life-threatening perils that heroes endure, that many people end up heroes by accident.[5] Purposely intending to set out on a hero's adventure is *not* one of the definitions of a hero story. Campbell uses the example of young men who are drafted into the military and end up becoming war heroes. Throughout history you find many stories of heroes who would have preferred to stay home and live their lives comfortably, but an idea or the needs of the people around them drew them into their adventures. The hero almost always starts out as a normal, everyday person. It is the adventure that transforms the person into a hero. Campbell's advice to would-be heroes is "to take it all *as if* it had been of your intention."[6]

In Charles Garfield's book, *Peak Performers: The New Heroes of American Business,* he tells of this type of hero in a story about his father, Ed Garfield, who was a sales engineer for a company that sold soldering materials.[7] This is a classic story of a person being faced with unexpected and unwelcome circumstances and responding *intentionally* in a way that "saved the day." Back in the 1950s, a customer placed a large order with his father's company. This customer was a cosmetics manufacturer who had just developed one of the first pressurized shaving-foam dispensers. Ed Garfield's company produced the solder that would be used to attach the valves to the cans of foam. Orders were pouring in. Then, suddenly, all orders stopped. Garfield's company got a furious call from the cosmetics company saying that the solder was no good and to send someone down to check what was happening. As anyone who has ever been put in that position can tell you, being sent into an angry customer situation like this is one of the most dreaded events in organizational life.

Ed Garfield was selected for the trip. When he arrived, he was greeted with the news that the cosmetics company had shipped thousands of cans of men's shaving cream to stores all over the country and were now getting calls that the cans were "erupting on the shelves." Shaving cream was spraying all over the other merchandise on the shelves as well as on any clerk or customer who happened to be standing nearby. Needless to say, the people at the cosmetics company were not happy. When Garfield walked into the conference room, he was almost physically attacked by seven mechanical engineers and top management. Accusations and threats of lawsuits were flying. Garfield described it as a war zone atmosphere. Depending on Ed Garfield's response at this moment, the situation could deteriorate into permanent damage that would hurt the soldering company's reputation throughout the industry.

Instead of flaring back at the angry, abusive group, Ed Garfield calmly started asking questions. After a short time, he discovered that cosmetics company was using the wrong type of solder to hold a vertical valve. They had been in a hurry to manufacture the new product and had rushed through the design phase, ignoring the consultation that Garfield's company had offered. Garfield knew how to fix the can, but it would involve recalling thousands of cans from the stores and adding a flange. He knew this suggestion would trigger a new round of tempers and yelling. But he calmly suggested it anyway. When the yelling started, he did not argue. He suggested they think it over, and then they could talk again. A few weeks later, the cosmetic company called and was ready to implement the suggestion with his help.

As Garfield points out, this was a crisis that in many companies would have ended up taking a great deal of senior management time and energy to resolve. His father was not in top management. He was a technical adviser. Yet, when he was faced with the customer's angry top management, "he took responsibility for the outcome and accomplished as much as anyone would have expected of the highest-ranking company leader."[8]

## Teams Can Be Heroes, Too

As many companies move into a focus on total quality management philosophies and use of interdisciplinary teams to get the work done more effectively, the definition of the hero as the rugged individual needs some rethinking. If the basic definition of a hero story is one that is about an adventure where something important or noble is accomplished, then there is no reason that a *team* of people might not be the main character of the story.

An impressive example of a team hero story was told in an article written for *Fortune* magazine about some employees at a General Mills cereal plant in Lodi, California. Over a picture of seven smiling people standing around a huge shipping box of corn flakes are the following words:

> If Harvard awarded MBAs to factory workers for their expertise, this team at General Mills would graduate with honors. They do just about everything middle managers do and do it well.[9]

This team was self-managed and did all its own ordering, scheduling, and other tasks that are normally left up to managers to do. Since the team has been working together, productivity had increased 40 percent.

Rubbermaid is another of many examples of hero teams in action. They created a cross-functional team composed of engineers, designers, and marketers to design a new device called an "auto office," a portable device that straps onto a car seat and contains office supplies and a writing surface. The team focused on going into the field and asking customers what features they wanted. Each professional on the team approached the research from a different point of view, but they managed to blend those perspectives to produce a product that was running 50 percent above projected sales.

If North American business and industry continue to move in the direction of increasing the use of continuous improvement and employee participation, team hero stories could eventually become the norm in organizations. One caution when telling a team hero story: when you lose the focus on a single individual, it is easy to lose the humor or drama that gives a story impact. When telling a team story, it is important that it still have the quality of an anecdote and not just the straight reporting of the facts. Remember, the key ingredients of a well-told story are the same whether the story is about an individual or a team. The following ingredients still need to be included for the story to be entertaining and compelling in a way that makes anyone want to retell the story:

| | |
|---|---|
| *Plot* | Have one central plot and do not confuse the listeners with lots of side plots. |
| *Characters* | The characters in the story need to be interesting and fun. Even though the story is about a team, there still needs to be "personality" in the story. Either the team can be described as having its own personality or the individual members can be described in the story. |
| *Action* | Lots of it. Build in suspense, if possible. |
| *Timing* | Keep it short. One to seven minutes is the typical range for a story. |

*Fluency*              If this is a story you will be telling more than once, practice
                       telling it until you have the sequence and content down
                       pat. When Charles Garfield tells his story about his father
                       at the soldering company, you can be sure this is not his
                       first telling. Important stories are worth practicing until
                       you are a skillful teller of the tale.

## Who Are the Heroes in Your Organization?

There are individuals and possibly teams of people in your organization
who have been the key characters in hero stories. Many times the founders
will have become the legendary heroes in the stories about the founding of
the organization. But there are new hero stories being created all the time
in companies. Any time there is a crisis, an exceptional opportunity, or a
major change, there is the possibility of hero stories emerging from those
events.

Think about the following questions and see if you can identify some of
the hero stories from your organization:

- Go back to the sacred bundle stories that you thought of for your organization in Chapter 5 and see how many of them qualify as hero stories. If
  the story is about an "adventure" that led to a accomplishment of something important or noble, then it is probably a hero story. This is especially true if the adventure involved sacrifice and great effort on the part
  of the hero in the story.

- Who are the people that you admire most in the organization? Why do
  you admire them? What have they done or accomplished that has earned
  your admiration? People, in general, admire heroes, so it is highly likely
  that the people you admire are heroes in some part of their work or personal lives.

- What are the major crises or turning points in your organization during
  your tenure there? Who has stepped forward at those moments to "save
  the day"? What did they do to rescue the situation?

- Who are the heroes that are not in the limelight? There is a tendency to
  think of the CEO or the founder of the company when asked to think of
  the organization's heroes. There are many heroes in organizations at all
  levels. If the only heroes an organization has are at the senior management level, that company is in serious trouble. The people closer to the
  front lines are usually closer to the customers, and their heroics can make
  or break the reputation of the company.

- How do you take care of your heroes in your organization? Do you celebrate them or shoot them? Many cultures have a tendency to shoot their heroes and then deify them after they are dead. There is a high tolerance for irritating innovators at 3M and a tendency not to shoot them. What could your organization do to at least tolerate your heroes?

- How frequently are your hero stories told? Who tells these stories? To whom are they told? Are there traditional times and settings where these stories are retold for newcomers to hear and for the veterans to be reminded?

- When have you been a hero in your organization? When have you been faced with an "adventure" and managed to accomplish something that mattered?

- As you think about your answers to some of these questions, keep in mind these words of Joseph Campbell:

  The adventure of the hero is the adventure of being alive. The big question is whether you are going to be able to say a hearty "yes" to your adventure.[10]

# 10
# Storytelling and the New Employee

One collection of stories that employees remember for as long as they work for the organization is the set of stories about events surrounding their hiring and start-up phase with the company. These events may be positive or negative in the minds of the employees and that tone will affect their attitudes toward the organization from the very first day on the job. A classic example of a positive story that has been repeated many times by an employee of Wal-Mart involves a truck driver named Bob Clark.[1] Clark started working for Wal-Mart in 1972 when they had only sixteen tractor trucks on the road. During the first month of work, Clark attended a drivers' safety meeting and Sam Walton was there, as usual.

Bob Clark remembers that day well. Walton got up to talk and, according to Clark, he said, "If you'll just stay with me for 20 years, I guarantee you'll have $100,000 in profit sharing." Clark says that he thought to himself, "Big deal. Bob Clark never will see that kind of money in his life." Twenty years have now passed and Clark says that the last time he checked he had $707,000 in profit sharing, and sees no reason why it won't go up again. He goes on to explain that he has bought and sold stock in the company and used it to build a house and buy lots of other things as well.

It is not hard to guess how this story that represents a part of this man's history with the company affects his attitude about working at Wal-Mart. He says, "When folks ask me how I like working for Wal-Mart, I tell them I drove for another big company for 13 years—one they have all heard of—and left with $700. Then I tell them about my profit sharing and ask them, 'How do you think I feel about Wal-Mart?'" If an organization wants to "manage" the morale and attitudes of its employees, one of the most important aspects of work to orchestrate very carefully is their initial entry into the organization.

What happens in the hiring process and during the first few weeks of work will form the foundation for their opinions and feelings about that organization for years to come. And those employees will go on to repeat their start-up stories many times. They will be the primary "trainers" of the new employees of the future and will pass on their attitudes about whether or not this organization is a good place to work.

## Storytelling as Training . . . Who and What Do They Believe?

Picture this situation. A new employee arrives at an organization for the first day of work. This person attends a formal orientation program that is elaborate, detailed, and well run. The employee hears from the president, learns about the history of the organization, policies and procedures are reviewed, and the culture of the company is described to the new employees. The next day, this new person goes to the work area and begins the new job. Later that day, two of the veterans from the department take this new employee out to lunch and spend the entire time telling stories about the organization. These stories can be put under the heading "Now, we'll tell you how it *really* is around here!"

If the informal stories that the new employee hears from the veterans do not match the more formal information that was given out at the orientation program, which set of information do you think that the employee is likely to remember and believe? I have asked hundreds of people that question and have never found anyone who would vote for the orientation information winning out over the informal stories. As described at the beginning of this book, stories are much more powerful communicators than any other form of information dissemination. The situation described previously with the new employee is a familiar scenario in many organizations.

Often the information that companies choose to present in an orientation environment is an idealized version of the way the company operates. It is important, of course, to emphasize the positive and to be clear with new employees about the direction, goals, and progress of the organization. It is, however, a setup for trouble when a formal orientation process gives the new employee an unbalanced, unrealistic view of the organization. In the first place, very few new employees are naive enough to believe that they are hearing the whole story, so they will be skeptical listeners.

The main truth they are learning is that this organization only wants to hear good things about itself. It also sets up the aforementioned situation, where the other employees in the departments will fill in the new employee on the "real story" in a way that almost totally cancels out the message from the more formal setting. If those veteran employees are cynical or angry with the organization, the new employee will be hit with a very negative view of the company, and it is being delivered in the most powerful communication medium. As social scientists would describe it, the new employee is being enculturated into the new environment through the use of stories. They are being given a picture of the organization that includes information about the values, rules of behavior, relationships, enemies, etc. And, in many cases in organizations, people are being "oriented" to a very negative picture of their new workplace.

## Improving the Orientation Process

A number of organizations are working on this problem by revamping their entire orientation process to include a long series of events over a one-to-two-year period of time. These events are carefully planned and managed so that the new employees' experiences with the company reflect the goals and values that the organization wants to encourage and protect. One of the key elements of many of these new approaches that seems to help close the gap between formal information and storytelling is the assignment of a buddy to the new person.

The buddy is a person who has been selected from the department to be the informal partner of the new person. The buddy is *supposed* to tell organization stories. The buddies are employees who will represent the organization in a positive way to the new employee, but it is never intended that these buddies will tell only the idealized version of life in the organization. The buddy is supposed to help the new person learn the ropes—both formally and informally.

Extending the orientation process over a longer period of time also gives the organization more opportunities to present *both* the ideal version of the organization and many of the current realities, both good and bad. There are a number of different events planned into the process that include many opportunities for discussion, not just one-way information dissemination. One organization has set up lunches for the new hires and invites some of the most well-known veterans to come and tell the old stories about the organization. This allows for predictable, planned opportunities for new employees to hear about the heritage of the organization in the words of a variety of employees from different departments and points of view.

No matter what type of orientation or training occurs in an organization, some type of picture of the culture of that organization will always be passed on to new employees. The question is, what is the content of the picture that is being passed on in your company? Some of the most significant and long-lasting learning takes place during the first few days and months on the new job. The picture that is formed in that person's mind at that point will be very difficult to change later.

## What Did They Learn *before* Their First Day of Work?

The second potential danger zone for a new employee's "training" in a new organization occurs *before* the person is hired or arrives at work for the first time. In my experience many, if not most, employees arrive for their first day of work at a new job already insulted and cynical. This is because of how they were treated during the hiring process. The interviewing and selection process is actually a story in itself. The entire series of events of being hired and adjusting to a new job is really a story in progress. It is one of the most important stories that employees will remember for the entire time they work for that organization.

How they are treated during this process is their first set of messages from the company of what to expect in other situations in the future. After years of working in hundreds of organizations in many different industries, I have reached the conclusion that the typical hiring process is often one of the most humiliating experiences that employees are forced to endure by the organizations where they work.

One of the predominant themes of many hiring stories that I have heard is the experience of being "left dangling"—not knowing what is happening next or when (or, even worse, being told what will happen next and when it will occur, and then having it not happen as promised). This is the famous "I will call you next week and let you know where we are on this job" comment from the hiring manager. The next week comes and goes, and there is no phone call. This is a form of lying, although many people prefer not to think of it that way. After two weeks the person interviewed can't stand it any longer and calls to find out what is happening. Three days later the employer finally returns the call. Then comes the famous apology line, "I'm sorry I didn't get back to you sooner, I have been so busy." A variation on that quote is, "I'm sorry I didn't call sooner, but we didn't know anything on the job yet." Usually several rounds of these types of phone calls occur.

What is happening as this story unfolds is that the employers are taking a person when he or she is most vulnerable and powerless, and they are abusing their power. There is a very clear message at this point to the prospective employee about what to expect from this organization—not much. This is not the kind of starting experience that produces enthusiastic, loyal employees.

One might assume that this kind of hiring treatment is confined to lower-level jobs. However, that does not seem to be the case. Many of the stories that I have heard were told to me by people applying for senior-level positions or key sales jobs. It seems to be the notion in some organizations that it is acceptable to be rude and lie to prospective employees. One example that is particularly appalling is that of a man who had applied for a general manager's position in a fast-growing chain of stores.

The employers narrowed the field down to two candidates for the position, and this man was one of them. Throughout the entire process of interviewing, the hiring manager never called to update the man when he said he would. When the applicant would finally call to find out what was happening, he was assured that everything was on track and he was one of the top candidates for the job. They were just so busy, it was taking longer than expected. Then they called him to cancel an interview less than an hour before the scheduled appointment time. He asked calmly why they were canceling. Had they decided to hire someone else? He was assured that the problem was simply timing.

The senior manager who was to meet him was just too busy that day, but would call back the next day and reschedule the appointment. By the following week when no one had called, the storyteller said he was sure something was up. He was angry. He called the company with gritted teeth to get a straight answer once and for all. A receptionist, who was innocent about the whole situation, had the misfortune of answering the call. When she was asked for the manager, her response was, "I'm sorry he can't come to the phone right now. He is training the new general manager."

Later, in response to a scathing letter that the teller of this story sent to the president of the company, the senior manager who had been involved in the hiring fiasco wrote back apologizing for the mix-up and assuring him that there might be another job for him with the company at some point. This man, who would have been highly qualified for a similar position in that company as they opened new stores, now puts that organization in the "I'd rather dig ditches" category of employment. This is a story that he has repeated many times to colleagues, and often finds that they have a similar story to tell about one of their own interviewing and hiring experiences.

Contrast that story to one that left the person enthusiastic and excited about the new job and the company that offered it. This one happened to me, so I know the story well. It was years ago, when I applied for my first job in the for-profit, corporate world. I had decided to try to convince Hospital Corporation of America that I could handle a training job in their financial information systems department. I had never seen a computer and did not know a debit from a credit, but I knew I was a good trainer and could learn anything if they would give me a chance. They called me for an interview shortly after I sent in my application. I was thrilled.

Before the interview, I had to go out and buy an outfit to wear, because I was coming out of jobs in schools and hospitals where I never wore suits and heels. I was very nervous when I arrived at the huge, glass corporate head-quarters, and walked in the wrong entrance—right into the middle of some work unit. Several people looked up and offered to help in a very friendly way. As they pointed me in the right direction, one woman called out as I was walking away, "Great suit!" I laughed and said thanks, knowing that she had no idea how much I meant it.

When I arrived in the department, I was greeted by the man who I would work for if I got the job, and spent over an hour with him. He said he knew that I was coming out of a different professional world. He had worked for a university in the past, so he took time to fill me in on how this place was different from where I had worked before.

When we finished our conversation, he said that he would introduce me to his boss, the assistant vice president. He smiled and warned me that this man was a computer-type person who could be intimidating at times, but was a "peach" of a guy. I went on to have what was one of the strangest job interviews of my entire career. I thought it was a disaster. He didn't seem to understand my language and I certainly did not understand his. I kept try-ing to reexplain myself but didn't seem to be getting anywhere. And he kept bursting into laughter when I had *not* meant to be funny. It was very unnerving. At the end of the interview, he walked me to the elevator and was very polite. He said someone would call within a few days to let me know what was happening on the job. I bit my tongue to keep from saying that I already knew what was happening to me as far as the job was con-cerned. Just to finish off the disastrous day, I discovered that due to my ner-vousness prior to the interview, I had locked the keys in my car. I considered permanently abandoning the car, but decided to call a friend to come bail me out instead.

Two days later the computer whiz vice president called. I could not believe it when he said that he wanted me to come in to talk with him again. I couldn't believe that I was going to get a second chance. I went out and bought a second new suit and showed up for interview number two. I prac-ticed for days how to talk about the job I was applying for in as much busi-ness/computer language as I could handle. Because of this, I was not happy when the first words out of his mouth were, "I want you to forget about that other job. I want to talk with you about a completely different job."

He went on to explain a consulting job that took much greater skill and knowledge than the education job. At that point I was so shocked, I lost all interviewee poise and started to laugh. I reminded him that I had never seen a computer and couldn't even understand the job description for this position. He waved off my comments. No problem, I'd learn fast. Then he took me to meet the person that I would be working for in this job. He spent time with me explaining what would be involved in learning the job and how the department operated. He was very clear about both the positives and negatives of the job. When I left, I told him that I wanted the job, and he agreed that he would think it over and decide if he thought it would work. Two days later he called and offered me the position. And I found out later that they had offered me the job at the same salary they were offering people with accounting and data processing backgrounds.

A few weeks later, when I walked into work on my first day, I thought I was one of the luckiest people in the working world. I was so proud to be working there and was determined to learn that job faster and better than anyone expected. Over the next year, I worked harder and endured more stress than I had ever experienced in my life. There were times when I did not think that I would make it. At those moments, my hiring story kept me going. If they were convinced that I could do the job, then it must be possible. Besides, it was a great place to work. I finally learned the job and was even offered a promotion to manage a team of people in the department. I am convinced to this day that the way I was treated in the hiring process—the politeness, the humor, and, most importantly, the honesty—was a key element in my ability to have survived that first year.

My hiring story was one that I told over and over to people in the company. It was also a story that I remembered later when I was in the position to hire people. I would think about my story each time I was interviewing people. I would remind myself to treat these potential new employees in such a way that they would walk in the door that first day of work feeling the respect and enthusiasm that I had felt several years earlier on my first day of work.

One observation about this hiring story that has always struck me as noteworthy is that the people who treated me so well throughout the process were not professionals trained in psychology, social work, human resources, or any of the "touchy-feely" professions, as they are often called. The people who treated me with respect and courtesy during the hiring process were "bean counters" and computer types. The many hiring horror stories that I have heard over the years do not seem to follow any professional pattern. The significant variable in the story seems to be the individual values of the hiring managers and the department's norms or expected behaviors from its managers.

In the department that hired me, everyone was treated well during the hiring process. All the managers in that department carried out the interviewing process quickly, called back when they said they would, told the truth when they called, and were fair about the salaries they offered. Whether people were hired or not, they were not left hanging. It was quite common in that company for someone to be turned down for one job and then later to be hired in another department for a different type of job. The hiring stories remain and continue to affect people's attitudes about the place they work long after the job interviews are over.

When people enter as new employees, they bring their own stories with them. These stories will eventually be added to the culture of the organization where they are now working. If the organization is small, with only a handful of employees, any single individual can have a significant effect on the content of the storytelling within that workplace. If that individual has significantly different values or characteristics, this may eventually end up changing the content of the organization's sacred bundle. For example, in a company with only ten employees, one new person with a different definition of what constitutes high-quality customer service may end up eventually convincing the other nine people to upgrade or change their behavior or procedures to be more customer-responsive.

In larger companies the impact of single individuals can be seen, but the effect is usually limited to the specific work group or department where the new person works. In a large company, an individual has to be in a leadership position to change a key characteristic of the entire organization. The important point is that one single individual can affect the important, basic elements of an organization's culture. Cultures may change slowly, but they do change.

An example of this is described by Carl Sewell, author of *Customers for Life*, a book about his career with Sewell Village Cadillac in Dallas, the top luxury-car dealership in the country. On the first page of his book, he writes this description of his entry into the company.

> I joined Sewell Village Cadillac full-time in 1967, after I got out of the army. Back then there were only three Cadillac dealers in Dallas, and we were third in sales and profits. That bothered the hell out of me. I wanted to be number one. I didn't know it then, but that decision represented the turning point for our company.[2]

He goes on to describe some of the key values that he brought with him into the company and his drive to build the most successful dealership in Dallas and eventually the best in the country.[3] In this case, the cultural changes were introduced by a new leader into a medium-sized organization. Sewell's ability to tell stories and to become the subject of stories himself was one of his most effective tools for changing the culture. He is a talented enough storyteller that he has ended up writing a book about the dealership which has become very popular in business circles as a story about how to turn a business into "the best" in terms of customer service.

In smaller organizations, something as deceptively simple as a change in the person who acts as receptionist can impact the key characteristics of the organization. This position is never referred to as a "leadership" role, but if that person brings a significant change in politeness, warmth, and efficiency to the job, it will affect the customers who call or walk through the door. And it will also affect the behavior of the other employees of the organization. If that person is exceptionally good at the receptionist job, people will not only change some of their own behaviors, but they probably will start telling some stories about the remarkable job the receptionist is doing. These stories become one small part of the organization's folklore, especially if the receptionist stays with the organization for a long period of time and creates a whole series of stories. Everyone is constantly shaping everyone else's behavior in any work setting.

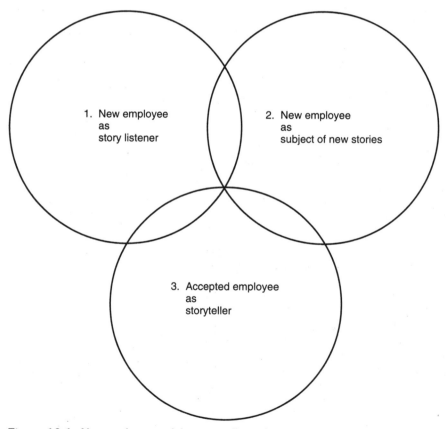

**Figure 10-1.** New employees and their storytelling role.

# Stories That Work and Those That Don't in a New-Hire Situation

There is one storytelling caution that is important for any new person at any level in an organization to keep in mind. The new person can begin to affect the culture of the organization immediately, but not directly, through the tool of storytelling. The way a new person affects the environment is by becoming the subject of stories that other employees tell about that person's behavior as in the aforementioned example of the receptionist. But if that new person tries to use the more direct approach of telling stories about "how we did it at the last place I worked," there will be trouble. No one in the organization wants to hear those stories at that point.

These kinds of stories tend to trigger the response, "If they liked it so much where they were before, why didn't they just stay there!" The reason that direct storytelling about one's past employment experience does not work for a new employee is that this person has not yet been accepted as a full-fledged member of the group. The new employee, even if the person is in a leadership role, is still an outsider. The group has not "initiated" that new person into full membership in the culture. Because of this, the primary role for the new person is to listen and learn about the culture of the organization. Later, once that person has been accepted into the group, a certain amount of stories from past jobs will be listened to and tolerated. But while the person is new, the appropriate role is story listener, not storyteller. If a person does not understand the role of listener when new to an organization, the employee may never be accepted as a full member of the group. This has been true for thousands of years in tribal settings and cultures all over the world. It is still just as true today in organizations. (Figure 10-1 shows the evolution of a newcomer into a fully integrated storyteller.)

# 11

# Storytelling and Relationships inside the Organization

## Folklore as the Internal Cultural Road Map

The folklore of an organization is made up of the stories and myths that have accumulated over the years and which are commonly known to employees. This collection of information gives employees a road map of the culture in the organization and helps them know how to handle situations and relationships they encounter during their day-to-day activities at work. Sam Keen uses the metaphor of computer software to describe the role of myths and stories.[1] The organization itself is the hardware and the collection of folklore stories is the software. According to Keen, it is the program that is run on the hardware that governs the way people see "reality." The stories define the rules of behavior and the goals of the group. If employees are familiar with the stories from the past, this information will answer some of the following questions about relationships in the organization:

- Who are the heroes?
- Who are the villains?
- Who is the enemy?
- Who are my helpers or guides?
- What is our purpose?

- What are my duties?
- What is taboo, and should be avoided?[2]

This "software" or road map is vital information for any employee at any level in an organization to understand. If a person is going to be able to function effectively in any group setting, the person must know the rules of the game or the norms of that group. Otherwise, the employee will be likely to make frequent mistakes—such as inadvertently insulting people, stepping on toes, or even behaving in ways that are interpreted as betrayal by the group. When serious violations of the norms occur, the group usually reacts strongly to the person who has stepped out of line. If the violator is a new employee or the violation is a minor one, the response from the group might be fairly mild.

For example, a number of years ago, before the smoking bans were instituted in many organizations, there was a large company that had developed very clear folklore about where and when smoking was allowed, even though there were no official policies or rules. One of the clearest messages from the stories was that no employee should ever smoke around the president of the company. He was a well-known health and exercise fanatic, and many of the stories about this man were tales of his numerous marathons and other athletic feats. This company was also famous for its track and workout facilities in the headquarters building and for paying employees monetary bonuses for logging in miles for aerobic exercise.

The folklore told an employee that it was perfectly acceptable to be seen taking time out of the middle of a busy workday to run on the company track or to jog through the nearby park. In fact, midday jogging was so prevalent, they finally had to issue a companywide memo asking people to quit coming and going through the formal main entrance of the building in sweaty jogging clothes. At times there seemed to be as many joggers in the lobby as corporate suits, so the memo suggested that joggers use the back door from that point on. There was even a joke around the company about the key role of exercising. The saying was that you could always recognize people who worked for the company because they had pin-striped suits tattooed to their bodies and were carrying gym bags. Smoking in front of the president was one of the fitness taboos in this organization, and any new person learned this very quickly. The word went out whenever he was coming through a department. All cigarettes were extinguished, and the air filters on every smoker's desk were running full tilt.

If a new employee for some reason had not received the word and made the embarrassing mistake of lighting up in front of the president, there would be a few uncomfortable stares in that person's direction, but no one would say a word. As soon as the president walked away, however, the colleagues of the new employee would deliver a quick and dramatic *"Don't* ever do that again" message accompanied by several marathon/health stories to explain the situation.

Think about the information that you just learned about the company described in this story. Without any further explanation, you now know that if you had taken a job in that company, you would have been wise to downplay your smoking or, better yet, to quit. You would want to talk about the sports or exercise that you participated in or keep your mouth shut if you were a couch potato. You also know that pin-striped suits and the conservatism that they symbolize is important in this company. If someone approached you during your first week of work to ask you to play on the company softball team next month when they took on one of their arch-competitors in town, it is not hard to guess what would be the culturally correct answer to give in this company.

By having heard one story about a company that you know nothing else about, you have received a useful lesson in the corporate culture of that organization. In this case, it is a cultural characteristic that might be considered relatively minor. It was possible to succeed in that company even if you were a nonexercising smoker . . . as long as you did not talk about it too much. But even a relatively minor cultural characteristic like this one is an important part of the road map for understanding how to function as a full member of the group in this organization.

Contrast that story to another one that represents an important cultural characteristic that brought severe punishment from the group when violated. This story took place in a financial sales company that is famous for putting high-producing salespeople at the top of the list of corporate heroes. In general, even if the salesperson is seen as something of a "jerk" in other ways, that person will still be held in fairly high esteem if the sales numbers are high enough. In this particular company, however, there were limits on how far the "jerk" behavior was allowed to go. One of the top salespeople in this company was a man who was famous for being arrogant and blunt. He was not particularly well liked, but was respected for his sales success. He pushed his arrogance too far one day, however, and the entire firm reacted. According to the story the employees told, he made a costly mistake on a client's account that was very embarrassing to the firm and to him personally. Instead of accepting the mistake, fixing it, and rolling on, he decided to blame his hourly wage sales assistant for the mistake and demanded that she be fired. She was a particularly popular person in the firm and was considered something of a saint for putting up with him on a regular basis.

According to the story, the management of the firm tried to ignore his demands, hoping it would blow over. But he was relentless and threatened to take his business elsewhere if the firm did not clear his name by firing the sales assistant. Finally, because of the revenue-producing power he had in the company, they caved in and fired her. The word went out through the entire firm, and people were furious. In a rare display of solidarity, the entire sales force and back-office personnel joined together to use one of the oldest forms of tribal punishment that has existed for thousands of years.

To use tribal terminology, the people in the firm "declared the man dead." They did not touch him or say a word to him. Everyone just started ignoring him and acting as though he did not exist. No one acknowledged his presence, spoke to him, ate lunch with him, or had anything to do with him beyond the bare necessities of the job function. This went on day after day, until he finally cracked, apologizing for his behavior and swearing he would never do it again. And he hasn't.

In this story, you learned a lot about the company. You learned about the importance and power of the high producers in the sales force, which may seem strange if you have never worked in a sales-driven company. When I tell that story to groups of people, some of the listeners often react by saying, "How could management fire that person! She didn't do anything wrong." Without exception, the people who make that comment have never worked in a sales-driven company. They do not understand the norms in those settings. People who have worked in sales environments may not always like the norms, but they do understand them and do not find this story particularly strange. This story also illustrated one of the taboos of this organization. The salesman went too far and the rest of the group reacted. *The formal structure of management could not stop his behavior even if they disagreed with it, but the collective punishment from the group was able to affect him and change his behavior in the future.*

Assume that you were interviewing for a job in one of the companies described in the preceding stories. Getting the interviewers to tell you a few of the classic stories about people and events inside the organization would tell you a great deal about whether you would fit into that particular culture. One of the most common mistakes people make when deciding whether to take a new job is that they do not learn enough about the internal culture of the organization. Whether your personality and style fits into a company or not is one of the key issues that will determine whether you are happy in the job. And yet most people spend very little time consciously collecting stories during their interviewing process.

## What Is the Folklore Road Map of Your Organization?

Every organization has a collection of stories that serve as a road map on the norms for appropriate behavior. If you were new to the company and a veteran told you 10 of the most important stories of the organization, you would be well on your way to knowing what you could and could not do in that setting. These stories would be invaluable in helping you stay out of trouble, as well as telling what you could get away with in the organization. Each story is usually filled with all types of information. In the two preceding stories, you learned more than one lesson about the company's expected behaviors in each of the stories. Stories are an efficient communication tool for sending multiple messages in a way that people remember and understand. What is the collection of stories that represent the road map for appropriate behavior in your organization?

Think of 10 stories which would represent a good road map for a new employee to guide that person's behavior inside the organization.

What are some of the stories about the founder's behavior or the CEO's way of doing things? For example, there was a story about the CEO/ founder of a company that met a newly hired manager who happened to have a beard. The CEO shook his hand and supposedly said, "Some of my best friends have beards, but none of them work for this company."

What are the stories that tell you who the enemy is, either inside or outside the company? What do these stories tell the listeners about the appropriate ways to deal with the enemy?

What are some of the famous stories in your organization or department about someone's "most embarrassing moment" inside the organization? Sometimes these stories tell about rules of behavior that were accidentally broken by someone.

What are the stories that tell employees about the important behaviors that will bring rewards, recognition, and hero status?

## What Does the Folklore Road Map Tell You about Employee Relationships?

If you look over the stories that you have just identified from your own organization or the two examples described earlier, you will find that some of the most important information that you learned was about the relationships between employees. Stories about events inside the organization almost always tell you the answers to the following questions:

- What is the status of various groups or individuals and how do they compare to each other?
- Who has more power? And how do they use the power?
- Who can you trust? Who will help you out? Who will tell you the truth?

- How formal or informal are we supposed to be with each other? What constitutes "polite" behavior in this organization?

- How much do people laugh at themselves and each other in this organization?

- How competitive are employees with each other? Is the competition inside the department, between departments, or with the outside competitors in your same line of work?

- How do people in the organization handle conflicts between individuals or departments? Is this a "sweep it under the rug" place or a "clear the air" culture?

- How long do people carry a grudge about old insults or injuries? Many organizations have a culture that harbors old grudges for years. Others are better at forgiving and forgetting.

All of these cultural characteristics will affect what it feels like to work in that setting. For the most part, there is no right or wrong in these characteristics, but for any individual employee the question of personality fit with the culture of the organization is a very real concern in terms of personal job satisfaction. The key issues that affect the types of relationships that people within a company form with each other are the following:

*Power.* Who has it and who does not?

*Trust.* Whom can you trust and for what?

*Formality.* How formally or informally do people treat each other?

*Humor.* Do people laugh a lot, particularly at themselves?

*Competition.* How much internal competition is there?

*Conflicts.* Who is angry at whom and how long does it last?

# 12
# Protecting Employee Morale

One of the key issues that affects the morale of a company is the types of relationships that employees at all levels have with each other. There are other issues that affect morale, such as the current financial performance of the organization, layoffs, cutbacks, major restructuring, etc. But even in these cases, often the reason that morale is affected is because financial issues and restructuring affects relationships in the organization. One of the most constant and ongoing impacts on the general morale of employees in an organization is the quality of the relationships between employees.

In Chapter 11, the following key issues that affect the types of relationships that people have were described:

*Power.*   Who has it and who does not?

*Trust.*   Whom can you trust and for what?

*Formality.*   How formally or informally do people treat each other?

*Humor.*   Do people laugh a lot, particularly at themselves?

*Competition.*   How much internal competition is there?

*Conflicts.*   Who is angry at whom and how long does it last?

In all but one of these characteristics, the primary concern in most cases is whether the employees' personal styles and expectations match the characteristics of the organization. If an organization is highly competitive or very formal in its relationships, and employees expect the behaviors to follow those patterns and they are fairly well suited for that type of environment in terms of their own personalities, then people will be reasonably satisfied with the place where they work and report that they feel fairly treated. The same is true for various types of power arrangements.

Authoritarian structures and power arrangements have a bad name these days, but I have seen many work settings with authoritarian patterns that worked well. One example was a finance department of a larger organization. The controller who was in charge of the department was very authoritarian in his style of operation. He personally knew almost everything that was happening in the department and controlled almost all of the decision making himself. The people who worked for him loved the man. They called him "the chief" among themselves, although they always used his surname to his face. I was a consultant in this organization and after several weeks of working with this client, I had to fire a fellow consultant from the project because she was making hostile, rude comments about "the chief" behind his back and stirring up trouble for everyone. When I walked back into the department after escorting the volatile consultant to the parking lot, I received a standing ovation from the entire employee group. These people were comfortable with their leader's style. The loyalty and the morale in that work setting was as high as I have seen anywhere.

Ross Perot is another example of a leader who is reported to use a more authoritarian style of leadership. During the 1992 campaign for President, his style of work was scrutinized and analyzed by many people. It was often described as militaristic. Some people reported that they would not or did not like working with him because of this characteristic. But, at the same time, Perot is reported to instill loyalty and devotion in many of the people who work for him. A typical example of the comments made about him was from a long-time employee who said "I'd walk through a brick wall for the guy."[1]

In most of these relationship characteristics of organization's cultures, the main issue is "fit." Do the people who work for the organization have expectations and personalities that fit the patterns of behavior existing in that work setting? There is, however, one characteristic that is an exception. This one characteristic seems to be a given in all environments. This characteristic seems to explain why authoritarian environments can work well. The characteristic which is necessary for high morale in an organization is *trust*. All the other characteristics seem to be negotiable, but this one is a given.

If trust is not high between employees at all levels in an organization, none of the other relationship characteristics can offset the damage done by this missing element. In fact, without high levels of trust, you often find that the other characteristics such as apparent cooperation or high degrees of humor in the workplace are just a hollow facade for what is really a tense and unpleasant environment. Behind closed doors in an organization where there is low trust between employees, the stories people tell are filled with cynicism and themes of "Watch your back around here and take care of yourself." When talking about the leadership in these settings, the theme of "They tell you that they care, but they don't" is almost always present.

## The Pivotal Role of Trust in Organizational Culture

The level of trust between employees at all levels in an organization is so pivotal to the morale of an organization that it may well be the cultural foundation stone that everything else in the company rests on, including long-term performance of the organization. Research done by Kotter and Heskett for their book, *Corporate Culture and Performance,* indicates that one of the key ingredients in corporate cultures that produces outstanding long-term financial results is the organization's ability to remain adaptable and flexible.

This characteristic determines its ability to change as the environment changes around it.[2] They contrast this to risk-averse environments with a "widespread emphasis on control that dampens motivation and enthusiasm."[3] They go on to quote Ralph Kilmann, an expert in organizational culture as saying, "An adaptive culture entails a risk-taking, trusting, and proactive approach to organizational as well as individual life."[4] They describe a setting where people support each other, share feelings of confidence, and believe that they can effectively handle whatever comes at them from the outside environment.[5]

What they are describing in the long-term high-performance companies is a high level of trust between employees and for their leadership. According to Kotter and Heskett, the leadership person's role in setting this atmosphere is of paramount importance.[6] Without trustable leadership, there will never be a high level of trust throughout the organization as a whole. There will be pockets of trusting relationships, but they will primarily be used to protect each other from the perils of the larger organization. This will not contribute to the overall performance of the organization.

Trust is a slippery characteristic that cannot be manufactured in any direct way. There is no way you can set out to increase trust in an organization and introduce it directly into the culture. As powerful a communication tool as storytelling is, it will not be effective at increasing trust in an organization just by changing the content of some of the corporate stories. Stories are, however, an excellent barometer for measuring the current levels of trust throughout the organization. By listening to the stories people tell about the organization in private, you will quickly get an accurate picture of the levels of trust or paranoia that exist in an organization. But if you try to artificially change the stories to trigger a change in the culture, the employees will ignore the new stories and go right on telling the ones that match the truth of their own experiences.

Trust is a *byproduct* and can only be produced by a long series of experiences that result in trust. If employees experience being on the receiving end of respectful treatment from other people in the organization for a long period of time, the byproduct of that respectful treatment is trust. That is the only way to arrive at trust between human beings, individually or collectively.

> *Respectful treatment over long periods of time leads to the byproduct, high levels of trust within an organization.*

There are times when I get calls from prospective clients asking me to help them increase trust in their organization. My reaction to that request is that I do not have any trust packages in my office that I can help them implement. There is no such thing. What I can do is help them operationalize their own definitions of "respectful treatment" in their company and help them begin to implement that. In the long run, if they stick with it, a byproduct of that effort will be higher levels of trust inside their organization. If there has been significant damage done in the past, this will be a very slow process.

Trust is, in effect, a gift that people give each other as a result of how they have been treated. Being trusted is not a right, it is a privilege or a gift. We can use the stories people tell in the organization as a tool for measuring progress and as a way of publicizing progress as the organization changes. But you cannot use storytelling as an artificial substitute for respectful treatment. People are too smart for that. They know what is really going on and the stories have to match that reality. If you want high morale in an organization, you have to have high trust levels and the stories that go with them.

## Building a Folklore of "Trust" Stories

The art of using storytelling effectively when it comes to trust is to create a folklore of "trust" stories that are based on reality. For example, if you are a new leader in an organization or a new manager of a department, one of your most important tasks is to build a sense of trust between you and the employees in that work group. One way to look at your behavior at work during that "new" phase is to view yourself as *creating* new stories about yourself in the minds of the people who work with you. All the events around you offer opportunities to create the plots and themes for stories that will be told by other people about you. You are creating a new folklore about yourself as a leader. This will be true whether you think about it or not. People watch a new leader's behavior very closely and they repeat what they see.

One of the primary questions that they are waiting to answer is whether or not you can be trusted. Nothing that you will say will have the power of your behavior that they see. They will go on to turn your behavior into stories that become a part of your leadership folklore. You can, of course, tell your own stories about yourself as well. For example, you could tell about how you handled different situations in other organizations in the past. But those stories will only be credible to the new employees with whom you are now working if they match the behavior they are currently seeing and the stories that they are telling about you themselves. Probably the most powerful stories you can tell about yourself that are likely to be picked up and added to the organization's folklore about you are your own personal sacred bundle stories. If your family heritage stories match the behavior they see, these stories will become key elements of the folklore about you.

## Watch Out for the Ripple Effect of Stories

There are two keys to understanding how to use storytelling as a powerful communication tool for the good of the organization. One is to understand that for stories to have any positive power in terms of inspiration or morale, the stories have to be perceived as true. The facts and details may have gotten exaggerated over the years, but the theme or message of the stories must be true in the minds of the listeners. The second key to understanding how to use stories effectively is to understand the power of the ripple effect of stories. The *ripple effect* of a story is defined as the number of times that story gets repeated. The more it is repeated, the more powerful the story becomes. To manage the effectiveness of stories around an important issue such as trust, it is important to hunt for the stories that truthfully demonstrate respect and trust, and then find ways to increase the number of times those stories are repeated. There are a number of ways this can be done.

One way is to create new opportunities for storytelling . . . more tribal campfires. There are many ways to do this. Often, you can use current group gatherings as a vehicle for more storytelling just by changing the format slightly. Using quick, simple ways of doing this is important in most organizations, because the time pressures are severe in most companies. Here are a few suggestions of how you might create more "tribal campfires"

around your organization. Build on these ideas and adapt them to your
own organization.

- Reformat current meetings to include some opportunity to tell a few positive stories each time. One or two hero stories or "we survived" stories every time a group gets together has a cumulative effect of highlighting the positive folklore in the company.

- Encourage informal get-togethers such as lunches or coffeepot stops, but be aware of the types of stories that you tell and encourage other people to make sure that at least a portion of the stories have some positive intent or message. If you cannot influence the kinds of stories other people tell in these settings, at least edit your own stories and deliver them with a positive message.

- Look at your orientation-related activities for new employees. Get some of the organization's veterans involved in telling stories about the company to the newcomers. This setting for storytelling is good for everyone who participates. It makes everyone stop and think about the key features of the organization that need to be emphasized.

- Find written formats for storytelling, such as company newsletters or E-mail systems. Use these settings to tell short versions of stories on a regular basis.

- Use the video technology to make short, in-house programs on a regular basis that update employees on the stories about progress on important projects or other activities. These can be done by interviewing employees and editing their stories into a quick 5- or 10-minute video that can be left in the cafeteria or lobby for informal viewing. People in companies still tend to see video as a medium that can only be used in a way that requires bringing in expensive outside technicians and producing very formal, slick presentations. That is not the approach to take if you are trying to use this medium as a regular ritual of a "tribal campfire" for storytelling. Homemade movies are more the model for what you are trying to create in this case, not slick advertising pieces.

- Get employees involved in customer interviewing and then have meetings to tell the customer stories and think about the implications. Both the praise and complaint stories can be used as positive stories with an intent of improving customer service.

- Make teams aware of the stories they already tell and encourage them to tell more in settings such as continuous quality improvement teamwork or other types of project teams. Stories are an excellent tool to help in clarifying a problem or needed improvement. Be sure the teams are listening to customer stories and not just their own stories. Sometimes the two types of stories do not match, and the customer's version of the stories is always the most important one to listen to carefully.

- If your organization has work shift changes where people meet to pass on information from one shift to another, use those settings to highlight the stories that are told. Make sure that you use your influence to increase the percentage of stories that are told with a positive intent or message.

Another way to increase the number of times positive stories are repeated is to get people in the organization to talk about the importance of an issue like trust, asking people to pay attention to and tell the group about events that represented trust in action to them. If you are the leader, make sure that you "edit" your own storytelling to emphasize the key issues that are important to you, and tell lots of stories on a few key themes.

This is another way to encourage a concentration on stories that enhance the organization instead of tear it down. No one can ever *control* the ripple effect of storytelling, but it can be influenced and guided in positive directions, if people in the organization stop to think about what messages and themes they want to emphasize.

Storytelling is such a potent form of communication that it only takes a small shift toward a more positive ripple effect to affect the morale of the organization or work group. This is often described as the *power of leverage.* The ripple effect of storytelling is a highly leveraged form of communication. With a small amount of change in the number of positive stories being repeated, you would see a substantial change in the morale and atmosphere of the organization. There are "terminally negative" people in every organization, and there always will be. If it was necessary to convert everyone in the place and all stories to a positive theme to get any useful results, storytelling would not be a particularly powerful communication tool. But the reality is that by encouraging as little as a 5 percent change in the message of the stories that are rippling through the organization, you can probably affect the morale of the organization.

Keep in mind that the stories must be true in the eyes of the employees. If they are told a story that they do not believe, they kill it immediately, and it never becomes part of the ripple effect. Or, worse yet, the disbelieved story is retold as a cynical story along the lines of "Did you hear the latest corporate propaganda?" Then the message of the story is a completely different one that tells the employees this is a dangerous place and warns them not to believe anything they hear. If you are not sure whether a story will be believed or not, stick to the stories that the employees witnessed with their own eyes and ears and know to be true. Or, better yet, tell stories about them that cast them in the role of "hero." Almost no one will turn that type of story into a cynical, untrue story.

# Forgiving and Forgetting . . .
# How Do People Repair
# Past Damage?

One of my frequent observations in my work with conflict situations in organizations is that you can damage a relationship with someone at work in about 30 seconds and then you will spend months trying to repair the damage that you did so quickly. This is particularly true if there is a history of previous damage between the people involved. In that case, 30 seconds is probably entirely too generous a time allowance. One glance or a few words spoken in an insulting tone is all it takes and the battle is up and running again. I often ask groups of people to estimate the length of the memory of people in their organization after having been jerked around by someone else who works there. I used to estimate that the memory ran about 13 years, because I had heard so many "I waited 13 years to get even with that person" stories. Not too long ago, a particularly astute client laughed at that estimate and responded, "No, no . . . *death* is when the memory ends in this organization."

Damaged relationships is just another way of saying that there is a lack of trust between the people involved. Both sides are usually more than happy to tell you an entire collection of stories about the reasons for the damage. "What those other people did" stories are a major category of stories that are repeated frequently and passed on from one generation of employees to another in organizations. If there are large numbers of damaged relationships, this will negatively affect the overall morale of the organization.

## Repairing Damaged Relationships

The first consideration is to try to repair the damage that has been done. If you can damage a relationship in 30 seconds, but take six months trying to repair it, it is important to know what are you going to do during the six months of repair efforts. In many cases, the answer seems to be "not much." There is an old expression that says "Time heals all wounds." I do not know who made up that expression, but that person did not work in many of the organizations I have seen. If anything, time seems to make the damage worse. Often new events continue to happen that reinforce the old damage. I am convinced that many people would not bother to carry a grudge for 13 years or to the grave unless new situations continued to occur that heap more damage on the old. This ongoing chain of events allows the wronged person to continually tell new stories about "what they did to me this time." Something has to happen to break the chain of negative events, and doing nothing rarely has that effect.

One of the easiest ways to think about trying to repair the damage that was done in a work relationship is to think of it in terms of stories. What you must now do is create a *new* collection of stories that are trust stories between the two of you, instead of damage stories. Because of the ease with which people understand stories, they seem to be able to picture the plot lines and behaviors that need to go into creating these new stories that will help to repair past damage. In contrast, try directly asking someone who needs to do some repair work on a damaged work relationship, "What do you need to repair this relationship?" That person is likely to throw up his or her hands and tell you that he or she hasn't got a clue what to do or where to start.

Even if the person is motivated to try to do some repair work, he or she often is baffled about how to go about it. But when that same person is asked to think of a chain of stories that could occur over six months that would help to repair the damage between the two people, most people can come up with many ideas for plots and stories. People are creating new stories all the time with their behavior whether they think about it or not. All the person is doing in this case is consciously thinking about what kinds of stories to create.

If, however, the person goes right on creating the same story line that matches the themes of the original damage story, the problems between the two people will continue to get worse. This seems to be what happens in many organizations. It reminds me of a song that I learned at camp as a child that went on and on, verse after verse. It had a line in it something like "Same song, twelfth verse, a little bit louder and a little bit worse," and then you would repeat the same song again. If this cycle of damage affects only the two people involved, then it might be considered just a private affair. But that is rarely the case.

If there are many of these damage cycles going on in an organization, then the effect will be devastating on the morale of the entire organization and will eventually affect its performance. Somehow, people need to learn to break the cycle and turn the pattern of damage into a new collection of stories. I am convinced many people are capable of this and even willing to do it. Often they either do not know where to start or do not think that they have the power to change their stories in the future. No one has the power to change the stories of the past, but everyone has the power to change their own stories in the future.

There are, however, some people who seem to be organically untrustworthy people who will never genuinely try to repair relationships with anyone. Unfortunately, they are present in every organization. They have probably been present in all tribes for thousands of years. In this case, the people who have been damaged will probably have to heal themselves with the help and protection of other people in the organization. If the untrustable people are seriously outnumbered and the other people in the organization put out the effort to keep the rest of their relationships in good shape, the situation is usually manageable. Those people will negatively affect the morale of the organization, but not in devastating proportions.

They become the lead characters in the villain and enemy stories that are used to teach other people how to handle them or avoid them. If the organically untrustable person is in a leadership position in your organization, find a new job. If they are powerful leaders and seriously untrustable, find a new job quickly. They can turn an organization into a living hell. There is no way to improve morale in this situation. People who work in that situation are in danger, and they know it at some level. If you are certain that you are working for Darth Vader, take your stories and go elsewhere. You deserve better than that.

Fortunately, this is not usually the case. In most cases the damage is done by normal, fallible people who really did not mean any harm. They do some relationship damage, and then they do not know how to repair it or do not bother to try. I often ask audiences of people from organizations to raise their hands if they can think of at least two or three people at work with whom there has been some damage. In most cases, everyone laughs and raises their hands. That is normal. That's life. The question is where do you go from there. The first part of the answer is to try to do some repair work. The second part of the answer is to forgive and forget. This may in many ways be the more important part of the answer to damaged relationships.

## Forgiving and Forgetting . . .
## Grieving and Healing

> Any sorrow can be borne if we can put it in a story.
>
> Isak Dinesen
> *Out of Africa*[7]

I hear so much about relationship damage and its aftermath in my work that I have come to the conclusion that one of the least developed skills in most companies is the ability to forgive and forget. This point struck home for me with one particular client group where there were some seriously damaged relationships based on past events. All of the people in this group were basically honorable people who were trusted by many other people with whom they had worked in other settings. The history of this particular grouping of people, however, involved a number of events that were handled in ways that left the people in the group wary of each other and the larger organization. I was asked to help this group begin to build some form of teamwork out of the damaged history.

During my interviews with each person in the group, two of the people told me exactly the same story about an event that had occurred between them more than a year ago. Both people, of course, told the story from their own point of view, so although the facts were the same, the interpretation of the events that had occurred was quite different. Each person had left this encounter feeling insulted by the other person. Both people explained that they had meant no harm in what had happened and that they had been misunderstood by the other person. Then both of these people went on to say exactly the same words, "I've tried ever since, but that person just won't forgive and forget." I was struck by the pain in this group of people and the history of damage and distrust they were carrying into their future. Some of the events that had triggered the problems even involved people who were gone from the group and the organization. They seemed trapped in that history with no way to recover and move on. In fact, almost every person in the group made it perfectly clear to me that they did not have the energy or interest in bringing all this out in the open to discuss it. They were not hopeful that anything could be changed.

Forgiving and forgetting is a simple expression in the English language that describes the last steps of what is usually a long complicated process of grieving and healing. Elisabeth Kubler-Ross and others have done a great deal of research about how this process works from a psychological point of view.[8] She divides the grief response into stages that make it easier to understand and help to illustrate that there is actually a very predictable pattern that most people go through. The first stages are immobilization when the negative event first occurs, followed by denial, anger, and bargaining. Then depression sets in. The stage of depression would be an accurate description of the state of the team of people just described.

Many of the damaging events had occurred some time ago, and there had been a great deal of denial, anger, and bargaining tried in the group. They were frustrated and sick of it at this point, and for the most part just did not even want to talk about it anymore. They were depressed. If a person cannot move on beyond the depression, according to Kubler-Ross, that person will never reach the stages of testing and acceptance of the painful situation that allows healing and rebuilding to begin.

At a psychological level, the question is whether the person can find some way to go through these stages and reach the end of the process. There is no way to skip the process, no matter how much one might want to do so. The only way out of damaging, painful events is to live through them and reach the point of healing. In the case of damaged relationships between people in the work setting, healing means much the same thing as the expression "forgiving and forgetting."

Storytelling plays a key role in helping a person to work through these stages of grieving. Grieving is not just a solitary, psychological event in an individual's life. It is a cultural event. Or at least it was historically. One of the most important functions that cultures have performed throughout history is to provide their members with a pathway for grieving and healing. Cultures have had rituals and ceremonies for this purpose. The cultures have also given their members guidelines on how to grieve appropriately. People have even been given a general pattern to follow for how long the grieving lasts and what to do after it ends. The movie *Dances with Wolves* demonstrated a classic example of this cultural role when the Sioux tribal chief announced to the young widow that her grieving time was over and she could remarry now. The rituals, ceremonies, and cultural events that help people grieve use storytelling as one of their main tools for communicating the appropriate pathway for grieving and healing.

In our modern-day organizations, and possibly society at large, we seem to have lost our cultural rituals, ceremonies, norms, and guidelines to help individuals find their way through this process. There is no clear pathway to follow anymore for grieving and healing. Each person is left alone to do the best he or she can. Grieving, healing, forgiving, and forgetting has historically *never* been a solo activity. Historically, it has always been a community activity. It was the group's responsibility to participate and help in this process. One illustration of the "solo" approach to grieving in our society at large is the messages that are sent to people who are grieving to "keep it to themselves." "Don't talk about it because it makes people uncomfortable."

Often, when people try to tell their grief stories about their pain, they are cut off. One of the most dramatic examples of this was a story told to me by a colleague whose two college-age daughters were both killed in an automobile accident when they were driving home from college for the wedding of the older of the two. This woman described the reactions that she got from many people when she would try to talk about her daughters and want to tell stories about their lives. People would act as though they did not hear her and would change the subject. She said these people preferred to act as if her daughters had never existed at all. The isolation and loneliness that this woman told of experiencing was one of the most painful descriptions that I have ever heard. And it was a cultural outrage that this was happening to her. This would not happen in a culture that still understood and remembered its responsibility to help its members grieve and heal. To work through the stages of grieving, a person must be able to tell his or her story. Often one must tell the story over and over until the intensity of the feelings begins to fade. It is the responsibility of the culture and the people in it to provide the settings for this storytelling and to listen.

Many times people will make the comment "I don't know what to say to the grieving person." That comment illustrates the level of misunderstanding about our cultural, community responsibility to the grieving person. The cultural role is *not* to say anything, but to listen, and then listen some more. Without this role being performed by the culture for its members, there will be wounded people walking around everywhere who are unable to heal themselves because it cannot be done alone.

And that is precisely what is happening in many organizations today. They are filled with the walking wounded. People have been damaged in some way and have no acceptable pathway to grieving and healing. They are stuck somewhere in the anger or depression stages of grief and cannot get out. There are no rituals, ceremonies, tribal campfires, or other organizational activities or settings for them to tell their stories over and over until they are able to begin reshaping the stories into a new form where they can move on into the future. They cannot find a way to forgive and forget.

Not only do most organizations have no structure in place to help people grieve and heal, many people in organizations seem to have a naive idea about the length of time this process takes. The exact length varies, of course, from one individual to another, and will also vary depending on the severity of the damage that was done. It is safe to say, however, that in all cases it takes far longer than many people expect. In a discussion with a group of people about managing resistance to change, a senior manager from one organization expressed her frustration with problems in her organization since a major reorganization had occurred.

There had been layoffs and significant restructuring of the jobs of the people who were still there. She expressed that she understood that this had been painful at the time; however, in her opinion, the time was long overdue for those employees to get over it and move on, but they were still talking about it and morale was still terrible. I asked her to define "long overdue" by telling us how long it had been since the layoffs and restructure had occurred. She responded indignantly "It has been *six months!*" I stood for several seconds, frozen, trying to swallow my overwhelming urge to scream, "People don't grieve on a six-month schedule!"

At that moment I caught the eye of two nurses who were sitting in the audience. They were watching my efforts to control myself and smiling knowingly. When they saw me look at them, they burst out laughing and so did I. That broke the tension and I turned to the woman who had made the well-intended comment and was able to respond to her in a way that she laughed, too. We went on to discuss that for a change that was as serious and painful as that one had been, six months was probably not enough time for most people to recover completely. A year or two might be a more reasonable time frame to expect. Then we went on to discuss whether the organization had given the employees any safe, appropriate pathway for grieving. There had been a few meetings and a few private discussions with supervisors right after the events had occurred and that was about it. Under those circumstances, it is highly unlikely that the employees will ever really recover.

Rosabeth Moss Kanter writes about this organizational responsibility in her book, *When Giants Learn to Dance,* when she describes the need for "managing the past: mourning the losses"[9] during major organizational transitions. "Issue number one in managing a difficult transition smoothly is to allow employees to mourn the past, to grieve over their losses."[10] She tells the story of the acquisition of Western Airlines by Delta Airlines as an example of where this was handled well. A period of mourning was encouraged to help people bury the past. This included testimonials that were written by long-time Western employees and distributed to all employees. They even had a funeral ceremony.

At this event, each of the Western people attending were asked to write down the three worst things that could happen to them as a result of the changes that were occurring. Also, they were each given several pieces of their former letterhead and business cards and were led outside and assembled around a wooden casket. As a band played the funeral march, one by one each person was asked to crumple up their statements, cards, and letterhead and toss them into the coffin. When they were finished, a hundred-ton paver came rolling around the corner. As it approached the coffin, the group burst into the singing of "On Wisconsin" and cheered as the paver rolled over the coffin, flattening its contents. As soon as this was over, the group was taken back inside, given caps and gowns to wear, and assembled for a "graduation speech." Each manager was then called forward and given a "Doctorate in Merger Management" and a share of the Delta stock as a graduation gift.[11] That is a classic example of a grieving and healing ceremony. The specific events of this company's ceremony might not be the same that you would use in your organization, but every company can create its own pathway for grieving and healing that matches their culture and style. The problem is that most organizations have no rituals or ceremonies. There is no place for the employees to go to vent their feelings, find support, or simply to tell their story to someone who is willing to listen.

The group described earlier that was suffering from past damage and pain is fortunate to work in an organization that is willing to make an effort to help people heal. That group was provided with a number of resources and allowed the time to go through the rest of the stages of grieving so that they could heal the old wounds. When they first started, they were not willing to talk about the personal histories of damage between them, so we concentrated on getting their work mission and goals back on track. They felt that they had been so worn out by their situation that their ability to accomplish the mission of the department was suffering.

They were still doing good work, but it was taking far too much energy and effort to carry out the number of tasks they had accomplished. They also began to talk openly as a group about their norms of behavior toward each other. They were able to acknowledge that they needed at some point to talk about what had happened in the past and that they had to heal themselves. Eventually, they went on to begin to open up these issues and try to work through them. They are beginning to heal. This is a fine group of people who have a tremendous amount of talent and energy to offer their organization. They are fortunate to be a part of an organization that understands it has a cultural responsibility to help its members find a pathway to forgive, forget, and move on into the future.

## How Does Your Organization Grieve and Heal?

Ask yourself the following questions to see if you can identify any ways that your organization takes on a cultural responsibility to provide the pathway for people to forgive and forget. If you cannot think of any answers to these questions, try to think of new ideas on how your organization could begin to do these things in the future. If you do not have the ability to influence the entire organization, just focus on your own work unit. There are subcultures within the larger organizational culture, and many times it is possible to have your own norms and rituals at the local level of the subculture.

- Think of a major organizational change that has occurred in your organization since you have been working there. What happened in an organized way to help people express their grief, anger, or fear about the changes?

- How long was it acceptable to talk about the past after the major change occurred?

- Was there any organized place to tell your stories about life before the change and about the pain of the transition? Where were the tribal campfires that could be used to grieve and heal?

- Was it a "career-shortening gesture" to bring up the past after the change had occurred? If so, how long after the change did it become dangerous to bring up the subject?

How do people in your organization resolve individual or team problems? When there is relationship damage between people, when and where do they have an opportunity to work out the problems? Who helps them?

Are there walking wounded in your organization? These are people who feel they have been insulted, betrayed, ignored, or mistreated in some way by others in the organization and they feel powerless to do anything about it.

The morale of your organization will sink lower as the number of these walking wounded increases. There is a direct relationship between these two factors. To have high morale, you must have high trust levels between employees at all levels. And to have high trust levels, people must have a way to grieve and heal after damaging, painful events occur. An organization cannot always stop the damage from occurring in the first place, but it can take on its cultural responsibility to listen and help people heal.

# 13
# Storytelling and Relationships with Your Customers

Listen to one of the stories that Carl Sewell tells in his book about his company:

> We have an excellent customer who lives half the year in Dallas and the other half in France. When she was coming back from Paris last year she called us up and said she planned to spend some time in New York before returning home, but she didn't want to rent a car there. She said all New Yorker rental cars were dirty and smelled of cigarette smoke. She wanted to know if we could rent a car for her in Dallas and have someone drive it to New York, and turn it over to her there. [Sewell goes on to finish the story with the words:]
> We could, and we did.[1]

If people hearing this story had never heard of Carl Sewell or his book, it probably would not surprise them to discover that the name of his book is *Customers for Life* or that the chapter this story is taken from is named "If the Customer Asks, the Answer Is Yes."[2] It would also probably not surprise them to find out that Carl Sewell is the owner of the most successful luxury-car dealership in the United States.

*Customers for Life* is actually one long story about how Sewell built and maintained this extremely successful business. Sewell and the people who work for him have been *creating* customer stories for years at his dealership. His friend Stanley Marcus, of Neiman Marcus department stores, sums up the effectiveness and the power of Sewell's storytelling when he says, "From reading this book, it's evident that Carl's mother 'raised him right.' If you don't learn something from this book, it's your fault."[3] The book is filled with stories and explanations of Sewell Village Cadillac dealership's Ten Commandments of Customer Service, including one whole chapter devoted to stories about the condition of the bathrooms at the dealership. It is difficult to turn to any page in that book and not find a story about the importance of customers and the service behavior that goes with it.

In another chapter, titled "There's No Such Thing as After Hours," Sewell describes their 24-hour-a-day service approach. This applies to the sales force who will make appointments at any time to meet a customer to show a car. He says that if a customer wants to show up on Sunday morning dressed in his pajamas to look at a car, it is fine with them. Even more unusual, however, is that the 24-hour availability also applies to their service department. As an example, he tells the story of a person who purchases a car at the dealership, comes out of work at five o'clock in the morning and discovers that a tire on the car is flat. There is a 24-hour telephone number that the customer can call at the dealership, and a service technician who is on call will get out of bed and drive over to fix the tire. And there is no charge for the service. Sewell explains that the biggest problem they have with their 24-hour service availability is that customers often forget about it or do not believe they are serious. They remind the customers regularly about the 24-hour number, but this level of service is so uncommon that people still often forget to call when they need help.[4]

Sewell goes much further than most businesses in the proverbial "putting his money where his mouth is" on the importance of customer service by paying everyone who works at the dealership on commission instead of salary or wages. This practice generates a number of stories of its own. Sewell tells one of his favorites about a man named Curley Crawford. He tells this story to highlight the fact that they do not cap people's income as is often done in commission situations. Often, if a commission-based person, such as a salesperson, starts to make too much money, the company will change the rules on payouts or redistribute the sales territories in a way that reduces the person's capacity to generate income. Sewell believes that type of changing the rules is counterproductive in the long run and he uses his story about Curley Crawford to illustrate the point.

Curley Crawford was a transmission technician who was promoted to service director and did an outstanding job of building the service department into a very profitable operation. When he started, he was making $27,500 plus 10 percent of all increases in profits. By the end of the second year, Curley was making $75,000. He told friends that the company would never let him continue to make that much and he was sure they would change the pay plan. Sewell heard about his comments and thought they were funny, because he had no intention of changing the arrangement. The next year Curley made $100,000, and told his friends that this year they would cut his pay for sure. Sewell called him into the office to talk and described Curley's body language as "I knew it! He's gonna be like everybody else. He's going to cut my pay." Instead, Sewell said to him, "I'm really proud of the job you've done and hope you make a lot more money next year."

Two years later he was making $150,000. Sewell called him in again and could tell that Curley was convinced this year the pay plan would change. Again, Sewell told him he was doing a great job and that everything would stay exactly the same in the future. At that point Curley said, "You aren't ever gonna change my pay plan, are you?" Sewell explained that there was no reason to change it. Curley may be getting 10 percent of all the increases in profit, but the dealership was getting the other 90 percent. Under those circumstances, it would not make sense to take away the incentive of a man who was doing such a great job.[5]

From the stories told here about Sewell's dealership, it is clear that the messages of taking care of the customer and taking care of the employees are both important in that company. In most organizations that produce excellent customer service over a long period of time, the culture of the company emphasizes both the customers' and employees' welfare. In fact, it is often difficult to tell where employee relations end and customer relations begin. They are actually both parts of one long chain of relationships and events that operate like a domino effect, ending in either high-quality customer products and services or poor ones. Sewell obviously understands the importance of both of these issues and knows how to generate a collection of stories which represent a powerful customer-service folklore. In most cases, the leader of an organization will not go so far as to write a best-selling business book about the organization as Carl Sewell did, but every leader and every organization can have its own well-known collection of customer-service folklore stories.

## How Important Are Your Customers . . . How Many Stories Do You Tell about Them?

I was working with the senior management team of a hospital a few years ago and started the project by interviewing each manager individually, as well as several board members and doctors affiliated with the facility. The interviews ran about 16 hours in total. One unnerving piece of information I reported back to the group was that in 16 hours of interviews about the hospital, I counted two times that anyone used the word "patient." They talked about market share, new buildings, revenue production, medical services to be offered, and even about the employees of the facility. But only twice was the patient mentioned. The family members who accompany patients to the hospital and sit through long hours of frightening anxiety were never mentioned at all.

How important was the customer in that situation? The mission statement said the patients and families were important. All the new services and buildings were intended to be used by patients and families. "Market share" was a reference to the number of patient admissions that the hospital would bring in during the next year. Still, if the patient was only mentioned twice in 16 hours of interviews, and the families were forgotten altogether, how important were the patients and families in that facility? The efforts the group made to answer that question changed the direction of the meetings that we were having and put the whole issue of customer service on the front burner for attention.

If you want to know which groups of people are important around an organization, simply count the number of stories that you hear about that group during a typical workweek or month. As you count the stories, be particularly watchful of the informal, off-the-cuff stories in the halls or over lunch in the cafeteria. The formal stories in speeches or at official gatherings are not as significant as the unrehearsed "This is what's on my mind" stories that you hear during normal daily activity. Counting the number of stories will tell you which employee groups are important, as well as which external groups (such as customers) matter the most.

If you took graph paper and plotted the stories for a month in the life of the company, you would see the pattern of whom and what this company pays attention to on a regular basis. *Customer-focused* is a phrase that is used a great deal these days and basically means "concentrating on the customer" or thinking about the customers. If the majority of people in an organization are concentrating on the customers and thinking about them frequently, it is almost impossible for them *not* to tell stories about the customers. People talk about and tell stories about what is on their mind.

In addition to simply counting the number of stories that you hear where the customer is the topic, the second indicator to look for is the content of the stories. What kinds of stories are the employees telling about the customers? Are the themes of the stories focused on "what a pain in the neck" the customers are? Or are they hero stories and "aren't we great with the customers" stories? Go back to Chapter 3 (which describes the different types of positive stories) to see if the customer stories that you are hearing fit into any of those categories.

This reminds me of a comment made to me by a Catholic sister who was a nurse in a different hospital than the one just described. We were discussing the resistance to the idea of "customers" in health care and the hostility toward training in customer-service skills. She smiled and said to me that the old attitude in health care was that the professionals who worked there were clinicians and technicians, and the *illness* was seen as the customer, not the patient. She said "If we could have sent the patient home and just treated the illness, everyone would have been much happier." We both agreed that the hospital staff would definitely have preferred to send the distraught families home. They were often viewed as severe interference in treating the illness.

This attitude had changed significantly over the past few years in health care because of increasing competition for physicians and their patients, but the old attitude described here is not an unusual one in many businesses and professions. "This place would be great if it weren't for those irritating customers" is a common theme heard in stories that people tell in many organizations. In a customer-service seminar that I was conducting in an insurance company, for example, one employee who answered the telephone to handle customers' questions about their policies and benefits spoke up at one point in the seminar and said, "Those customers are just going to *have* to understand that we can't always . . ." I let her finish her tirade and then pointed out that there is one thing on this earth that no one has to do, and that is *understand*. Customers, in particular, do not ever have to understand the employees' problems. That mindset will never produce high-quality customer service, and it will not produce customer stories that are positive and lead the company in the right direction when it comes to satisfying the customers.

In the case of the senior management team described earlier, they spent the time in their interviews talking about what was on their minds. There were very few stories told in any of the interviews. The information was given in a factual manner listing the successes and problems. The focus was on marketing and the strategic plan for the future. All the information provided was useful and accurate. The problem here is a typical one when people in business decide to talk markets and strategies. In many cases, the customers get lost somewhere along the way. They become "statistics" and "market share" instead of *people.*

There is no reason that strategic planning or marketing has to be this way. It is quite possible to talk about statistics, market share, *and* include stories filled with customer and employee experiences. But for some reason, it is common that the facts and figures grab more of the attention of senior managers, while the customer stories slip into the background. My guess is that this occurs because these people do not spend enough time face-to-face with the customers. Therefore, they do not have their own stories to tell. Nor do they spend much time listening to the employees tell their stories about customer-service experiences. Without either their own customer stories to tell or their employees to learn stories from, these managers do not have a customer folklore. When they talk to me using facts and figures, they are simply recounting what is on their minds. They have no stories to tell.

In his book, *The Customer-Driven Company,* Richard Whiteley talks about how to "saturate your company with the voice of the customer."[6] The key to being able to do this, he goes on to explain, is that everyone, including the leader, must gauge every action against customers' needs and expectations.[7] He suggests that you get to know your customers better than they know themselves, and that you measure everything constantly against the expectations and needs of the customers.[8] If anything remotely close to this level of customer-driven activity is going on in a company, there will be large numbers of stories about the customers floating all over the organization on any given day.

## Listening to the Customers' Stories

"Saturating" your organizations with the voice of the customer may be the ultimate goal, but the first question to ask is whether you really know what the customer wants from you or what the customer thinks of your organization. More and more organizations are beginning to ask, which is a great start. But asking does not always mean that you are really getting the answers.

One time a woman came up to me to tell me about a problem that she was having with a new customer-service effort that they had just implemented in the company where she worked. Their new technique was to call a few days after that person had purchased a product from the company to ask them if they had been satisfied with the service and the product they had received from the organization. Her frustration was that no one was complaining about anything. Everyone just said, "It was fine" and hung up on her. She knew everything could not have been "fine" all the time, so she was justifiably suspicious that the data she was gathering was worthless. I asked her to tell me exactly what she was saying to them on the phone, and for the most part her approach sounded good. She was, however, only asking them to tell her about problems or complaints that they had with the company's products or services.

This company was in a small town in Wisconsin, which is an area of the country heavily settled by Scandinavians, and it would probably qualify as one of the politest places in the United States. She was asking them to be complainers, which is not a role that most people relish. Some do, but most people find it uncomfortable. I suggested that she change her wording and start asking people for their advice, instead of asking them to complain. People, in general, love to be asked to be advisers.

When you give advice, you do not have to say that what happened was bad. You are simply making suggestions on how it could be made even better. In her cultural environment, she was much more likely to hear real customer stories if she asked her questions in this way. As soon as I made the wording-change suggestion, the woman's eyes lit up and she laughed. She said that she was sure that using the word "advice" would make a big difference in what people told her. She was genuinely looking for customer stories. But she had to ask in the right way if she was going to get what she was looking for from her customers. Depending on your business and the cultural backgrounds of your customers, you will have to ask in different ways.

The heavy reliance on paper-and-pencil surveys to get information from customers is too limited as a communication tool for learning about the customer. Those surveys are fine if they are used as a starting point, but you will never really get to know your customers by reading the tick marks they make on a survey—or even by the short phrases that they write in the "Comments" section of the survey.

If you want to hear the stories that they have to tell, you have to talk with them, at least on the telephone. And it is much better to talk with them face-to-face. That is the purpose of focus groups. They give customers a chance to sit around in a group and tell their stories with someone from the organization listening. The group setting is usually helpful, because they can get each other warmed up on their storytelling. Another way that some organizations gather customer stories is to actually send employees out to the customers to visit them on-site where they work or live. This gives the employees a chance to see what their customers do with the products and services that they sell them. It is often easier for customers to tell their stories if they are on their own turf where they are comfortable. If the only people who ever make these visits are senior managers or customer-service coordinators, then the visits will be almost worthless in bringing customer stories into your organization in any large scale. As many of the frontline employees as possible need to make the visits and see for themselves.

Part of what makes people want to tell stories about customers is because they actually know those people and have some type of relationship with them. A large number of the employees in a company need to know some of their customers well enough to be able to describe what they look like, how they talk, where they live, who their families are, and what their personalities are like. If most employees cannot describe a few customers this way, then you do not have enough customer stories floating around your organization to maximize the customer service that you could be providing.

## What Are You Learning from the Stories Customers Tell You?

What do you do with the customer stories once you have gone out and gathered them? Many times I have heard these stories discussed inside the company with the primary purpose of explaining away the complaints or short-comings that were highlighted in the stories. If a customer made a suggestion for an improvement, the employees discussing the story will put their energy and eloquence into explaining why that suggestion cannot be done. Or, if a customer complains about how some service was handled, the employees will focus on what the customer did wrong or will explain away the problem as an exception based on unusual circumstances. If this is how customer stories are handled, it would have been better if those stories had never been told at all. The only thing these types of discussions do is to reinforce the poor customer-service behaviors. "We are justified, so we continue." A much better way to listen to and discuss customer stories is to find your own organization's version of Carl Sewell's motto, "If the customer asks, the answer is yes."

If the customer wants you to improve something, improve it. You will have to find a way, of course, to improve it that you can afford and that is doable in your setting, but do something, even if it is only a partial improvement. If you cannot think of any way to improve the situation now, keep it on the agenda and keep discussing it until you do think of some way to respond to the customer's concern. Worst-case scenario: fail at finding a way to improve the situation, but *never* take a customer concern and just explain it away. When this happens the power of storytelling has turned against you and will become a deadly force to maintain the status quo in terms of customer service.

An acquaintance told me a story about going to the local hardware store on the main street of the small town where he lived. He asked for a particular item that he needed for some repair work that he was doing at home. The clerk shook his head and responded: "No, we don't carry that item. It's funny, people come in here all the time asking for that thing." This is not an isolated event in organizations. I have heard many different versions of the comment: "The customers keep telling us they want it, but we don't offer it." In most situations, this is a classic case of ignoring and refusing to listen to the customer. My friend who told me this particular story owns a small business himself and told me he yelled back at the clerk: "Are you nuts! If people keep asking for it, start stocking it!"

---

*Listening to your customers' stories is the single most important use of stories. NEVER IGNORE THEIR STORIES AND JUST EXPLAIN THEM AWAY.*

---

When you are listening to customer stories, positive or negative, the key diagnostic question to keep asking yourself is, "What are they telling us in this story about their definition of quality?" The only definition of quality that matters is the customer's definition. It is always possible, of course, to take the customer's definition of quality and build on it, making the product or service even better than what the customer expected. This is what is meant when companies talk about not just satisfying their customers, but surprising and delighting them with the quality of the service they receive. The point is, however, that the starting point for defining quality is with the customer stories and point of view.

There are two parts to this diagnostic question that you are asking yourself. The first part is to analyze the stories to understand the customer's definition of your product quality. If you are a service organization, think of the key services that you sell as products. What content, features, and results do your customers want from your products?

The second part of this diagnostic question is to analyze what the stories are telling you in terms of service quality. What did the customer like and not like about every minute of the time that he or she was in contact with your company, from the very first telephone call to the paying of the very last bill? The product component of this question focuses on *what* you sell and the service component focuses on *how* you sell and service it. For example, there is a specific service problem that has become very common in companies today. These companies have excellent products for their customers that produce high levels of satisfaction in terms of the quality of the product itself. These same companies, however, are driving their valued customers nuts with a voice-mail system that takes the customer in an automated loop from one recording to another until the customer slams down the phone in total frustration.

I know, for example, of one small business that ended up making a decision about which long distance telephone company to use for Watts line service based heavily on which company answered their telephones with human beings within a reasonable period of time. And that is a telephone company! They are selling a high-quality Watts product, but are not providing high-quality service to their own customers when it comes to the use of their telephones. Storytelling is a particularly valuable tool to use in gathering customer information when you are trying to understand these service issues of how the product is being provided. Because the "how" issues usually involve more intangible elements that cannot easily be seen, held, or measured for quality, stories are often one of the few ways that you can find out about service problems.

## Diagnostic Questions to Understand and Use Customers' Stories

1. What is the customer telling you in this story about the quality of the product (*what*) you are selling them?

2. What is the customer telling you in this story about the quality of the service (*how*) you are providing?

*Warning:* Do not ever use a customer story to explain away the problem or complaint. Contrary to popular opinion, the customer does not "just have to understand that you can't . . ."

Listen, learn, and respond in some constructive way to what you learn in a customer's story.

## Customer Stories Are Essential in Continuous Quality Improvement Work

When an organization is using Continuous Quality Improvement (CQI) methods to work on improving processes and systems, it is essential to listen to the customer stories at every step in the team efforts. This may sound like a statement of the obvious, but from my experience with CQI teams this is one of the most common mistakes they make. The teams will often pick the wrong problem to work on because the *employees* decided which part of the process is the highest priority to fix, instead of listening to the *customers'* points of view.

I witnessed a recent example of this in a hospital setting where a team of employees was working on improving the patient flow process for women who came to the hospital as a follow-up on a positive result from a mammogram. This means the woman will be having biopsy of a breast lump as an outpatient. Needless to say, this is an upsetting and frightening experience for any woman. The team members were very enthusiastic about their work and committed to improving the process. They had done extensive research and data gathering about the current system and had identified many areas that needed improvement. They were now deciding which problem to work on first. They were leaning toward picking a problem related to the patient waiting time that occurred at one of the steps in the process.

At that point, I overheard a conversation that occurred between one of the team members and a nurse who had just gone through the process as a patient. She was telling the team member what an awful experience it had been and that she was glad they were working on improving it. The CQI team member told her which problem they were going to tackle first—waiting time. Her response was to immediately start shaking her head and saying, "No, no, that's not the worst part at all." She went on to explain that the worst part was having to walk through the middle of the public lobby in the hospital gown to get from one department to another during the testing process. She explained in detail how embarrassing that was. She pointed out that this was a small town and people who knew her saw her in the lobby and that was the end of her confidentiality about the procedure that she was having done. She then went on to highlight several other problems, but none of them involved the waiting time.

The fascinating part of this conversation for me to watch was the reaction of the CQI team member to this customer's story. She tried her best for the first few minutes to ignore it. The momentum of the team efforts were already going in another direction; she did not want to hear stories that might require them to stop and think about what they were doing. I interrupted and asked the team member if they had done any customer interviewing after they had analyzed the process before picking a problem to work on first. She said that they had interviewed people while studying the flow of the process, but not at the point of deciding which piece to work on first. At the end of the conversation, the team member seemed to be convinced that the customers needed to be heard in this decision process. Now, she had to go back and convince the team to stop and reconsider their plans.

## Using Stories to Sell Your Ideas and Products to Your Customers

Stories are an excellent communication tool for keeping the customer on the minds of employees and for learning about the wants and needs of customers, but their customer value does not end there. Any top-ranking salesperson in any field can quickly tell you the value of a good story when you are trying to sell a product or service. Storytelling by salespeople may well be the most common use of stories in many organizations.

When screening and hiring for sales positions in many companies, one of the key factors that the recruiters are looking for is the verbal, interpersonal skills of the individual who is applying. Even if the product is financial or technical, the potential salesperson's ability to communicate at a relationship or interpersonal level is as important as the ability to understand and handle the technical information effectively. This interpersonal or relationship type of selling includes the ability to tell stories effectively.

A classic example of the use of storytelling in the selling of an extremely "factual" product is in the investment field. When an investment salesperson talks to a client about the purchase of a particular stock, most salespeople want to have some type of story to tell about the company. This may be a story about the CEO, a new product that they have just developed, or an interesting item about the history of the company.

Whatever the specific story is, having a story to tell will increase the odds of getting the customer's attention and persuading him or her to buy the product. This, of course, is not necessarily as true if the broker is talking to another securities professional, such as a portfolio manager from a client company's pension fund. In that case, the two financial professionals tend to talk in much more succinct facts and figures. There is no need to spark the interest of the other professional in the way that there is with a non-professional client.

And there is no need to find a way to help that type of client understand the value of the product. But with the typical investment client, a story is usually helpful to get the person's attention and to help them understand the value of the product. This goes back to the original explanation of the reasons that stories are such a powerful communication tool. They are *memorable* and *believable*. In a sales setting, both of these traits are extremely important.

Another great story was told about the CEO of one of the long distance telephone companies back when it started in competition with AT&T. They were erecting towers in a number of locations and, in one particular spot, the best location was on the property behind the home of an elderly woman. She was not at all convinced that she wanted that ugly thing in her backyard, so she refused to give them permission to build it there. Several people from the company had tried to sell her on the idea, but had gotten nowhere. Financial incentives just did not impress her.

Finally, the CEO, who was known as a great salesman, decided to give it one last try himself. He went to see her and, in the process of the conversation, managed to get her excited about the idea of the tower decorated with lights at Christmastime to look like a huge Christmas tree. He promised that if she let them erect the tower in her backyard, he would personally assure her that every Christmas the tower would be decorated at the company's expense. He kept his promise for several years, and then he left the company. After he left, someone decided to discontinue the Christmas decorating of the tower. The elderly woman never said a word or complained to the company, but the next time the contract came up for renewal on the tower, she would not sign. The company had to go in and remove the tower and go to the expense of relocating it.

## Mini-Negotiations . . .
## Everyone Is Selling Something
## in Organizations

Although only a small percentage of people in the work force are in jobs that are defined as sales positions, the reality is that almost everyone who works in an organization spends a large percentage of their time selling or persuading. When I talk with people about negotiation skills, I am quick to clarify that I use the term to mean any conversation that includes an element of persuasion or problem solving between two or more people.

When the conversation involves some effort to reach a meeting of the minds, this conversation is a form of negotiation. Many of these conversations in organizations may last only for 30 seconds or a minute, but they are still a negotiation conversation. I call these *mini-negotiations*. The same skills needed for elaborate, formal negotiations apply in these smaller, briefer settings. When I use this definition of mini-negotiation and ask audiences to estimate the percentage of their work conversations that would qualify as a mini-negotiation, I rarely get a vote from any individual of less than 75 percent. The majority of people vote in the 80–90 percent range. Some people swear that at least 98 percent of their conversations at work are some type of mini-negotiation. I usually tease these people about whether they ever engage in enough social chat to even say "Good morning, how was your weekend?" to their colleagues. In any case, the percentage of persuasion-based conversations among working people is very high. These conversations are a form of selling.

By watching the skills and behaviors of a talented salesperson in action, many non-sales professionals would learn some communication skills that would serve them well in their own setting. One of the skills that they would observe in this talented salesperson would be the ability to tell a great story. This salesperson has the ability to paint a verbal picture for the client that is added to the factual information to increase the odds that the client will take an interest in and understand the product. Anyone in any role in an organization can do the same thing when they are in a mini-negotiation conversation.

For example, assume that you are a supervisor of a large number of people who handle a service such as telephone customer service. You are having trouble with scheduling during a particular week, and you have to find some way to persuade at least one more person to come in and cover a particular shift. You could, of course, just order someone to come in using the power of your position, but you have found in the past that it works better to use persuasion, rather than power, whenever you can. In the long run, everyone is more cooperative that way. You are about to approach one of the employees to ask that person to come in to work for the shift you need covered. You could walk up to the person, state the facts, and explain that you need five people to cover the Tuesday shift and you only have four.

You may even be able to add the facts by offering to pay overtime for the work. These are all facts, and they might work to persuade the person to help you out. Now add to the facts that the reason that you only have four people for this shift is because of the flu epidemic that has hit the area. John is out sick and two other colleagues are out taking care of sick kids. What happens to the persuasive element of your request for help? Now, add a third piece by asking the employee to respond and tell you a story. Ask about the employee's situation to find out what the person may want in return for helping you out in this situation. Maybe this employee does not have sick children at home, but wants another day off later because of some personal plans.

By adding the second and third pieces of this conversation to the factual piece in the beginning, you have increased dramatically the odds of success of persuading the person to help you. You have personalized the situation and turned it into a story about the lives of several of the employees, including the person that you are trying to persuade. Notice that by adding both the second and third pieces to the conversation, you are balancing the stories. One story is intended to talk the person into helping you out. The other story is intended to find out what that person may want back from you in return. If you include both types of stories whenever possible in persuasive conversations, it will help you avoid falling into the trap of manipulation. Manipulation is a lopsided negotiation conversation where you make the other person feel good at the moment about doing what you want, but the person usually figures out later that there was nothing offered in return. This is not a good long-term strategy for persuasion. It will only work a few times. If you are going to use stories to turn a mini-negotiation into a more personalized persuasion, be sure that you are prepared to both tell your story *and* to listen to the other person's story.

## Stories as Verbal Persuasion

Stories are used for verbal persuasion in many different settings, including everything from simple work conversations to dramatic world events. Some of the most inspiring statements of persuasion used by leaders throughout history have actually been mini-negotiations in the form of brief stories. The speaker has used words to paint a visual picture for the listeners and inspire them in ways that the facts alone could never do. One of the masters at this was Winston Churchill. One of the most dramatic and inspiring portions of any speech he ever made was only one paragraph long. It is basically a visual picture that he painted for the people of England to inspire them to courage and hope at their bleakest time during World War II. It is a masterpiece of verbal persuasion.

> Even though large tracts of Europe and many old and famous states have fallen or may fall into the grip of the Gestapo and all the odious apparatus of Nazi rule, we shall not flag or fail. We shall go on to the end. We shall fight in France, we shall fight on the seas and oceans, we shall fight with growing confidence and growing strength in the air, we shall defend our island, whatever the cost may be.

> We shall fight on the beaches,
> We shall fight on the landing grounds,
> We shall fight in the fields and in the streets,
> We shall fight in the hills;
> We shall *never* surrender.[9]

Another famous example of a speech that used eloquent visual imagery was Lincoln's Gettysburg Address. The entire speech lasted only two minutes and was three paragraphs long. In that short amount of time, Lincoln managed to remind the nation what the United States was all about and produce one of the most well-known speeches ever given. Here are a few excerpts from that speech:

> Four score and seven years ago our fathers brought forth on this continent a new nation, conceived in Liberty, and dedicated to the proposition that all men are created equal . . .
>
> We are met on a great battlefield . . . to dedicate a portion of that field as a final resting place for those who gave their lives that this nation might live . . . But in a larger sense, we cannot dedicate—we cannot consecrate—we cannot hallow—this ground. The brave men, living and dead, who struggled here have consecrated it, far above our poor power to add or detract . . .
>
> It is rather for us to be here dedicated to the great task remaining before us . . . that these dead shall not have died in vain—that this nation, under God, shall have a new birth of freedom—and that government of the people, by the people, for the people, shall not perish from the earth.

## Success Can Make You Stop Listening to Your Customers' Stories

One of the most dangerous habits that an organization can fall into is to stop listening to its customers' stories. One of the most common traps that can trigger this mistake is success itself. If an organization is on top and doing well, there is a strong human tendency toward arrogance. In both individuals and companies, there seems to be a fine line between confidence and arrogance. The dictionary, however, makes a clear distinction between the two terms, defining *arrogance* as "exorbitant claims" and *confidence* as "trustworthiness or reliability." If you look at these two words from the point of view of the customer, they are dramatically different.

Being the customer of an arrogant company would in no way match the experience of being the customer of a confident company. Yet there seems to be a tendency for companies to react to short-term success by slipping toward arrogance and forgetting that it was their customers who gave them that success. The people in the organization stop listening to the customers' stories. The organization lets go of the very behavior that made it successful in the first place. The reasoning seems to be that if they are that good, they do not need to listen anymore. The status quo is very comfortable, so the people inside the organization gradually relax and settle in for a smooth ride. But in business, the ride never stays the same, so the environment keeps changing and within a relatively short period of time the status quo products and services are no longer what the customers want.

Long-term success requires long-term listening to customers. Once the company is successful, the listening is geared toward hearing the new wants and needs of the customers. One of the best sources of stories to help you stay in the lead with your customers are positive stories about your competition. If you listen to your own customers as well as their customers talk about what they like about the competition, you will often pick up valuable ideas about new products or services that you should be offering. Copy their ideas and use them to improve your company's products and services.

Count on the fact that the competition will copy you too. If you develop a new idea that no one else is offering, within a short period of time the competition will have heard about it and be offering it, too. Carl Sewell gives an example of this at his dealership. It was the first dealership in Texas to provide free loaner cars for service customers and to be open all day Saturday for service. For a period of time this service gave them a tremendous advantage over their local competition. But the lead did not last.

The competition started offering the same service. Sewell upped the ante by staying open until 8:00 p.m. when other dealerships were closing at 6:00 p.m. Again the competition matched them. Sewell then started sending secretaries to drop off and pick up the loaner cars to customers, so they did not have to make a trip to the dealership for service. The competition did the same. He says, "When will these improvements to our service program end? They won't. If we want to attract more customers—and keep the ones we have—we need to keep giving them more reasons to do business with us."[10] According to Sewell, if you are not constantly getting better, then you are getting worse. The customer-service environment is a moving target. The only way to know what is happening is to listen to your customers, listen to your competition, and listen to your employees. The stories they tell will be filled with information about the future, if you are willing to listen for it.

Fortunately or unfortunately, depending on your point of view, life has a way of self-correcting for arrogance in individuals and in organizations. When this happens to companies, it shows in their bottom line. Wisdom can be measured by the ability to take preventive action to head off the arrogance and stay in touch with reality. Listening and responding to your customers' stories is the most powerful protection any organization can have against arrogance.

## Questions to Ask about Your Organization's Customer Stories

Ask yourself the following questions to examine your organization's customer stories. The two important areas to examine are:

1. Do you tell large numbers of positive stories about your customers?

2. Do you listen and respond to your customers' stories?

- How many stories can you remember telling or hearing in the past month in your organization that starred the customer?
- Of the customer stories you remember, were the customers cast in a positive light or a negative, pain-in-the-neck role?
- How many times in the past month have you personally listened to a customer's story about the product or service that person received from your organization?
- If you did listen to any customer stories, what did you do with the information? Did you ignore it, explain it away, or try to change something in response to their story?
- What methods does your organization use on a regular basis to gather customer stories (surveys, telephone calls, focus groups, on-site questions, etc.)?
- What does the organization routinely do with the information that they learn from these customer stories?
- Can you list the recent new information that you have learned about your organization's quality in the following areas:

  Product quality

  Service quality

What have you done about what you have learned in each of these areas?

- How well do you use stories in your mini-negotiation conversations that you have at work? There are two ways to use stories in a negotiation conversation:

  Tell stories to explain your need and to persuade.

  Listen to the other person's stories to learn what to offer for a balanced negotiation.

- If your organization is in a successful phase at this point in time, how high is the arrogance factor running right now? Are you still listening to the customer stories and constantly changing and improving to respond to their needs? Or have you quit listening? If you have relaxed into your success, worry. Your customers will be moving on without you soon.

# PART 4

# Storytelling as a Tool for Managing Change

Hope is a memory of the future.
GABRIEL MARCEL[1]

# 14
# The Folklore
# of Organizations
# Built for Change

## The Role of Storytelling
## in Cultures Built for Change

In most organizations, storytelling is used to reinforce the old ways of doing things. The stories are based on the past and are used to communicate "tradition" or the historical way of behaving in that culture. Because storytelling as a communication tool is generally used to solidify the old, it would appear that the storytelling in an organization would act as an impediment to change and flexibility. And often, this is true. Many times storytelling is used to discourage or stop change. It is used to justify the past and make a case for continuing the past behaviors in the future.

Storytelling is, however, a neutral communication tool. Like any form of communication, it can be used for many purposes. It can be used to encourage people to think or move in any direction. It all depends on the motivation of the storyteller and the setting in which the person tells the story. When considering the issue of change through storytelling, an important question to ask is, "How do these adaptive cultures define the word *tradition*?" Does it necessarily mean "doing things *exactly* the way they have always done them in the past"? Or, as in the case of adaptive cultures, does the definition of tradition include a set of values and norms that tell people to keep changing and evolving new ways of being successful?

The word *tradition* is defined in Webster's dictionary as "the handing down of opinions, doctrines, practices, rites, and customs from ancestors to posterity by oral communication." In adaptive organizations, their cultural opinions, doctrines, and practices are geared toward encouraging and tolerating change. The oral communication that they use to pass on this tradition are stories that include a heavy emphasis on heroes and successful events around major changes or developments in the company's history. These organizations usually have founder stories or origin stories that reinforce this message of adaptability and risk taking.

For example, there are many stories about Sam Walton, the founder of Wal-Mart, that carry the message of his willingness to constantly adapt and change the ways the company did business. Walton wrote his autobiography, *Made in America*, shortly before he died. The book is actually the autobiography of Wal-Mart from its birth to 1991. One of the stories that he tells in the book about the early days of the company begins with these words: "As good as business was, I never could leave well enough alone, and in fact, I think my constant fiddling and meddling with the status quo may have been one of my biggest contributions to the later success of Wal-Mart."[1] He then goes on to tell about his running competition with the Sterling Store, run by John Dunham, across the street. He heard through the grapevine that Sterling was going to buy the lease for an empty building next to their existing store and expand it to be much larger than Sam's store. Although Walton admits in the story that he had no idea what he was going to do, he managed to talk the landlord into leasing the building to him instead. He then went on to add a small department store of his own. Now he had two stores on the same street in Newport, Arkansas. "I would run up and down the alley with merchandise. If it didn't sell in one store, I would try it in the other."[2] This is one of many stories of Walton's "ingenious" style and his willingness to always try something new, even if he was not too sure what he was doing. This attitude is one of the constant themes found in all of the Wal-Mart folklore.

> *In adaptive organizations, tradition and the folklore that supports it encourage change and risk taking.*

These sacred bundle stories about change are always present in a culture that values adaptability and innovation. If a company says it values change and risk taking, but you do not hear any stories in current events or historical "traditions" of valuing change, then be suspicious. Believe the themes and heroes of the stories, rather than the official statements that the company makes about itself. Brass plaques on walls may contain illusions or misrepresentations, but the collection of stories that make up the folklore of the company never do. The facts of the stories may have been exaggerated or changed over the years and may have lost some of their factual accuracy, but the themes and the cultural messages about key values will be as true and as accurate as they ever were.

## The New Story Line . . . Adaptive Cultures Built for Change

The conventional wisdom about change is that organizations hate and avoid it, and their corporate folklore usually reinforces this attitude. Even though this is probably still an accurate description of the attitudes and behaviors in most companies, there are some organizations that seem to handle change more easily. In these organizations, you will hear a common theme of "change is normal" in the stories people tell. Ralph Kilmann, author of *Gaining Control of Corporate Culture,* defines these adaptive cultures as having a "risk-taking, trusting, and proactive approach to organizational as well as individual life. Members actively support one another's efforts to identify all problems and implement workable solutions. There is a widespread enthusiasm, a spirit of doing whatever it takes to achieve organizational success."[3]

An often-cited example of this type of company is 3M. The company folklore is filled with stories about how 3M consciously works to encourage a culture that can handle change effectively. They found innovation and support risk taking at all levels in the organization. For years, 3M has had a goal of keeping at least 25 percent of its current product lines less than five years old.

A classic example of a 3M story that illustrates its nonbureaucratic style of operating is told about a *Wall Street Journal* reporter, Ames Smithers, who was writing an article on the company in the late 1950s. He was interviewing the president, and asked at one point to see the organizational chart. The president ignored him and changed the subject. The reporter repeated his request several times and was ignored each time. Finally the reporter interrupted and asked, "From your reluctance to talk about or show me an organization chart, may I assume that you don't even have one?" The president replied, "Oh, we have one all right," reaching into his desk drawer to pull it out. "But we don't like to wave it around. There are some great people here who might get upset if they found out who their bosses are."[4]

## Four Key Topics in Change Stories

One of the characteristics of adaptive organizations is that they have managed to incorporate a positive view of change into the key values of the company. The company expects change, looks for change, and sees it as a source of their current and future success. People who work in these companies are repeatedly told to expect change and are rewarded for introducing change into the organization. There are several different types of changes that take place regularly within these organizations. Organizations with adaptive cultures are usually changing constantly in all of these categories. There will be many stories circulating through the organization about frequent changes in all of these areas.

1. *Structural changes.*   Reporting relationships, divisional structures, location of offices, and work sites.

2. *Product changes.*   Development and introduction into the marketplace of new products on a regular and frequent basis.

3. *Strategy changes.*   Changes in the plans and execution of strategies in areas such as marketing, R&D, or service procedures.

4. *Technology changes.*   Finding faster or better ways to produce old products or services as well as development of new methods.

For example, during the years that I was employed at Hospital Corporation of America, the company was a classic example of a young, growing company in constant flux. There was a continual stream of new stories about changes within the company, with a particular emphasis on structural changes that occurred on a frequent basis as the company grew. Organizational charts were something of a joke because they were updated and changed so frequently.

Some of us used to suggest that we should post one of those large magnetic boards in the lobby of the headquarters building for the organizational chart. The idea was that everyone could have their name on a small magnetic chip, and then whenever the reporting relationships and titles changed again, all we would have to do is go out and reshuffle all the chips around on the board. In my five years with the company, I personally worked in six different offices, in five different buildings, and within three different subsidiaries of the company. And that was not considered particularly unusual at the time. Many of us used to claim that our best corporate skill was packing and moving from one office to another. A common theme of the stories that many people told in the company carried the message that if you did not like the way things were arranged now, don't worry about it because it wouldn't stay this way long.

Another example of a company that has built change into its culture is NSA (National Safety Associates), which is another young, fast-growing company that operates as a network sales organization and markets smoke detectors, water filters, air filters, and other environmental products. The people who work for that company are conditioned to expect the addition of new products to their lines on a frequent and regular basis. If there were not constant change in that company, the employees would see it as a sign that something is wrong. Stories about *lack* of change could hurt morale at NSA.

Hewlett-Packard is another company that seems to have fostered this expectation of positive change and has been able to maintain that key characteristic over the years as it has grown and become a mature company. Hewlett-Packard was founded in 1939 and, during the decades since its start, the culture of the organization has managed to change as the environment around it changed. The famous "HP way" has actually changed significantly over the years with more specialization of employees, lessening emphasis on cradle-to-grave employment, and fluctuations back and forth in the flexibility of procedures and management styles.

There is, of course, a great deal of controversy inside and outside the company about whether all these changes are good. But there is no question that Hewlett-Packard is highly skilled at changing itself in relatively short periods of time. When asked why they are not more resistant to change, the answer given by George Newman, the treasurer, is typical of the opinions your will hear inside the company. He talks about the objectives that were set by the original founders Hewlett and Packard at the beginning of the company's life. "They were not very specific. Instead they represented more of a general philosophy of how to be successful—the value of profit, satisfied customers, a good environment for employees, and the like."

According to Newman, the collective commitment to these types of key values has worked better to help keep HP more flexible than firms that have very specific key values such as "maintain an AA bond rating." He goes on to say that HP encourages employees to step to the plate and have a "radical idea" once in a while. "That helps to keep us from getting too set in our ways."[5] This is an example of a company that tells stories about itself using the theme that change is a normal and positive aspect of the work life.

## Risk Taking and Innovation . . . Do the Company Stories Emphasize These Values?

Although organizational cultures that are built for change are still in the minority, there is a keen interest these days in understanding how these cultures work and what caused them to develop in this direction. The environment today in almost every industry is changing so rapidly that there is a very real concern about whether most companies are equipped to keep up with the demands that these constant, rapid changes force upon them.

To examine how and why the adaptive organizations work, it helps to begin by looking at some of the key characteristics of their culture. The most significant characteristic of any culture in any setting is its values. All the other characteristics of a culture are rules and methods for attempting to carry out that culture's values. Values are, in effect, the hub of the cultural wheel, and all other characteristics such as norms, language, rituals, taboos, etc. are the spokes of the wheel, connected to and leading back to the key values. If you were going to study the key values of a culture such as a traditional tribe of people, one of the key areas that you would study is their religion.

Their religion and the elaborate network of stories associated with it will tell you about many of the basic tenets that they live by in that particular tribe. This does not mean, of course, that every individual always lives up to every value perfectly. People everywhere are human and there are many lapses away from the key values in any culture, whether it is a traditional tribal setting or a corporation. The key values represent the goals of the group and the direction in which it is headed. They tell you where you are going and, in general terms, how you are supposed to behave along the way. The other cultural characteristics add more detail to the picture, but the values are the controlling feature.

Current research indicates that one of the most consistent characteristics of adaptive cultures is a central value that states "Change is good for the organization." The examples given previously are several stories of this key value in action at companies such as Hospital Corporation of America, National Safety Associates, or Hewlett Packard. This does not mean that these companies or the people who work for them necessarily believe that change is always fun. You will find plenty of stories in these companies about what a pain in the neck and how frightening a lot of these changes are. It also does not mean that everyone in these companies agrees with the wisdom of every change that is made.

## Change Stories Include Controversy

There is usually a great deal of controversy about most major changes that occur. And some of the changes turn out to have been bad moves. They do not produce the intended results. The attitude, however, is to keep moving forward and to keep changing, even if you sometimes stumble. One of the attitudes that Franklin Roosevelt was famous for when he was first elected president at the height of the Depression was to *do* something. Try a new approach by changing something, even if you were not sure that it would work. If it does not work, change it again and keep changing until you get it right. This is a mindset similar to one you will find in many adaptive companies. They do not expect perfection. In fact, one of the other key characteristics of adaptive companies is that they encourage risk taking and can tolerate failure or changes in direction if the original idea does not work out as planned.

An example of this philosophy is the story told at 3M about the development of masking tape and eventually Scotch Brand tape at 3M. The man responsible for these developments was Dick Drew, a 3M employee in charge of selling sandpaper to automotive customers. He noticed that his customers were having trouble painting two-tone cars, because they would cover one color with newspaper and library paste and the new paint would often pull off with the paper.

Drew took a risk and promised that he would develop a tape that would solve the customers' problem. All his early attempts failed, and the 3M president became concerned that these failures would hurt the company's reputation in the automotive industry, so he told Drew to quit working on the new project and go back to his project working on sandpaper. Drew's next assignment was to work with a flexible crepe-paper backing for sandpaper. Drew could see that this paper had possibilities for adhesives that would work for the tape he had been trying to create, so he went to the lab to experiment with it. About that time, the president walked through the lab and saw what he was doing. The president asked Drew if he was aware that he had been ordered to stop working on that project. Drew admitted that he did know about the order. The president went on to ask if Drew knew how to follow orders. In response, Drew explained to the president why he believed the stretch in crepe paper would make the tape peel away, and how important it was to their customers. The president decided to let him continue. After hundreds of failures, the crepe paper worked and customers were ordering the new tape by the truckload. Drew went on to invent Scotch Brand tape five years later.[6] These products are two of the most successful and profitable products 3M has ever invented.

The key cultural issue is that change, risk taking, and tolerance for failure are parts of the sacred bundle of adaptive organizations. If you want to find out whether a company holds these values near and dear, just listen to the stories they tell. Listen to the informal folklore of the company and listen to the sacred bundle stories that are repeated over and over through the years.

If the heroes of the stories are people like 3M's Art Fry of Post-It Note fame and Dick Drew who defied authority to create masking tape, then you have a company with a history of valuing change and risk taking. No one at 3M claims that the president was pleased as he walked away from Dick Drew that day. In fact, Drew probably gave him a splitting headache and left him worrying the rest of the day about unhappy automotive customers. But in spite of the fact that he was not enjoying himself at the time, the president did walk away and let Drew continue on his renegade project.

## Stories about Cultural Norms and Rules That Support Change

There are many other cultural characteristics that back up this key value of tolerance for change that show up in the organization's favorite stories. One that is closely tied to values is the set of norms that the culture adheres to in its behavior, policies, and procedures. As described in earlier chapters, many corporate stories are intended to be instructive, explaining "how we do things around here." *Norms* are defined as rules for acceptable behavior. Each culture has its own rules that govern all types of behaviors from simple definitions of courteous behavior all the way through to complex definitions of ethical or honest behaviors. What may be considered legitimate in one culture may be heresy in another. The following examples of norms that encourage change are often found in adaptive organizations. Listen to the stories in your company to see if people regularly tell stories that carry these themes. Are they a part of the folklore of the organization?

- Rules support monetary and nonmonetary rewards for risk taking and innovations.
- People in the organization follow the motto "It is easier to ask for forgiveness after the fact than to ask for permission beforehand."
- Following your intuitions is allowed, even when it is considered a waste of time by others.
- Risk taking and successes in handling change are likely to get you promoted.
- If there is a policies and procedures manual at all, no one knows what it says and, besides, everyone lost their copies years ago.
- People believe that if you are not making some mistakes along the way, you are probably not doing anything very important.

If you want to know what the rules or norms are in an organization and whether they encourage change or not, listen again to the stories people tell in the organization. In this case, listen particularly closely to any of the stories that tell you "what pays" around here. The folklore about who gets ahead and why will tell you a lot about the norms in the organization as they are perceived by the employees. Also listen for taboo stories. These are the stories that tell you what an employee could say or do that would be a career-shortening gesture in that organization. In one organization it might be taboo to take a risk and fail, but in another organization it might be taboo to interfere with an employee who wants to take a risk.

There are hundreds of taboos, large and small, in every culture. In a change-oriented culture, behaviors that would discourage risk taking or discourage change in some way are likely to be taboos. For example, the famous statement, "But we've always done it that way" could be a taboo comment in a change-oriented organization. This could cause the person making the comment to be branded as a person who is short on thinking skills or lacks the courage to make a change. Another taboo could be to become known through stories as a manager who punishes employees who take risks and make mistakes.

The taboos in any culture are actually the reverse or opposite of the norms or rules of appropriate behavior. If, for example, you worked in a company that could never "find" its policy manual, you would be violating a taboo in the organization to show up at department meetings carrying your copy of the manual. If you then proceed to quote from memory out of the policy manual during the meeting, your job is probably in jeopardy. Your comments will, at least, be greeted with cold stares and silence from the other people in the meeting.

## Cultures Built for Change Hire People Who Are Attracted to Change . . . The New Storytellers

One of the key practices that seems to be present in many of these companies that foster change is that they hire people who can handle change and who are risk takers. They are aware of their key value of encouraging change and actively look for new employees who represent a good cultural fit. New employees are often referred to in organizations as "an infusion on new blood." In many ways, this expression refers to the new events and the stories about those events that these new employees are expected to trigger. Their attitudes, mindsets, and experiences will influence future events and create new stories in the organization.

The issue with recruiting new employees who are receptive to a change-oriented environment is not to determine whether the prospective employee *loves* change and finds it fun, exciting, and not the least bit frightening. Anyone who claims to feel that way about change is probably either lying or is completely out of touch with a portion of their own feelings about the change process. It is a perfectly normal human characteristic to find change difficult and frightening at times. The variation comes in how people respond to the painful and fearful parts of change. Do they have a history of running from it or avoiding it for as long as possible? Or do they have a history of managing those feelings and pushing on into the future and new adventures? There are many of both types of people in the world. The interviewers tell stories in the interviews that give the prospective employees the picture of the values and norms of the organization in terms of change. They listen for and ask for stories in the interviews that will tell them if the individual has a personal history of handling change well. They also tend to promote and reward the people who are the best representatives of this type of behavior.

Adaptive organizations know how to look for people who can manage the change and push on. Individual characteristics are dangerous to clone when recruiting new employees. If you get too many of one type of person in the organization, it can be damaging to the performance of the organization, because no one wants to do the tasks that all the cloned employees hate doing. The propensity for handling change well is an exception to this rule about the dangers of cloning. In the organizations with a history of adaptive cultures, it appears to be a policy that works well to clone themselves with new employees that match their own history of adaptability to change.

## Stories Focusing on Change as Improvement

There is a general mindset or habit of thinking in adaptive organizations that is important to the ability to sustain growth and innovation through the years. That mindset is to view change in general as a process of continual improvement. This is the core of the message of the Total Quality Management revolution that has been sweeping through American business and industry during the past decade. Whether all these formalized TQM efforts will produce all the results that people are hoping for still remains to be seen, but the core idea behind the movement is a stunningly simple statement about change.

The message is that true, long-lasting change in an organization does not have to be accomplished by large, sweeping, glitzy changes that cost millions of dollars and are spectacular enough to make the front pages of business journals all over the country. The real heart and soul of change in an organization is a much quieter series of events that takes place in the trenches of the organization every day. Change is the cumulative total of hundreds and even thousands of incremental quality improvements that are implemented by individuals and teams of people who define change as continual improvement. This means that *everyone's* stories are important. The cumulative total of all the stories from all over the organization adds up to the company's autobiography of continuous improvement. Every story matters and needs to be told.

As Kilmann says in his definition of an adaptive organizational culture, its members "actively support each other's efforts to identify all problems and implement workable solutions." That is a definition of change that most people can understand as worthwhile. It is also a definition of change in which more people can actually see themselves having a role, compared to the type of change that requires high-profile risk taking and charismatic personality traits to be able to pull it off successfully. The habit or mindset of thinking of and talking about change as incremental continuous improvement seems to be the clearest path toward productive change for adaptive companies. This is also one of the keys for how change-resistant organizations can find a pathway toward forming new habits of tolerating and encouraging change. In a "continuous improvement" culture, the teams of employees working on incremental improvements should be one of the key sources of stories. The team members become the most important storytellers in the organization. Even when it is the leader telling the stories, these stories are about these teams of people and their accomplishments. One example of this type of team story comes from the University of Michigan Hospital, a leader in the health care field in implementing continuous quality improvement methods. One of their teams decided to tackle the problem of an inefficient patient admission and discharge system. Because discharges were not being done on a timely basis, the incoming patients were spending an average of three hours waiting to be admitted to the hospital. The team discovered during their work that the problem spanned many different departments and was extremely complex. The cross-functional team did eventually manage to make some major improvements, such as consolidating several key departments under one administrator and giving the housekeepers beepers to let them know quickly when rooms opened up and needed to be cleaned. They were able to cut the average admission waiting time from three hours to eight minutes! But the team's story is not over yet. Their goal is to cut the waiting time to zero minutes. They are working on a way to have someone waiting at the hospital door to direct each patient directly to a room.[7] The retelling of this story will effect new work teams as they approach similar challenges.

## Is Your Organization Adaptive? Listen to the Stories It Tells

Answer the following questions about your own organization for clues about whether or not it has an adaptive culture. Think about both the organization as a whole and your own department or work unit specifically. Both are important to consider. Each department or division in an organization can work to become more adaptive and flexible in the same ways that the overall organization can make these efforts.

- How does your organization define *tradition* in the stories they tell? Does it mean doing things the same way they have always been done in the past? Or is the term used to mean that your organization has a tradition of constantly changing and improving the way it does its work?

- Are there frequent stories about people being encouraged and rewarded for taking risks, even if those risks sometimes lead to failures? If they are rewarded, what types of rewards are they given?

- Who are the heroes in your corporate stories? Are they the change agents, innovators, and risk takers? Or did people get ahead in your organization by conforming and not making waves?

- Are the people in senior-level positions people with professional autobiographies of being risk takers and change agents?

- Does the organization make a conscious effort to recruit and hire people who are receptive to change? What are the new story lines that are arriving in the organization on a regular basis with the new hires?

- What are the stories about your organization's history of success or failure with implementing major changes? No organization is 100 percent successful in implementing change, but adaptive cultures usually have a good track record, with most change efforts ending up a success. Part of why adaptive cultures have a better track record on successful change implementation is because they adapt and change the implementation plan as they proceed through the change process.

# 15

# The Role of Storytelling in Creating an Adaptive Organization

Kurt Lewin, pioneer and expert in the field of organizational dynamics and change, states: "If you want to truly understand something, try to change it."[1] Most organizational cultures are not as adaptive as they need to be to survive and prosper in their fast-changing environments. One of the most pressing concerns of many people in leadership positions is how to overcome the resistance to change that exists in their organizations. The old culture may have served the organization well in the past, but the environment has changed and their old ways of operating do not fit the new circumstances anymore.

Northwest Airlines is often cited as an example of a culture that fit its environment well in the past, but did not serve it well after the deregulation in 1979.[2] It had a cost-cutting, financially oriented culture that worked reasonably well in the regulated airline industry. After deregulation, the increased competition between airlines made customer service an increasingly important factor in an airline's economic performance. Northwest's financially driven culture did not help it adapt as rapidly to this change in priorities as some of the other airlines were able to do. Using their perspective of a financially driven operation, the solution that they saw to their problems was a major acquisition of Republic Airlines. This move hurt their performance even more. In the months after the merger, customer-service problems reached nightmarish proportions for both travelers and Northwest employees in airports all over the country. During that period of time, frequent business travelers, who are notoriously harsh in their opinions about airline service, nicknamed the airline "Northworst." Their earnings dropped from $430 million in the 1970s to only slightly more than half that in the following seven years.[3] Gradually, during the 1980s, Northwest has managed to catch up to some extent, but there is no question that its old culture was a barrier to its ability to adapt in the 1980s to a very different regulatory and competitive environment.

This is not an isolated example of one company. It is, in fact, probably one of the most common problems that a majority of organizations face at some point in their existence. Their culture "fits" well during the founding and growth era and contributes significantly to their success during that phase. When the environment changes, however, these mature companies are not adaptable enough to shift quickly into new strategies, products, or services that are needed in the new setting.

## Telling Stories That Build the "Habit" of Expecting Change

In many organizations there is a silent agreement during profitable, successful times to pretend that the world will always stay the same. The assumption is that the current phase will last forever. All the stories people tell are about the past and the present. If they tell stories about the future at all, they tell them with the assumption that the future will be approximately the same as the present.

But present conditions do not last forever. The most casual review of the writings on world history makes it perfectly clear that no era of human existence has lasted forever. This is a basic truth of living that everyone probably knows at some level. And yet, during the good times in an organization's life, you will rarely hear day-to-day references to what will happen *after* the current glory days. It is one of the amazing examples of collective "group think" in action. The ability to rationalize and ignore the obvious until it forces itself upon the group is one of the most common mistakes that groups of people make over and over.

Here are a few examples of some comments that have been made in business circles which represent this assumption that things will not change too much in the future. In 1943, Thomas J. Watson, chairman of the board of IBM, said, "I think there is a world market for about five computers." In 1962, a recording company executive turned down a contract with the Beatles saying, "We don't think they will do anything in this market. Guitar groups are on the way out." In 1968, *Business Week* wrote, "With over fifteen types of foreign cars already on sale here, the Japanese auto industry isn't likely to carve out a big share of the market for itself."[4]

## Being Your Own Futurist . . . Stories about Change

If an organization's goal is to become more adaptive and flexible in dealing with change, one of the first things that the people in the organization must do is face the fact that there will be change and start telling stories about it. This is particularly crucial during the successful eras, when there needs to be a continual dialogue at all levels of the organization about what is likely to come next and ways that the organization might be able to respond to these future stories. No one, of course, knows with certainty what the future will look like. With the expertise inside most companies, however, there is usually the knowledge and skill to create plausible scenarios and think through the options of how the company could respond.

This process is a mental exercise that keeps people's thinking flexible. It also helps people deal with the fear and dread that inevitably accompanies major change. One ingredient of the fear of change is a feeling of losing control. People were skillful and competent at the old way of doing things, and now they are thrown into a new situation that leaves them feeling incompetent and out of control. Anticipating possible directions that the future might take and thinking through ways to respond and "gain control" over these future events helps people manage their fear. The key to dealing with fear and dread is to face it and figure out what you are going to do to regain a sense of control over your part of the events around you. Creating future story lines and thinking through how you will handle these scenarios is one way to do this.

Thinking about and telling stories about the future eras of the organization needs to become an organizational habit that occurs regularly, in both formal and informal settings. One of the ways that some organizations do this is to bring in futurists, who are often economists, to help them think through the possible future scenarios for their business. These consultants are basically sophisticated professional storytellers focused on the future. My impression from hearing clients talk about having participated in this type of exercise is that these futurists are helpful in shining a light on the future and giving people some ideas about what to expect and how the company might respond. Going through this type of exercise is a good start, but that is all it is.

Let's assume that the futurist spends a day or two with the senior management of the company, and everyone finds the experience enlightening. What people are talking about a week after the futurist is gone is the real evidence of the impact of that interesting experience. Once-a-year one-day events will never change an organization's culture. To change a culture, the new way of thinking must become an organizational habit that occurs every day. A once-a-year event is a good springboard to get started, but the forming of the daily habit has to be triggered by the people inside the organization, beginning on the day after the futurist leaves. There must be an ongoing dialogue of stories about the future and the expectation of constant change.

> *Form the organizational habit of expecting change and telling stories about the future that reflect these changes. No business cycle lasts forever.*

## Getting Employees Involved in Telling Stories about Change

The second concern that must be addressed if you want to change the culture toward adaptability is to consider how to involve everyone in thinking about the future. Even with the organizations that bring in the futurists, often the only people who are invited to participate in these conversations are a select group of top management. No one else is invited, and no one else ever hears the stories from these discussions. For example, this was the case with one Fortune 500 company that had a practice of bringing in these types of consultants to help the leadership in the company think about the future. The senior management would rave about how helpful these meetings were and how enlightening the discussions were. If, however, others in the company who were not a part of this elite group asked for details about what was discussed, they were told that the information was confidential. It was competitively sensitive information that could not be shared broadly for fear the competitors in the industry might get their hands on it.

As a communication and cultural change consultant, my reaction to hearing this was one of my less-than-reverent "Are you nuts!" comments. This "confidential" policy is a cultural change disaster. This type of storytelling about the future should never be a private affair for only a few members of the organization. In the first place, in this particular company, people at almost all levels were highly educated, knowledge-based professionals who found the "confidentiality" answer to their requests for information insulting. If they could not be trusted with information about the future of the company, then many of these people drew the conclusion that they apparently were not really a part of this organization in any significant way.

The second and more important part of the problem with the confidentiality approach is that the *leaders are not leading* when it comes to creating a habit of thinking and talking about future changes and looking at how everyone in the company will need to adapt to those changes. The leaders are going off on their own to contemplate future change, but they are not taking anyone along with them. In most cases, this will result in an organization with an employee population that thinks strictly in terms of present and past stories and is very resistant to a vision of the future that has not been shared with them. The leaders are trying to *drag* the organization into a changing future instead of leading it.

## The "Hit the Ball and Drag Charlie" Syndrome

This reminds me of an old golfing joke that I often repeat to clients which has the punch line "hit the ball and drag Charlie." The joke is about an avid golfer named Tom, who played golf every day with his best friend Charlie. When he came home late from golf one day, his wife asked how the game had gone. Tom responded, "Terrible; Charlie had a heart attack on the fourth tee and dropped dead." His wife was shocked and responded that it must have been awful. Tom nodded and said, "Yes, it was. From that point on, it was hit the ball and drag Charlie the rest of the way around the course!"

It is a silly story that has been around golfing families for decades, but many times in organizations the punch line comes back to me as I watch leaders try to lead change. No one is following. Those leaders have to "hit the ball and drag Charlie" the entire way through the change. If you have an organization with hundreds or thousands of employees, there are a lot of Charlies to drag. It is, in fact, impossible to drag that many unwilling people effectively through a major organizational change. If the leader is powerful or charismatic, that person may be able to get the majority of employees to nod in agreement while standing there face-to-face. But I am certain from hundreds of interviews that I have conducted in many change-resistant organizations, the minute that leader walks away, most of those employees will turn their thoughts to figuring out a way to ignore the message without getting caught. And from the stories that I have heard, they are very skillful at doing this. If the employees are not allowed or encouraged to participate in an ongoing dialogue about the future and the need for constant change, they will be focused on the present and will not see the need for the change. It just sounds like a lot of trouble and inconvenience to them.

One of the most extreme examples of this "nodding and ignoring the message" that I have witnessed occurred several times in organizations where the business office employees were involved in implementing a new computer system. This was back at the time when the employees were being asked to give up their trustworthy manual systems and replace them with computers that were highly suspect from the employees' point of view. Numerous times, we discovered that there was an elaborate pretense being played out by these employees. They would nod compliantly and agree to use the new procedures. But if you walked in on them unexpectedly or opened the "wrong drawer," you discovered that they were still maintaining the old manual tracking system on the side. Whenever a customer called, needing information, they always relied on their old reports.

With one group that was particularly stubborn about ignoring the new data coming out of the system, I teased them one day telling them that I had come back to the office during the night and hot-wired all their old filing cabinets. If they touched any of those drawers, their hair would stand on end. With that colorful image that appealed to their sense of humor, they were willing to strike a deal with me to try the new reports a few times to see if they worked. Fortunately, the reports worked well for them and gradually they began to switch over to the new system and abandon their old manual procedures. During the entire process, however, I never deluded myself by thinking I could order them to make the switch. I had to find a way to get them to be willing to give it a try. In that case, a funny story about the nut who claimed to have hot-wired their file cabinets did the trick.

By the way, the company that had the confidential meetings with futurists is no longer a Fortune 500 company. The environment changed and the company was not able to move its thousands of employees fast enough to keep up. The layoffs were massive, and the collective corporate pain was far greater than any ongoing change and evolution ever could have been.

## Creating a Shared Vision of the Future through Storytelling

Once you start to develop the organizational habit of both thinking and talking about future changes, the second issue to consider is whether everyone is headed in the same direction toward the same future. If the habit of talking about the future took people in the organizations off in hundreds of different directions with different stories about what the future will be and how the company should shape itself in the future, there would be chaos and endless frustration. The essence of teamwork is a shared vision. There are many other bells and whistles that are associated with great teamwork, but if the group does not have a shared vision of where it is headed and why it is going there, there is no teamwork. In other words, the people in the organization all have to tell stories with a shared message and theme. The plots and characters may vary from one department to another, but the underlying purpose or direction of the story is the same.

Peter Senge gives a compelling description of shared vision in his book, *The Fifth Discipline.*

> A shared vision is not an idea. It is, rather, a force in people's hearts, a force of impressive power. It may be inspired by an idea, but once it goes further it is no longer an abstraction. People begin to see it as if it exists.[5]

The shared vision is the goal of what the people in this organization are trying to create and how they want to shape their future. They cannot control external environmental events, but they can control their response to those events and what they create out of the future that is handed to them. The famous story of Steve Jobs and the cofounders of Apple is a classic example of a group of people with the shared vision to move the power of computers into the hands of masses of people.

The vision must be inspiring in the sense of creating something new and making something important happen. Having a shared vision is similar to what is meant by the old-fashioned term of having a "calling." The calling is a commitment to accomplish something that is larger than profits or earning a living. Beating the competition is not an inspiring enough vision to stand the test of time and trigger enthusiasm and commitment from large numbers of people. The vision must come from the inside out and focus on accomplishing something that is exciting or important, rather than just responding to a requirement imposed from the outside by the competition or survival pressure.

For example, AARP (American Association of Retired Persons) is the largest nonprofit association in the United States that was founded around the motto "To Serve, Not to Be Served." The founder's story included a vision that centered around the value of older people and what they had to offer. Over 50 percent of people in the United States over fifty years of age are members of AARP. This is more than 35 million people. Apparently, a lot of people are interested in the vision of this organization. Not only do they have a huge membership, but thousands of older people volunteer their time to work with AARP on their various projects. These volunteers represent the motto, "To Serve, Not to Be Served" in action.

When you interview people who work at AARP, many of them tell you at some point that they love working there and have no intention of leaving. One man told me that he knew that he had limited his career growth and earning potential by staying there over the years, but was not at all sorry about that decision. The employees in this association, as in most organizations, will readily tell you about the shortcomings and the irritations that occur in the organization, but when asked if they are thinking about leaving, most of them look startled and shake their heads. There are a number of reasons that employees want to stay with AARP, but the single most common thread in the explanations they give is that they believe in what the organization stands for and is trying to do, and it is reflected in the stories they tell.

## The Vision Cannot Be Private Property

In working to create a shared vision in an organization, the word "shared" is the key. If the vision is the property of one leader or a small group of the elite, you are back to the "hit the ball and drag Charlie" syndrome. Under those circumstances, the vision will never work to inspire the employees to gear up and expend the energy necessary to accomplish great feats. People cannot be ordered to share the vision. It is a voluntary process. An organization must have many settings that encourage employees at all levels to talk with each other, to exchange ideas and stories which focus on how to make the "vision" an active, genuine part of the organization's work life. There are many ways to do this. Here are a few examples:

- Build a few minutes of storytelling into your regularly scheduled meetings, such as department-head meetings, unit meetings, planning meetings, etc. Focus this storytelling on examples of how people are putting the vision into action.

- Build storytelling into your orientation process using experienced employees as the tellers. This serves a dual purpose of educating the new employees and reminding the older employees of the heritage of the company. Use both inspiring and funny stories to illustrate how the vision of the organization is played out.

- Organize lunchtime gatherings that center around storytelling, focusing on specific topics about the future of the organization.

- Use newsletters, bulletin boards, paycheck stuffers, and other forms of print to distribute employee stories throughout the company.

- Use videos to record storytelling and display them in public locations such as the cafeteria or lobby.

One thing to keep in mind is that people cannot be tricked easily with stories that do not represent the truth—at least not for long. If they are told that the vision is to create a great product, but soon discover that the real goal is to make sure that the senior managers get their year-end bonuses, there will be trouble. Under those circumstances, it will not work to try to sell them a new vision the next year, because they will not be fooled again. Instead of generating stories about creating great products, the employees will be likely to tell stories about being too smart to be duped. "Don't trust the leadership" will be the underlying theme of their stories. This is one of the problems that has created the anger and cynicism toward American politicians. They repeatedly try to sell a great vision of the future, but appear to have no real intention or ability to follow through and actually do the inspiring things they talk about. After a few rounds of that pattern, people are very skeptical of fancy promises and visions of a better future.

If shared vision is something that people must come to voluntarily, then the process of getting there is dialogue, as people tell and exchange the stories. Talking together and thinking through the possibilities is the only way to create a voluntary coalition around a vision. The process can be guided by the leader's vision within the framework of the key values of the organization and the external environmental realities, but it cannot be forced. Different individuals will take different amounts of time to reach a commitment to the shared vision, and some will never join. But there must be a constant, ongoing exchange of ideas and storytelling that creates a picture of the vision in action.

## Changing an Old Vision Requires a New Story Line

The new story line is particularly important when the old vision needs to change significantly. An organization may have been traveling down one path successfully for a number of years, and now the environment changes in a way that means the organization must change its direction. This is not a change that can be made without discussion and many meetings around those "tribal campfires" that were discussed earlier. If the organization has a history of being in the habit of thinking about and talking about changes in the future, it will help them to have open dialogue and exchange of ideas about shifting directions. An organization with this habit will move much more quickly to develop the new story lines than one that is shocked and surprised by the need for change.

> *If the goal is to have a shared vision, the process for getting there is dialogue. Shared vision is a voluntary agreement.*

## Listen to Current Stories before Trying to Change the Culture

So far in this chapter, the focus has been on the future: how to move toward an organizational culture that has a habit of talking about future changes and working toward a new story line of what the organization's role should be in that future. Another key element that is essential to successfully change an organization's culture is to look at the present. If you are going to change a culture, you need to be very familiar with what currently exists.

You need to understand both the future vision of where you are headed and the current reality of what exists, so that you have a clear understanding of the gap between the two. That gap between current reality and the future state you want to create will give you a starting point for knowing what needs to change and in what order to address these changes. If your goal is to move toward a more adaptive culture, then it is important to know in detail exactly how adaptive or nonadaptive the current culture is. One of the most effective tools for producing an accurate diagnosis of the current culture's characteristics is to listen to the current stories floating around the organization.

## Questions to Ask When Listening to Current Stories

When you are looking for the patterns of behaviors and opinions within the organization, the following questions deal with important topics about which to gather data. They are diagnosis questions intended to help you think through the current state of your organization's culture. Listen for stories around your organization that tell you the answers to these questions.

1. Is the organization geared toward *collective, team-oriented* behaviors or does this organization prefer *"lone ranger" style* of operating? Who are the heroes in the popular stories about your organization? This characteristic is an example of a norm, or cultural rule, about what constitutes appropriate behavior. If you work in an organization that has a norm of "lone ranger," independent action, you are breaking the cultural rules if you keep asking for instructions or help on projects. Likewise, if you work in an organization that has a norm of collective, team action, you are breaking the cultural rules if you launch out on your own all the time, never asking for help.

2. Who takes *risks* in the organization? When do they take them and why? Does it pay to take risks, either monetarily or with other rewards? Again, these are norms or rules for "how things work around here." An organization that has risk-averse norms will be much slower to change than one that values risk taking and does not punish its members for taking risks

and failing sometimes. Many times these stories are examples of "We survived" or "I know the ropes around here" stories.

3. Who has the *power* in the organization, both formally and informally? Both of these groups are important during a major change. Either group can block a change, if enough of them are against it. The "I know the ropes around here" stories will often provide you with a road map of who the power people are, as well as telling you when and why they use their power.

*Formal power* tends to be organized around budget control, project assignment control, and the capacity to order people to do things.

*Informal power* is centered more around influence. People with informal power sources are persuasive, are trusted by their followers, and are usually quite articulate.

4. Where are the *strong personal relationships* in the organization in terms of friendships and high trust connections? These may not be personal, outside-of-work friendships, but they are people who trust and rely on each other in the work setting.

5. What is the *management style or styles* in the organization? Do the managers use highly participative or hierarchical methods? Is this a setting where there is a great deal of hands-off management with people working independently, or does everyone usually wait for instructions? Do the managers speak out and say what they think freely around the organization, or do they wait till they get out in the hall and talk quietly among themselves about their true opinions?

6. Who are the *internal enemies* in the organization? It may be key individuals who are at war with each other, although often the battles run more along departmental or professional lines. For example, the sales force rarely gets along with the operations or production people. Doctors almost always irritate nurses in a hospital, and the feeling is usually mutual. Finance people usually drive everyone else crazy on a regular basis. Where are the battle lines in your organization?

7. What is the common *language* used in stories in your organization and is it compatible with the vision and goals of the change? Language is a cultural tool and represents a quick and easy way to measure how the organization sees itself and what is "on its mind." An organization may tell me officially that the customer is important, but before I believe this statement I listen to their day-to-day language in their stories to see if it includes frequent and varied references to customers. The same is true with the mission. If the mission really matters, people talk about it all the time. Some of their stories may be arguing or debating about the mission. Some controversy and debate is not necessarily a problem. But if no one ever mentions the mission at all in meetings and other settings, it is not a shared vision.

It is also useful to do a vocabulary count of the number of different words the organization uses for key topics in the organization. This will help to tell you how much importance is really placed on the topic. Organizations who are obsessed with the customer, the production of quality products, or innovation will have many different words and phrases to describe what these concepts mean. This is very different than hearing a vocabulary about rules, regulations, and policies in the stories people tell. Sometimes they build up such a lingo of jargon among themselves to describe these topics that an outsider has a difficult time figuring out what they are talking about.

8. Who are your *natural storytellers*? These are the people with the talent to entertain and educate people through the stories they tell as a daily part of their working lives. They often have a good sense of humor and a dramatic flare. They represent an invaluable source of help as you launch into your change efforts, particularly in the area of creating shared vision. It helps if they are long-time veterans of the organization and can play the role of "tribal elder." Their stories carry a greater credibility when they are seen in this light in the organization. They also have the potential to be formidable adversaries if they turn against the change. Remember, storytelling is the most powerful form of human communication. If the talented storytellers are opposed to the change and spin their tales in that direction, the change effort is in serious trouble.

These cultural characteristics represent some of the most important issues to investigate about your current culture as you embark on any large-scale change. Once you know the answers to the preceding questions, it will provide you with a wealth of information about where your organization is currently receptive to change and where the resistance is likely to occur. By understanding the current environment in the organization, you will have a clearer picture of the gap between the current state and the goal of the future state that you are trying to achieve. The answers to these questions will also give you ideas about the roles that people can play during the change process.

## Old Stories That Tell the "New" Message

Do not assume there are no old stories floating around the organization that carry the "new" theme. Old stories told by in-house storytellers can be an excellent tool to use for shining a light on the important new themes that need to be emphasized. Locate the old stories from the organization's history and current events that are examples of what the whole company needs to be doing on a larger scale in the future. Once you find them, tell the stories over and over in different ways all over the organization. Encourage people to create new stories with these same themes. Have them write or tell the autobiography of the organization. Put them on video, create oral histories, write your organization's autobiography or at least pieces of it that highlight the stories that emphasize the key values or goals in the new direction. Find the talented storytellers in the organization that are interested in the new themes and will consciously work with you to find the old stories that match those themes. Use these old stories as a springboard for creating new stories that build on those themes.

If, for example, you are trying to develop a more customer-driven culture, find specific individuals or departments that have a historical reputation for excellence with their customers. Once you find them, tell their stories to the whole organization, reward the heroes of the stories, promote them, talk about them constantly, involve them in advisory groups, be seen in the halls stopping to talk with them, write about them in the company newsletter, etc.

Find every way you can to turn them into the new organizational heroes. Move the power, both formal and informal, in your organization into the hands of the people and groups who are the walking, living, breathing examples of the new direction. A shift in formal power structures and informal power, through access and influence, is *always* noticed in organizational life. People get the message that this new direction is serious.

## Find the Current Stories That Are Supportive of the Change

When facing a major change, many times an organization's leadership focuses primarily on all the people and groups in the organization who are not in favor of the change or do not have the willingness or skills to move with the change. This is exactly the reverse of what they should be doing if they want to maximize the potential for a successful change. At some point, you do have to deal with the negative forces in the organization, but this is not the first place to focus your attention. Spend your energy paying attention to the people and the stories that are positive embodiments of the new themes. If you do this, a good portion of the resistance will disappear on its own and you will have few negative forces to deal with later.

For any key value that is embodied in organizational change there are always at least a few individuals and stories floating around the place that are current examples of the new direction. It does not matter whether you are talking about valuing the customer, innovation, improving quality, or moving faster, there are some employees and managers out there who believe enthusiastically in those issues and are willing to help make them happen on a wider scale in the organization. The job of the people leading the change is to go out and find those people and recruit them to help with the change process. If someone tells me that there is no one in the organization who represents the values embedded in the new direction, I am doubtful. It is likely that what this really means is the person who makes that statement does not know the people in the organization very well. They are there somewhere in the organization, although they may be hidden.

If there really is *no one* in the entire company who is interested or enthusiastic about these types of values, I would recommend that company halt its change effort, and take a serious look at its recruiting practices instead. But I have to say, in 18 years of working in and with organizations, I have never found a company that fits this depressing scenario.

Paying attention to current stories about people who are receptive to the new ideas is particularly effective if the story is about someone who is usually a naysayer. For example, there is a large corporation that is famous for experimenting with the latest new ideas in management styles and organizational theory. Several years ago, when this company jumped on the Total Quality Management bandwagon, the familiar groan went through the organization. "Here we go again, the latest new religion." This was the expression people used in the company to describe what they thought they were seeing. But this time it turned out to be different. Usually the senior management of this company ignored most of the fads that passed through the place. They certainly did not fund these ideas to any great extent and did not create a power base for these new ideas and the people who were promoting them. This time, however, senior management got involved and were trained themselves. They created a whole new group within the company to organize and lead the Total Quality Management effort. This group was very well funded. And they went out and recruited a prestigious person from the field to head the effort. The message was quickly sent out through the organization that when this person spoke, people in the organization listened, including the leadership.

About two years into this effort, I had an opportunity to talk with one of the long-time veterans of the company and ask him what he thought of the whole thing. This man is probably one of the people who helped to originate the expression "the latest religion." He is not an easy convert by any means, so I was curious to see what he had to say. When I asked him, he just smiled and shook his head. Then he said, "You know, I was very skeptical when they started this whole thing. And the verdict is still out. But I think there is actually the possibility that they might stick with this one and make it work." Then he laughed and said, "I can't believe I'm saying that." We both laughed and agreed that his uncharacteristic optimism might just be the result of indigestion from something he had eaten for lunch, but the real message of this conversation was that the company was going about this change in a way that a hard core "prove it" person was inclined to believe. In that company, when you heard a story about this man taking the change seriously, you would be likely to take notice. He was not an easy sell, and everyone who knew him was aware of that fact.

## Include the Informal Leaders as Storytellers

It is important to make sure that your change plans include the informal leaders, whether they are advocates for the change or not. If you try to ignore informal leaders who are naysayers at the beginning of the change process, they will not go away. If you try to threaten or intimidate them, they will go underground and continue to spread their negative stories. Keep in mind that even if the informal leaders look like they are standing alone, they are not. There is a network of supporters somewhere backing them and protecting them. Underground systems work because of massive support from large numbers of people. Neither the Underground Railroad of the Civil War or the French Resistance during World War II could have survived with only a few people supporting them. If either had been isolated or supported by only a few people in the two countries, the whole operation would have fallen apart. The same is true in an organization. Informal leaders *are* leaders because they have a strong following of listeners.

If you find that many of the informal leaders in an organization are in favor of the changes and embrace the new direction, the challenge is a relatively easy one. All you have to do is find a role for them in the change process. These roles can be anything from storytellers to handlers of detail logistics of the change. Just make sure that the role is a real one. Do not put an informal leader in a pseudorole that has no real power or purpose. That person will figure this out in no time, and will be insulted and angry. Then you have taken a likely advocate and turned that person into an angry adversary.

Keep in mind, as you look for these informal leaders in your organization and try to find useful roles for them, that this is an effort that can easily be blinded by prejudices. You could easily miss one of the most enthusiastic informal leaders, who would be invaluable to the change effort, because that person is a frontline worker in housekeeping or the kitchen. If you are accustomed only to looking within the ranks of people whose names are printed on the official organizational chart, you will never be successful at finding the majority of the powerful informal leaders of your organization. Even if you do manage to find them, the prejudices may cause people to resist giving them significant roles in the change process.

People often ask how one goes about finding the informal leaders. There is no one answer to that question, but the most straightforward way to find out is simply to ask frontline employees. The questions to ask are the following:

- Whom do you respect and trust?
- To whom do you listen?
- Whom do you consider to be one of the leaders among the employees?
- Who has the nerve to speak up and say what a lot of other people are thinking, but not willing to say?

People often assume that there is some mysterious process to learning about how an organization's culture functions. I am often asked, when working in a company, how I found out all those things about the people in the organization. And I invariably respond, "I ask them!"

## Persuading Reluctant Informal Leaders to Participate in the Storytelling

There are the informal leaders, of course, who are not receptive to the change. It is important that you track down these people and make every effort to involve them in a productive way in the change. If you follow this strategy only with the cooperative or receptive informal leaders, you are leaving dangerous loose cannons operating in the organization. The negative or resistant informal leaders must be drawn into the process as well. Once these people are located in the organization, the first thing that you need to be prepared to do is listen to them. Get them to tell you their stories about why they are leery of the change. Find out *why* they are resisting the change. It may be because of something about this specific change, or it may be that they resist any type of change.

There is often a lack of trust on the part of resistant informal leaders. Many times, part of why they are resisting is because they do not trust the motives or the truth of the messages that they are hearing from the leadership in the organization. If this is the case, persuading them to become involved in the change will require some repairing of the damaged relationship. There are three questions that have to be answered with the informal leaders who are resistant to the change. By the way, these same issues are important to consider with the people in formal leadership positions as well. It is, however, more likely that it will be the informal leaders who are overlooked.

- What would have to happen to prove that this situation is different than what they have experienced in the past in this organization?

- What role could they play in this change that would be useful in moving the organization forward in the new direction?

- What's in it for them? If these people are resistant to the changes, they are less likely to be inspired by the idea of the change and the possibilities that it holds for the future. In most cases, more immediate, short-term benefits will be a better motivator with a resister. These benefits could be anything from the recognition they receive for being in a key change agent role, to being sent for training in a new skill area. It needs to be something that person perceives as a benefit.

There are also several important issues that you avoid with resistant informal leaders. They have a great deal of organizational power and cannot be ignored. Their legendary stories can be very destructive if they are cast in the role of victim. This legacy can last long after the person is gone from the organization. On the other hand, they do not and cannot be allowed to control the organization.

- Do not ever bargain with the resistant informal leader about whether or not the change is going to take place. It *is* going to happen. The bargaining is about how to involve them in the change, not whether it is going to happen.

- Do not threaten or appear in any way to mistreat them. All of their supporters are watching how you treat these informal leaders. There is no such thing as a private encounter with an informal leader. If you appear to have attacked these resistant informal leaders, the story will circulate and you will solidify the resistance of everyone who supports that person.

- Do not make these people's participation in the change process optional. I am not suggesting that you order the person to participate. And it is possible that in the final analysis, some of them will stonewall you and refuse to participate. But do not approach them and discuss their role in the change in a way that communicates an "I could care less" message about their participation. Let them know their participation really does matter. Assume that they are going to participate. If you do this genuinely, this may be all it takes to get them to join in and be willing to participate. Their lack of trust is often based on the feeling that they have been excluded or ignored in the past.

## Stories about Informal Leaders Who Refuse to Participate

There are some informal leaders whom you will never persuade to work with you on changes. If you are trying to create an adaptive culture, these people could eventually become such a barrier that they can no longer stay in the organization. If an organization is serious about being change-oriented, there is bound to be some turnover of people who cannot stand working in that kind of environment and need to find somewhere else to work that is more suited to their style. There are several issues to consider if you think you are reaching the end of the line with a resistant informal or formal leader.

- It is not necessary to have every single informal leader in the organization converted to a change enthusiast. If a majority of key people in the departments that are essential to the change are with you on the new direction, that is enough to create the momentum that will sweep everyone else along with you.

- Be sure that you do not push out the useful dissenters. These are the people who often take an opposing stance on changes, but they do it in a way that forces people to think through the changes more clearly or more creatively. They may be a pain in the neck, but they are playing a valuable role in the change process. Try to develop a sense of humor about them and concentrate on listening to them, instead of avoiding them.

- If you end up asking some people to leave or they choose to go themselves, make sure that you handle their departure with the greatest of care. Any standard of fairness or humane treatment that the organization has will be under intense scrutiny when an informal leader is leaving an organization. Even the little things matter.

For example, there was a case of one large company where a manager who was an informal leader in one of the divisions was leaving the company by his own choice. There had been several serious run-ins with two of the senior management people in the division shortly before his decision to leave, and this had contributed to the decision to leave at that time. The run-ins had involved resisting changes that the senior managers were trying to implement. In his battles with management, the informal leader had represented the opinions and feelings of the majority of the employees in that division at that time. All the supporters knew this. Some of the run-ins, in fact, had occurred in division meetings where this informal leader had spoken up and answered the senior managers' questions about the employees' feelings concerning a new project. Everyone had been afraid to say that they thought it was a mistake, because the person in charge of the division had a reputation for being vindictive and finding ways to punish anyone who crossed him. The informal leader's willingness to take on this person had served to increase even further the hero status he had long held among employees in the division. There were a number of similar confrontations, and eventually the informal leader decided to take a job with another company.

The division senior management was, of course, relieved to see him go. On the surface, everything was handled very professionally, but the senior management group decided not to hold a going-away party on this person's last day of work, which was a tradition in the department. The man who was leaving noticed, but did not care. In fact, he was relieved not to have to go through the event. People in the department, however, were angry and bitter about the way that man's departure was handled. It was the common feeling in the division that this experience confirmed again what everyone believed about that senior management group. "You cross them, you pay." The irony is that by not having the division's usual "funeral" ritual (the going-away party) they had actually extended or exacerbated the grieving process for the people who continued to work there. The ghost of the informal leader would have faded faster if they had allowed the organization to go through one of its usual rituals of letting go. The stories about a person like this can become corporate legend in a way that presents a real problem for the leaders who are cast in the role of the villains in the legend.

## How Long Does It Take to Create a New Story Line?

The general wisdom about timing on large cultural changes is that it takes five to seven years to complete the change so that the new way of operating becomes "just the way we do things here." The organization is creating a whole new story line that takes time for the events to occur and the stories about those events to be told and retold. Obviously, the larger and more complex the organization, the longer it tends to take. The complexity of the change is also a factor. Changing one system in the organization, such as the performance appraisal system, is likely to be absorbed into the organization relatively quickly. Compare this to a change as complex as implementing a Total Quality Management philosophy and methodology throughout the entire organization. Five to seven years is a realistic time frame for a change of that magnitude. An attempt to change the organization into an adaptive culture is a massive shift in attitudes, skills, and systems throughout the organization. That sort of change takes at least five to seven years to accomplish.

Many people find these time frames discouraging because they are so long. Because of this, it is useful to think about the change as a dual track, short-term and long-term. Some experts suggest that organizations work on both seven-month and seven-year tracks in planning for and evaluating the progress being made. The seven-year time frame is the long-term vision of the new organization after the change has been fully and successfully implemented. The seven-month time frame is the realistic plan for the details of what will be implemented within the next seven months. The seven-year vision stays relatively constant, but the seven-month plan changes constantly. It is important to have stories about both time frames. Long-term stories take more the form of fantasies or dreams for the future based on the goals of the change process. Short-term stories are more likely to be based on real events as they unfold during the current phase of the change. In my experience, if you talk about both the long-term and short-term view of the change, it helps to clarify the entire process for the employees in the organization. The long-term vision is difficult for some people to picture or to believe in if they cannot see any specific, detailed action that is occurring which is tied to the vision. For other people, the short-term actions make no sense unless they are grounded in a long-term picture of where this whole thing is going. Talking about both seven months and seven years at the same time seems to help everyone understand what is happening. This dual thinking is also helpful in evaluating whether the organization is staying on track in terms of direction and speed of the change.

For example, in one organization that has just begun an implementation of Total Quality Management, the managers and employees involved in the start-up have decided that their seven-year goal is to implement the TQM process all over the organization, with most employees trained in the philosophy and tools, and a number of teams functioning at any one time. Their seven-month plan is to offer four seminars (eight hours of training) to all managers and employees who volunteer to participate and to pilot two interdisciplinary teams, whose goals are to learn the team process and to work on a relatively simple system issue. Knowing both sets of information makes the entire plan clearer and easier to understand for most people in the organization.

Bob Gough, an economist and futurist, quotes an old Indian adage that was told to him by theologian Ravi Zacharias. The saying goes:

Whatever you are filled up with will spill over when you are bumped.

This saying is one of the best descriptions I have heard to measure how long a major change will take and how difficult the transition will be. It all depends on where you are starting from when you launch the change. If the organization is trying to become more adaptive and already has many departments or individuals who are flexible and handle changes well, the transition will be quicker and easier than in a company that has a hierarchical, command-and-control culture consistently throughout all departments. "What you are filled up with" will turn into the topics and themes of the stories people tell. Continue to listen to the stories change over time, and they will offer you an accurate chronology of the progress your organization is making in becoming a more adaptive culture.

# 16
# Using Stories to Communicate Effectively during a Change

## Using Storytelling to Communicate Effectively *before* the Change Arrives

As the change is being planned, storytelling can be an invaluable tool from both the telling and listening point of view. Telling stories is an excellent way to paint a picture of the future that is being created and will exist after the change is completed. This is the way stories are used to help build the shared vision that was described earlier. Telling stories is also an excellent way to demonstrate the need for the change in the first place. Many times it is difficult for people to understand why anything needs to change at all. From their point of view, everything seems just fine as it is now.

One option for demonstrating the need for change is to wait for disaster to strike. At that point, everyone will understand the need for the change, but it may be too late to make the change fast enough for the organization to survive. Because of this, the crisis mode of demonstrating the need for change is quite dangerous. Stories, on the other hand, may let people live through the crisis in their mind's eye without having to actually experience it in reality. In this way, it can have the effect of jolting an individual or a group into action before it is too late for the action to do any good. The "kick in the pants" stories described earlier are one version of this type of storytelling.

One simple version of this was told to me by a colleague who was frustrated because he could not seem to make his healthy, but aging, mother understand the importance of carrying some type of long-term health insurance coverage in case she ever needed nursing home care. He had patiently explained all the facts and figures to her several times, but her responses made it clear that she did not understand and, furthermore, did not want to talk about it. She would respond that she had plenty of health insurance and, besides, she was never going to need to go into a nursing home.

Her son finally gave up. He went on to tell me that, much to his surprise a few weeks later, his mother called to tell him about what had just happened to a friend of hers who had suffered a stroke. The friend needed nursing home care, but the one that the family wanted to place him in cost over $3000 a month. Her friend had an adequate income for regular monthly expenses and had adequate health insurance, but that insurance did not cover nursing home care, and his monthly income was not nearly enough to pay for this bill. The family was very upset. They still had not decided what they were going to do. Then my colleague's mother announced to her son, "I need to get long-term health insurance!" Her son swallowed the impulse to point out that he had been trying to tell her that for the past year, and simply offered to help her find what she needed.

This is an individual's version of how a dramatic story can drive home a point about the need for change when facts and figures will never accomplish that task. The same is true in organizations. In some cases, hearing what the competition is doing with new product development or speeding up customer-service processes is just what it takes to jolt a group into action. This is also the reason that a well-designed simulation game can sometimes jar people into looking at their environment in a different way and trigger their ability to see the need for a change in the way they currently are doing business.

A simulation game creates an elaborate story line in the form of a game or exercise. Participants control many of the specific actions as the game proceeds, but they are operating within the story framework that was set up by the creators of the story. The game can, for example, project a group into the future and let them see what happens to their sales or profits, given a change in conditions in the environment or with their competition. Based on this artificial experience, the group can see the need to prepare for or protect itself in some way from the potential disasters they witnessed in the game.

Everyone learns best from personal experience. The problem is that you do not necessarily want individuals or organizations to have to "learn the hard way" about the consequences of not being prepared to change to meet a new future. Storytelling, whether in simple oral form or sophisticated computerized simulations, represents an effective way to allow people to experience the future consequences of decisions and actions that they might make.

## Stories Help Employees Understand the Changes

If an organization is going to develop the companywide habit of anticipating future business cycles and trends and strategizing about ways to handle these changes, everyone has to participate in the habit of future-oriented storytelling. Granted, there are some competitive issues that cannot be shared with everyone in the organization at early stages, but there are vast amounts of future information and ideas that can be shared. The outside futurists may be too expensive to keep on-site for enough days to hold meetings with everyone in the organization. That is understandable. But someone inside the organization needs to play the role of storyteller about the future and carry that message throughout the company to make sure that it is discussed frequently in many different settings. When the future changes and possible strategies are discussed, these events need to be *discussions,* not lectures by the CEO or anyone else. The point is that people need to be drawn into having an interest in the future and to develop the skill of thinking about and planning for changes. Being lectured at, particularly more than once, will not accomplish this. Shared storytelling, on the other hand, almost always triggers both understanding and interest in the issues being discussed.

According to Tom Fee and Johanna Thomas, consultants at Booz-Allen Health Care, effective storytelling can facilitate the complex education, planning, and communications required in the hospital reorganization process. They use storytelling as one of their techniques for communicating restructuring plans in a way that helps people understand the need for change in their client organizations. Fee says "numbers and graphs simply cannot address the values-oriented reasons for fundamental change. But, a good story will provide a vivid image of the barriers that staff face every day in serving the customer . . . Storytelling was the perfect vehicle for communicating the frustrations and anxiety that everyone faces day-to-day, as well as a vivid way to portray a better future." They use an activity they call "imagineering." The exercise walks people through a series of events that helps them think through the following issues in sequence:

1. See and experience the problems firsthand.

2. Tie current problems to underlying values.

3. Show how the "system" and work practices create barriers to meeting values.

4.  Let management see that the inefficiencies are due to systems, not people.

5.  Demonstrate that there are more heroes than villains in the organization.

6.  Tie the vision to organization values by showing the values-oriented solutions.

7.  Learn how to tell an effective five-minute story with a memorable punch line.

They go on to describe how the good stories that are told by the employees in this exercise circulate throughout the organization in a matter of days. From a top-management point of view, storytelling allows them to tap into the grapevine to send fundamental statements of values and vision throughout their organization relatively freely.

## Telling the Truth in the Change Process

The single most important communication "technique" to use during a major change, whether in the form of storytelling or factual memos, is telling people the truth. It may be a statement of the obvious to say that communicating effectively requires that the communicator tell the truth. Everyone has heard since childhood the old adage, "Honesty is the best policy." It is also true that if you ask people whether they generally tell the truth, most people claim that they do most of the time. And yet, in spite of all these statements about the importance and common practice of telling the truth, one of the most common complaints that I hear from employees in organizations, especially during major changes, is that they believe they have been lied to, misled, or in some way not told the whole truth about what was really going on in the organization.

This reminds me of some research that I read about a few years ago where large numbers of people were asked where they thought they ranked in terms of physical fitness and general physical attractiveness. Something like 75 percent of the people who were asked this question placed themselves in the top 20 percent of fit and attractive people. It does not take a statistician to figure out that there is something wrong with these percentages. There is no way that 75 percent of the people can fit into the top 20 percent category. There is a gap between reality and perception somewhere in this situation.

The same seems to be the case with telling the truth. Most people in organizations claim they tell the truth, and yet it is a very frequent complaint that people claim they are not being told the truth. How large is the gap in this case between reality and perception, and what can be done about it if you are trying to lead change in your organization? There is no question that if people in the organization believe their leaders are lying to them, they will not follow willingly and enthusiastically. The best that is likely to occur is reluctant, wary compliance. Because of this, it is important to do something about the problem if there is a general feeling in the organization that the truth is not being told.

There are three commonplace communication habits that are responsible for triggering much of the gap in perception about truth and lying in organizations. The people behaving in these ways do not see themselves as lying, but the people on the receiving end of these communications do not feel that they have been told the truth.

## Withholding Information for Too Long

Withholding information too long is probably the single most common mistake made by leaders and change agents in organizations. The people leading the change know information about the plans for change and withhold that information rather than pass it on. This is particularly likely to occur if the information is seen as "bad news," such as downsizing, product changes that affect the content of people's work, or relocation needs. Sometimes the reason for withholding information is because it is seen as competitively sensitive.

One typical version of withholding information for too long occurred in a corporation that has about 15 different divisions and multiple sites all over the United States. They had a communication "habit" of passing on information in a fairly timely way down through the vice president ranks. In many cases, the message would be given to the vice presidents that the information was confidential and not to share it with people in their divisions.

What happened at this point is that some vice presidents would "selectively" pass on the information to some of their subordinates, and other vice presidents would not say a word. If the information was hot news in the company, it usually took approximately two to three days for a variety of mutated versions of the story to travel through the entire company from coast to coast. There was one small division, located at a remote site, whose vice president took the "don't talk" message very seriously. Because of this group's size, function, and location, they were invariably the last to hear the news.

This was a constant source of irritation to the people in that division and a source of amusement to employees in other divisions who delighted in letting their uninformed colleagues know what was really happening around the company. Often, these people would learn about important changes affecting their division's future work from employees in other divisions long before they heard it from their vice president. The joke around the division was that they were suffering from a severe case of "information constipation" in the division.

There is no doubt that some information cannot be broadcast throughout a company at certain points in time, but in most organizations far more information is withheld than really needs to be for company survival reasons. It is my estimate that as little as 10 percent of information that is withheld is really imperative to keep confidential. The rest is based more on the organization's historical habit of using a highly controlling approach to managing information flow. Power is closely linked in organizations to how much you know, so if I know considerably more than you, I am significantly more powerful than you at that moment. There is also the natural desire to avoid being the bearer of bad news, so people often convince themselves that it makes sense to put it off as long as possible.

There are several problems with withholding information too long. The primary problem is that in most cases people find out anyway through other sources. There is an old expression that if two people know a piece of information, it is no longer a secret. It will spread. Life in organizations proves this old expression to be accurate on a daily basis. When people hear information from a secondary source, they quickly conclude that the primary source who "should" have told them is not to be trusted anymore. This damage will affect that person's ability to continue to lead the change process effectively after that point. No one may say anything directly to the leader, but the followers will be wary from that point on. They will certainly make an effort to fine-tune their alternative sources of information, since they have now concluded that the leader cannot be trusted to keep them accurately informed on a timely basis.

The second problem of withholding information, particularly bad news information, is that people's imaginations are usually much worse than reality. If, for some reason, they do not have a secondary source where they can find out the truth, they make it up. They guess. Remaining in a suspended state of the unknown is something individuals or groups of people are likely to do for only a few hours or days at most. If they are forced to do so, they fabricate or guess what the plans are, and because no one will tell them the truth, they usually conclude that the truth must be terrible. Their guesswork, therefore, tends to be worst-case-scenario storytelling. These exaggerated stories spread like wildfire through the organization and are difficult to correct once they get started.

### Not Keeping Promises
### Made during the Change

Failing to follow through on what has been promised is a second way that the perception of lying can be created. This is one of the keys to keeping people committed during a change process.[1] When Delta Airlines acquired

Western Airlines, one of the things they did that contributed to a smooth merger was to follow through and do *what* they said they would do *when* they said they would do it.[2] One of the reasons they were able to do this was because they did not use the "ready, fire, aim" method of planning and implementing the changes. They were methodical enough to ensure that they did not have to backtrack and change their minds or cancel one set of plans to replace them with a corrected version of what needed to be done.

A common mistake that is made about keeping promises has to do with timing. People often think that as long as they do what they said they would do, it does not matter very much when they get around to doing it. Unfortunately, this is not the case. If you are not able to follow through and do what you said you were going to do at the time you said you would do it, then it is imperative that people are updated and informed about the change in timing. If the expected date of action arrives, nothing happens, and no one is informed about the delay or change in plans, the people who are left waiting are likely to conclude that they were lied to in this situation.

I recall a time when I was brought in to work with a management team during a major change in an organization. One of the first things they had me do was to interview each manager individually. The purposes of the interviews were to gather input about their ideas for change and to clarify the key aspects of the plans for change. It was clearly stated to each person that it was not the purpose of these interviews to evaluate managers, and that it was not my role to make recommendations about changes in roles or elimination of positions.

People were leery at first, but the interviews went well and gradually people relaxed and talked more freely about their ideas and concerns about the changes that were coming. Much to my surprise, when I returned to the organization two weeks later to present the summary of the ideas and suggestions from the managers, I discovered that about 25 percent of the people I had interviewed had been terminated two days after the interviews. When I recovered from my uncharacteristic speechlessness, I asked when they had decided to terminate those people and was told that the decision had been made several days before my interviews. They had not wanted to postpone the interviews, so they had decided to proceed with everyone who was still there on that day. When I asked why they had not told me about this decision, they said that they had not told anyone and, besides, they thought it might have affected my interviewing if I had known who was staying and who was being terminated. I controlled my impulse to yell that they were damn right it would have affected my interviews, because I would not have done them at all. I made an effort to calmly explain to them what they had just done to both their credibility and mine on this project by their handling of the situation.

It was doubtful, however, whether they ever really did understand the implications of that series of actions. They certainly did not perceive of their behavior as a form of lying. They saw their decision to terminate those employees as a management prerogative that they had the right to act on at any time they deemed necessary. Although this was a fairly extreme example of not keeping a promise, the perception is that it is not necessarily an unusual one, according to the stories that employees tell around many organizations.

## Bad News Is Not Good News . . .
## Don't Try to Pretend It Is

The third common communication mistake that leads to the conclusion that people are not being told the truth is to try to cover up bad news by making it sound like good news. Even though it is true in many ways that every problem may well be an opportunity in disguise, it is questionable whether it is always a wise idea to present the information in that way. There are painful changes that all organizations must go through at times. Many times they involve cutbacks in personnel or budgets. Sometimes the organization must restructure in ways that drastically changes employees' functions or work teams. Sometimes products or sales strategies need to change because of competitive pressures or changes in the environment around the organization. These changes are intended to ensure that the company survives or, in some cases, continues to grow. The key point is that for the employees who are on the receiving end of these changes, many of these changes are "bad news," at least in the short run.

There is no problem with explaining the reasons for the changes and the hope for the future that these changes represent. Employees at all levels need to hear that message. But they do not need to hear the pain and losses of the transition made light of, glossed over, or sugarcoated in any way. If the employees are feeling the pain of the change and hear only the message that they are in the midst of an "exciting opportunity," the reaction will be intense and hostile. They will not only perceive this message as a lie, but they will also see it as an insult.

## The Role of Storytelling
## in Telling the Truth

Storytelling is one of many communication tools that is available in the effort to tell the truth about major change in organizations. It is, however, a form of communication that can be abused or distorted in a way that leads to an accusation of lying. All you have to do is stop to think about the connotation of the phrase "Have you been telling stories again?" to know that stories are often used to try to camouflage lies. Particularly if the talker is a talented and persuasive storyteller, that person may be able to temporarily distract the listeners from the reality of what is happening around them.

One way this is done is by focusing on the future in the stories and creating a picture of what is going to happen or what life will be like after the change. There is no problem with focusing storytelling on the future—just make sure it is an accurate picture of the future. This does not mean, of course, that you are able to predict exactly what the future will look like after the change. It does mean, however, that it is very dangerous to describe a future that is substantially different than the direction that you know the organization is headed toward, just to soften the blow. For example, do not paint a picture of career advancement and new opportunities when you know that the plan is a change in direction that will cut costs, staffing, and mobility for most employees.

I have seen organizations, for example, put people in temporary management positions and lead the individuals to believe that these temporary positions represent real career opportunities. They are led to believe that they will either be kept in the position on a full-time basis or moved into other outstanding opportunities, when this is not true. The company is actively recruiting outside the organization to fill the position and has no intention of leaving that person in the position or moving them into any other similar opportunity in the company. They are using the person to fill a need at the time and, either out of convenience or in an effort to be "kind," they do not tell the person the truth about the situation. A false story line is being created in this situation that is told to the whole department. When everyone realizes that the person is not staying in the position, and was probably never seriously considered for it, it puts that individual in a humiliating position and makes the managers who handled that situation look like liars.

---

*Telling the truth in organizations requires three things:*

1. *Tell employees as soon as you know.*
2. *Do* what *you said you would do* when *you said you would do it.*
3. *Don't try to make bad news sound like good news.*

---

## Face-to-Face Storytelling during the Change

There is no substitute for face-to-face communication. Memos, letters, videotapes, newsletters, electronic mail, and other forms of communication are all useful, and some of them even lend themselves to the use of storytelling within the medium. For example, a videotaped presentation can easily incorporate storytelling as a part of the presentation. None of these approaches, however, can take the place of the impact of communicating with people in person, particularly in small groups or individually. One reason for the potency of face-to-face communication is that the emotion of the speaker comes through most intensely if you are near the person and can actually see and hear both the verbal and body language of the person. Video comes close, but it still loses some of the intensity when the presentation is transferred to the flat, taped medium.

The more important reason, however, that face-to-face communication is more effective is because it allows for two-way communication. The presenter is no longer necessarily just a speaker. That person can become a listener and responder as well as a speaker and storyteller. This, of course, is much easier to do in a small group format of twenty-five or fewer people, but it can be done in large audiences, too, if the leader of the "discussion" has good facilitation skills.

This two-way storytelling is particularly important when you are discussing major changes. Any change can be a continuing evolution of ideas, identification of barriers, problem solving, and constant improvement on the original plan for the change. In fact, even if you wanted the original plan to be implemented in the exact format as first conceived, it would be almost impossible to make this happen in a large, complex organization. People adapt and adjust the plan as it is implemented whether or not they are authorized to make these changes. If this adaptation is done in a coordinated way, based on ongoing dialogue among leaders, managers, and employees in the organization, the evolution of the change is likely to produce a better end result because of the adaptations. If, however, everyone is off in their own world, talking to no one else and adjusting the new plans to fit their own needs or agendas, there is the danger that the change will end up fragmented and ineffective in producing the results it was intended to accomplish.

One of the difficulties with face-to-face, small group dialogue about change is that, in a large organization, a single leader or even a small group of top leadership people cannot possibly be in enough places at one time to accomplish the task. There is simply not enough time, even if this was the only project the leader had to spend time addressing. Because of the time involved in leading these ongoing discussions among employees at all levels, there needs to be a much larger group of "facilitators" than just the official leadership of the organization. In some form that fits within the organization's structure, any organization going through major changes needs to have a group of in-house people who are trained and authorized to lead these types of discussions face-to-face with employees throughout the organization. They are, in effect, your in-house storytellers who carry the change message throughout the organization under the guidance of the key leaders. They are also the people who listen and bring back to the leaders information about ideas, barriers, and possible improvements on the plans.

These people play a role similar to that of the facilitator of a focus group, that of bringing customers together to talk about their experiences with the company. The difference in this case is that the "storyteller" in these employee groups is a more active participant, giving information and telling stories, as well as listening to the comments and stories of people in the group. These facilitators are also colleagues and participants in the change process. Facilitation is an excellent role for the informal leaders to play in the change process.

Even if an organization were small enough that its leader could manage the time to lead all the discussions personally, it would be better if that responsibility were shared with other people in the organization. Ownership of the change is such an important issue in the success of any new effort that getting people involved in helping to "lead" the change is crucial for encouraging commitment to the new direction.

## The Role of Gossip in the Communication of Change

*Gossip* is a term that has several meanings and is interpreted differently by different people. This was pointed out to me in a discussion with a client group when the topic of gossip was mentioned. Everyone agreed that gossip is a form of storytelling, but beyond that common definition the interpretation of the word varied considerably. Some people in the group defined gossip as a term that had exactly the same meaning as "the grapevine." This definition identified gossip as any information that flows informally through the organization outside of official company communication mechanisms. Others in the group were adamant that gossip had a more specific meaning than this. According to these people, gossip is informal talk about other people and the talk has a negative intent. This definition of gossip is very similar to the word *slander.* After this conversation, I looked up the word in several dictionaries and discovered why we were confused about the exact definition of gossip. Even the dictionaries do not agree. For the most part, they defined the word in ways that matched the first, more neutral, definition of the grapevine. The dictionaries used words such as "idle talk" or "light, familiar talk." But in other cases they threw in words like "scandal." The one theme that was consistent in all the definitions, however, was that gossip was "talk about other people."

Gossip is a common word in the English language that we apparently use to mean a number of different things. This confusion makes it less likely that we will understand its role in an organization or know how to work effectively with gossip as a communication tool. Let me use the elements of the definition about which everyone seems to agree and go from there in the examination of the role it plays in communicating change effectively. In this case, *gossip* would be defined as informal talk that focuses on the subject matter of people's lives.

Using this definition, I would be hard-pressed to explain how gossip is any different than informal storytelling. The stories could be told with negative or destructive intent. On the other hand, they could be told to make a constructive point or even simply to entertain. In fact, stories that qualify as gossip are probably the ones with high entertainment value, regardless of the negative or positive intent behind the stories.

If you want to find ways to capitalize on the power of gossip for encouraging change, the approach would be similar to the one described earlier about using stories in general to communicate change. First, go out and find the gossip that is floating informally around the organization which has positive messages about the change that is occurring. This might be in the form of hero stories about key players in the change process who tell about their efforts and successes. They might be survivor stories about how everything went wrong, but the individuals involved survived and got things working after all. Or they might be stories about who got rewarded for participating in the change, what they received, and what exactly they did that earned them the reward.

After you find the gossip stories that carry a positive message about the change in progress, the second step would be to find every way possible to increase the exposure of these particular stories. Repeat the stories yourself, and use every communication vehicle available to you in the organization to play up the gossip that carries a positive message about the change. If you put these stories in official communication channels, such as a newsletter, the story, of course, is no longer gossip because it is no longer informal "idle talk." It has now become a more formalized story. But who cares?

The point is that it does not matter whether a story is defined as gossip or not. What matters is the same thing that matters with all stories. Is the message behind the story and the impact of the story positive or negative? When you are trying to encourage participation in a change and communicate productive information, any story that carries a positive message about the change is useful. It does not matter what label that story carries. Call it gossip if you want. It is still a positive story worth repeating.

## Using Stories to Talk about Sensitive Topics

One specific use of stories to encourage change is when dealing with sensitive or controversial topics. A story, particularly if it has humor in it, will help people look at these sensitive issues without getting as defensive as they would if they are given a lecture about the need to change a particular behavior. One example of this use of stories comes from the work that I do with organizations based on my book, *Tribal Warfare in Organizations*. This book deals with turf battles and lack of cooperation between professional groups and departments in organizations. This is usually a touchy topic, and certainly one that people in the organization do not usually find entertaining or amusing.

My goal when I talk to groups about these issues is to get them to change their behaviors with each other and work together more cooperatively. If I took the approach of lecturing at these groups about the inappropriateness of their current behavior, this would be likely to trigger a mixture of reactions from open hostility to boredom. But if I can find stories about their organizations and turn them into funny tales that entertain them, they will laugh, loosen up a little with each other, and talk in a more cooperative way with each other.

An example of one of my favorite stories from this work comes out of the field of health care. I tell it frequently to groups of hospital employees, and it always triggers laughter, head shaking, and jokes among the group. This is not a topic that is usually seen as funny by any of the groups involved. In fact, in many hospitals it is one of the long-standing battlegrounds between professionals and their different views about what is best for the patient. This is a story about two groups of professionals whom I refer to as the "two famous health care tribes, Nurse and Pharmacist." When talking to a health care audience, all I have to do is mention these two groups and people start to roll their eyes and look at each other, laughing. They are not sure what is coming, but if it is about those two groups, it is going to be good. Here is the story as I usually tell it.

**The Nursing/Pharmacy Story.**    This story was first told to me by a pharmacist I was interviewing in a hospital the day before doing a seminar with the entire management team of the organization. In our discussion, I asked him the question that I always ask people to get them going in the interview: "Who drives you nuts around the hospital on a regular basis, and what do they do to get on your nerves?" When I asked this question, the pharmacist who had been relatively quiet and sedate until that moment, slammed down his pen on his desk, his eyes flashed, and he responded, "Those nurses . . ." I knew that I was about to hear a tribal story, because that is how they always start. "Those people . . ." So I said, "What? . . . What are they doing?"

The pharmacist went on to say, "They *are* driving me nuts and they have been for 10 years. That's how long I have worked at this hospital, and that's how long they've been driving me nuts." He shook his head and went on to say, "I've tried everything and nothing works. I can't get them to stop." Then he glared at me and said, "And don't think you are going to get them to stop either, because you won't." I nodded and asked again, "What are they doing?"

He responded, "They hoard drugs up on the floors! That's what they are doing! And I cannot get them to stop. I plead, I beg, I threaten—nothing works." He leaned forward and said in a lower tone, "I even come in late at night when there aren't many of them around to sneak around the floors hunting for the drugs. But it doesn't do any good. The minute they figure out I've found their hiding place, they just start a new one."

Now let me pause here to tell you that at this point when I am telling the story to health care groups, the nurses in the audience seem to be having a great time. As soon as they hear the words "hoard drugs up on the floors," they start laughing, rolling their eyes at each other, and punching each other with their elbows. I always point out to the group that this elbow-punching behavior among tribal members is a physical mannerism that has great anthropological significance. When members of a tribe use this elbow action with each other, it always means that the tribe has no intention of changing its current behavior such as hoarding drugs. When I say this, everyone but the pharmacist bursts out laughing.

The story from the pharmacist continues as he goes on to say, "I was hired in this hospital to protect the safety and the accuracy of the flow of medications in the hospital, and I can't do it when they have this under-ground system going up on the floors." I sympathized with him and asked what he was trying to do now to get the problem under control. A satisfied smile crossed his face, and he pulled out a document from his desk to show me. He started to explain that this was a new control sheet that he had designed to use to track medications. He was going to get those nurses under control one way or another.

When I went on to ask the nurses about their side of the story, they indignantly told me that the reason they keep extra medications up on the floors is because the pharmacy was entirely too slow. They could have a patient in the bed in pain, and the pharmacy would take three or four hours to get the medications up to the floor. "They are down there doing their paperwork!" the nurses told me in a withering tone. They said they had tried over and over to explain the problem to the pharmacy and to get them to speed up, but they would not do it. The nurses readily admit that their underground system is far from ideal, but if the pharmacy will not cooperate, they will do what they have to do to take care of the patients quickly. A vice president of nursing (a tribal chief) who heard me tell the story at one meeting, came up to me later and said, "Any nurse worth her salt, if that happens to her one time, she will make sure it never happens again."

After telling this story (and after the laughing dies down), we use it in a discussion to illustrate that neither group is really wrong *if* you focus on the mission of what each group is trying to accomplish. Each group, in fact, is actually working hard to do exactly what they were hired to do. Safe, accurate medication distribution and speedy care and comfort for the patients are their two missions. On the other hand, both groups are wrong if you look at their procedures and behaviors for handling their missions. Because they cannot or will not negotiate effectively with each other, the quality and safety of the care for the patient is potentially in danger. In most hospitals, getting these two groups together in a room to discuss the problems often results in arguing, and sometimes even yelling at each other about which group is wrong. The classic health care accusation is "You don't care about the patient!" Both of these groups use this one on each other. This, of course, is extremely insulting to both sides and actually lessens the possibility that the two groups will be able to negotiate effectively with each other in the future. If they can find some way to be respectful of each other's mission, even if they disagree with the methods, you have a starting point for negotiations to occur between the two groups. But if all they do is exchange mutual insults, it would have been better if they had never met or tried to talk with each other about the problem at all. The "insults" conversation does more harm than good.

This message and the work that follows to get groups to negotiate with each other more respectfully is based on the audience reaction to this story. I tell many similar stories to entertain, make people laugh, but ultimately to make them think about their own behavior and look at the need for change. There is no lecture that I could deliver that would leave behind as great a possibility of change as the stories I tell. Stories are memorable and believable. They are the single best method of persuasion, especially when dealing with sensitive topics.

# 17
# Using Storytelling to Manage Resistance to Change

*Harvard Law of Animal Behavior:* Under the most carefully controlled conditions, organisms behave as they damn well please.[1]

## Storytelling Used to Encourage Both Stability and Change

In most cultures, storytelling is used heavily as a communication tool to encourage people to learn, remember, and take to heart the important themes of the culture from the past. When tribal elders sit around the campfires telling tribal stories, the intent of those stories is the teaching and passing on of the traditions of the culture. Continuity and stability are the underlying purposes of most cultural storytelling. Keep in mind, however, that storytelling is a neutral communication tool. It can be used for a wide variety of purposes. There is nothing inherent in storytelling that limits its use to encouraging only stability and the status quo. Storytelling can be reshaped and used to illustrate the need for cultural change and to help people make the transition from the current status quo to a new way of doing things in the group.

In his book, *On Becoming a Leader,* Warren Bennis relates a story that was told to him by James Burke, the chairman and CEO of Johnson & Johnson. James Burke was the person primarily responsible for the outstanding way that Johnson & Johnson responded to the Tylenol poisoning tragedy several years ago. This story Burke tells is about his early days at Johnson & Johnson and is a classic example of a story that could be told to encourage change and more risk taking from employees who work for the organization. Or the same story could be told as an example of a valued tradition at Johnson & Johnson that must be protected and continued if the organization is to be successful in the future. Either purpose for telling the story would be perfectly appropriate and would be valuable to the organization's culture. It is the same story in both cases, but one context for telling it would encourage change and the other would encourage stability and continuity of a valued tradition. The story itself is neutral. The difference is in the intent of the teller and the explanation that is given with the story. Here is the story.

Burke tells of an experience that he had in his earlier days at Johnson & Johnson before he was CEO. He made a serious mistake that cost the company over a million dollars. It was a new product that Burke developed which failed badly when it reached the market. He says he was sure he was going to be fired. General Johnson, the head of the company, called him in and said, "I understand you lost over a million dollars on that product." Burke responded, "Yes sir, that is correct." At that point General Johnson stood up, held out his hand, and said, "I just want to congratulate you. All business is making decisions, and if you don't make decisions, you won't have any failures." Johnson went on to tell Burke that the hardest job he had was to get people to make decisions. He added that, of course, if Burke made exactly the *same* decision wrong again that he would fire him. Then Johnson said, "I hope you'll make a lot of other decisions, and that you'll understand there are going to be more failures than successes."[2]

In Bennis's book, he uses this story to illustrate that one of the common traits of leaders is that they have learned some of their most important lessons from their mistakes. So in this case, the purpose of the story was to illustrate a leadership trait. But that is only one use for this particular story. How many times do you think James Burke has told and retold this story over the years of his career at Johnson & Johnson? It is safe to assume that his telling of this story to Warren Bennis was not the first time he had recounted those events.

On the different occasions that he has told the story, he may have had a different purpose or moral to the story. The story stays the same, but the context changes. Sometimes he may have chosen to tell that story to encourage the continuation of a valued Johnson & Johnson cultural characteristic of encouraging risk taking and tolerating failure. The message, in this case, would have been that this is the way J&J people treat each other and support each other. In another case, Burke might have told the story to encourage individuals or groups within the company to move ahead and make some fundamental change in the way the company does business.

Now the purpose of the story is to push people to stir things up and try something new.

The key in telling any story like this one is to clearly understand your purpose before you start telling the story. What is the moral of the story? Why are you telling it? Make sure in your telling of the story, and your editorializing before and after the story, that you make your purpose clear to the listeners. Use your storytelling to balance the messages of stability and change within your organization in a way that fits the industry environment in which you operate.

## The Status Quo Is Not All Bad

Every culture has built-in mechanisms to protect and maintain its current ways of doing things. The term *status quo* often carries a negative connotation, meaning stagnation and stubborn refusal to change outdated or useless old habits. At times this is true, but there is also another side to the status quo story which deserves mention when examining the issues around resistance to change. For any culture, whether it is a community, a religious group, or an organization, there is the need to create and maintain some level of stability. It would be impossible to live or work in an environment that was completely fluid and constantly changing on all fronts.

The purpose of predictable values, rules for behavior, use of language, and rituals is to keep individual and group life orderly enough on a daily basis so that people can accomplish more than just covering their basic survival needs. In a culture with no ability to protect the status quo, it would be impossible to use one's energy or intelligence to concentrate on any type of complex or creative tasks. Taken to extreme, it is quite likely that this type of environment would not be safe. There would be so few rules of behavior that you could count on people to follow that life in the group could be dangerously unpredictable.

There is a children's game, that can be adapted for adults, to illustrate what it feels like to try to function in a chaotic, constantly unpredictable environment. This game is a metaphor or story that is used to make a point about life in fast-changing organizations. A group of eight or ten people stand in a circle, and the leader explains that the "task" of this group is to throw three balls around the group in a consistent, predictable pattern so that each person always throws each ball to the same person and receives it from the other person who is also the same each time. After the pattern of throwing is established and practiced with one ball, the leader adds a second ball, and eventually a third.

At this point everyone in the group is scrambling to keep up with their assigned throwing and catching, but usually after a little practice the group functions fairly well. Then the leader announces that the throwing needs to go faster and speeds up the throwing to the maximum speed the group can handle. At this point, the leader starts adding disruptions, such as pulling two throwers out of the group because of "downsizing" or having someone walk through the middle of the group to interrupt one of the throwers to ask a question. The leader might also announce some throwing pattern changes as well. The whole time that these disruptions and changes in routines are occurring, the leader continues to remind the group that it needs to try to match its fastest throwing speed.

Of course, everything goes haywire. Balls are flying everywhere, bouncing off people's heads and across the room out of the circle. Eventually, everyone gives up. The only difference between this scene of chaos and confusion and what many people describe as their experience in some fast-changing organizations is that everyone usually laughs hilariously through the entire ball tossing experience. Real-life chaos usually is not so funny.

Protecting the status quo, therefore, is a rational response for any group of people trying to ensure stability and safety for its members. People who resist change and question the need for it are often playing a useful cultural function of pulling the group toward stability and continuity that is necessary if that culture is going to survive over an extended period of time. The challenge, however, is to balance this need for stability with a need to adapt and change as the world around the group changes and places new demands on it. As the twentieth century draws to a close, the balance continues to shift toward faster and more frequent change. An adaptive organizational culture, as described in Chapter 14, is one that has managed to maintain a stability/change balance that fits well within its industry.

The most adaptable company, however, still must put a great deal of emphasis on stability and continuity from the past through to the present and into the future. If it does not, the organization would not be flexible and adaptive. It would be chaos and filled with continual confusion. People would not know what their jobs were supposed to be or what the company was trying to accomplish. People who resist change are often viewed exclusively as problems which negatively impact the organization's future. It is important, however, to keep in mind that resistance to change is a two-sided issue. The productive, useful side of resistance to change can be the valuing and protecting of stability for the organization. The key issue here is balance in a way that matches the pace of change in the organization's industry. (See Figure 17-1.)

## Reducing Resistance by Getting People Involved in the Change

Even though resistance to change is a normal part of every group's existence, there are times when it interferes with the implementation of

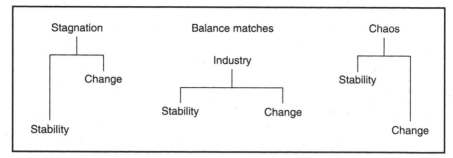

**Figure 17-1.** Impact of stability versus change on an organization.

changes that are needed for the future survival of the organization. Many people do not necessarily weigh and evaluate carefully the merits of each change that comes along and resist only the ones they believe are unwise. Instead, they resist all changes as a matter of habit.

> The most highly developed instrument of humanity: The human mind's ability to criticize.[3]

Because of this tendency to resist change whether or not it is useful or important to the organization, one main component of any change process is dealing with resistance in a way that minimizes its damaging effects. The most effective overall strategy for managing resistance to change is to get the people involved in the change process. There is a common business expression that is known by the abbreviation, NIH. It stands for *Not Invented Here* and means that if a new idea is your idea instead of mine, then it may be a good idea but it is not mine (Not Invented Here). If it is not mine and I have no connection or involvement with making the idea work, then I do not care a great deal whether it succeeds or not. On the other hand, if the idea was mine or I am heavily involved in figuring out how to make the idea work, then I feel some ownership of the idea and I am very interested in seeing it succeed. If the idea fails, it will reflect badly on me. If it succeeds, I will share in the credit and the pride of success.

When implementing a new idea, it is very important to avoid the NIH syndrome. Getting people, especially the resisters, involved as early as possible is the first line of defense against resistance to change. Sydney Pollack, Oscar winning motion picture director and producer, tells his story about the importance of getting other people involved and how he learned this important lesson the hard way by experience. Pollack says, "The first time I ever directed anything, I acted like a director. That's the only thing I knew how to do, because I didn't know anything about directing."[4] Pollack thought his job was to direct, defined as taking control and being in charge.

He claims that if there had been a megaphone around, he would have used it to order people around.

Now, after years of experience, Pollack is famous for creating a team of at least one hundred people where everyone is participating in the process of making the movie. He describes this part of leadership as an art. He claims that the trick to making it work is to avoid creating situations that trigger contests of egos. He says, "Oddly enough, the more willing you seem to be to let people participate, the less need they have to force participation. It's the threat of being left out that exacerbates their ego problems and creates clashes."[5]

## Getting the Resisters Involved to Create a Shared Story

When using employee participation as a strategy for reducing resistance to change, it is important to consider *who* is getting involved in the process. The first consideration is to get as many of the active resisters involved as possible. If they are willing to volunteer, then it is simply a matter of finding an appropriate role for them to play. If they are reluctant to become involved, then it is a more difficult task of selling them on giving the new approach a chance and persuading them to get involved so that they exert some control over how the change is implemented. Often, the best persuasion method for accomplishing this is to identify exactly why they are resisting and ask them to get involved in a way that will help to ensure that problem does not happen this time. For example, one typical resister's complaint in an organization trying to implement a Total Quality Management approach is that no one will listen to the ideas for improvements that are suggested by the teams. The teams will be ignored, and nothing will end up being implemented. If this is the complaint, then get one of the complaining leaders involved in the steering committee which provides the leadership for setting team guidelines and approving the implementation plans the teams develop. Your goal is to turn the resisters into positive storytellers about the change because they are now a part of it themselves.

> *The most effective way to handle resistance to change is to get people involved in the change and create a shared story.*

The second consideration when using participation to reduce resistance is to involve *groups* of people whenever possible, not just a few scattered individuals. It is very difficult to expect individuals to go away from training or planning meetings, excited or committed to a new idea, and then have to go back to their work units to create a "shared story" by selling the idea to everyone else. It can be done, but it is a difficult job that requires excellent persuasion skills. It is much easier—and more likely to succeed—to bring work groups into the process together or large numbers of employees from many different departments. These groups will have a common experience and their own shared story about the change. If you have a critical mass of employees actively involved in the change, they will have a much easier time convincing the nonparticipants that this change is worth supporting.

## Understanding People's Past Stories about Change in This Organization

The second set of actions that help to handle resistance to change is to let people tell their stories about the history of change implementations in your organization. By listening to these stories, you will usually be able to determine what experiences people have had in the past that make them leery of this change now. The following topics are common areas of past experiences with change that have left people wary of the next change. Listen for these topics in the stories people tell.

- Were the changes in the past short-lived bursts of enthusiasm about a new idea that died out quickly and were never fully implemented?

- Do people feel that they were lied to during past changes?

- Have past changes adversely affected their quantity of work, type of work, or amount of pay for their work?

- Was the purpose of the change not made clear?

- Do people believe that major changes in the past have been motivated by political self-interests, instead of for the good of the company?

- Do employees believe that they were not treated respectfully during the past changes?

Getting employees to talk and tell the stories of their experiences during past changes is an important first step in reducing resistance to change. Be careful when the employees tell their stories about the past. Do not respond by becoming defensive and trying to explain away past shortcomings. If that happens, the resistance will turn to granite and will be difficult ever to wear away. Once you find out which of these issues are hot spots where employees feel that they have been hurt in the past, concentrate your efforts on reducing the possibility that these same problems will be repeated again during this change.

When change involves bad news, allowing people to vent their feelings and treating them respectfully may be the only tools available at that time for handling resistance. Trying to cover up these bad-news situations only manages to add a second set of problems on top of the original problem. Now they will have to deal with the bad news and the fact that they were lied to about it. Listening and understanding the employees' stories about their history of experiences with change in the organization is the key to getting people involved. When trying to handle changes effectively, how well you listen to stories is much more important than how well you tell them.

## Going Back to the Original Story

"We've *always* done it this way" is one of the most commonly heard statements that accompanies resistance to change. It is also one of the most frustrating statements to handle. When people are faced with a change in procedures or organizational systems, they will often express their reluctance to go along with the change using this common refrain. This statement carries a warning of sorts. It cautions that the old way has worked for a long time and was "ordained" many years ago as the right way to do this particular task or activity. If it is changed, who knows what the consequences might be? In many ways, the sentiment behind this phrase is very similar to the age-old tribal desire to avoid making the gods angry. Long ago, the gods proscribed the way the tribe should behave and to change those patterns of behavior now is very likely to make them angry. No one really knows for sure when or why the group's traditions started, but it is assumed that these rituals and patterns are sacred and must be maintained.

There is an old story illustrating this type of tradition that has been passed on from one generation to another until the true origin of the behavior is lost. The story is about a young woman who had recently married and decided to bake a ham using an old family recipe. Her husband noticed that before she put the ham in the roasting pan, she cut off about a third of the small end and pushed it aside. She put the rest of the ham in the pan and continued her preparations. Her husband asked why she was discarding the small end of the ham.

She looked up in surprise and said, "That's the way my mother always prepared a ham." This did not seem logical to him, so the next time they were visiting her parents, the husband asked his mother-in-law why she always cut off the small end of the ham before she baked it. "I don't know," she responded. "That's the way my mother always baked a ham." The husband was still not satisfied with the answer, so the next time they were visiting his wife's grandmother, he asked her the same question.

"Grandmother, why do you always cut off the small end of the ham before you bake it?" The grandmother looked up with a startled expression and said, "I don't anymore. I used to years ago when the children were young because the only roasting pan I had at the time was too small to hold the whole ham!"

If you trace back to the origins of many traditional patterns of behavior, you are likely to find a pragmatic explanation for the "ways we do things" that made perfect sense at the time. The original reasons have gotten lost along the way, but the behaviors remain. They become comfortable, familiar habits. To exchange these predictable habits and the skills that go with them for unknown, untested new ways of doing things seems suspect at best. The change is a great deal of trouble and, besides, there must have been a good reason for doing it the old way.

## Demystifying the Old Story

One way to reduce some of the power that the old ways have over people is to have them trace back and find the old story about the origins of the behavior in question. Who first started doing it this way, when did it start, and why? Many procedures and systems in organizations are built around specific personalities or limitations of equipment or technology at the time. I have even seen communication systems that have developed so that two people who intensely dislike each other do not have to speak to each other. The two individuals may have long since left the organization, but the complicated communication system is still operating in the same old pattern. It is a form of inertia. Once the pattern is established, it is easier to just keep doing it the old way.

Consultant Daryl Demos was the person who first pointed out to me the value of going back to the origins of a procedure or system to "demystify" it. His company provides consulting services to help financial services companies improve their internal operations strategies, so he comes up against "the way we've always done it" frequently in his efforts to convince people in these organizations to change their procedures.

Demos tells one story about working with a bank where they discovered the processing methods used to pass accounting information back and forth between departments was outdated and inefficient. It was costing the bank a lot of money to continue using this old process. There was reluctance to change the system, even though people expressed frustrations with the system as it currently functioned. They were, however, quick to point out its positive attributes whenever the subject of change was discussed.

Demos and his colleagues were able to trace back to the origins of the current system and found that parts of the system went as far back as the 1800s. Certainly much of the system was designed in a different technological era than the present. Once the story about the system's past was told, the decision makers recalled with disbelief that they had worked with this same system in their early years at the bank. It had changed very little in all that time. They decided that a system "that old" must be outdated and allowed Demos to help them implement an updated approach. The bank ended up saving themselves a considerable sum of money because of the changes.

Demos also points out that sometime the stories from the past work to your advantage in other ways when trying to implement change. He recalls the time that they were working with a loan-servicing company that had implemented an internal audit system during a time of rapid growth when accuracy and compliance to balancing procedures had been a problem. The system was very cumbersome and involved keeping audit functions broken down into separate units so that they could be monitored more easily. This compartmentalization was no longer necessary because the company had stabilized and had adequate capacity now to monitor its auditing procedures, but they were reluctant to let go of the old system.

In trying to convince the company of the merits of changing to a simpler system using a new telephone technology, they went back to the original policies and procedures manual that was written when the company was founded. This was long before the explosive growth era. They stumbled across the original organizational chart and realized to their surprise that the structure that had been used at the time of the company's founding was the same simplified approach that they were recommending now. The forgotten past, in this case, was now used to lend "historical legitimacy" to their recommendations for current internal audit procedures. The plan was now viewed as a "back to basics" approach and was accepted by the company.

In most cases, once a group of people can see that "the way we've always done it" was a pragmatic or idiosyncratic decision made at a particular point in time by people very much like them, they are more willing to consider letting go of that old pattern of behavior. There are still the hassles of learning new procedures and maybe even new skills, but at least they do not have to face the age-old worry that to abandon the old ways might make the gods angry.

## Letting Go of the Old . . . Finishing the Story

Letting go of the old is an important part of being able to accept the new. Some type of ceremony or ritual that symbolizes the end of the old way is an organization's version of a funeral. It serves the same purpose that a funeral serves for a family or community. For those readers who are old enough to remember 1963, when John Kennedy was assassinated, think back to the days and weeks that followed the announcement of his death. Try to imagine how different those days following his death would have been if there had been no funeral. Almost everyone who was living then can remember exactly where he or she was when they heard the news that Kennedy had been killed.

What if that was all there had been? One announcement followed by the changes in Washington, D.C., and then nothing more was said or done in reference to the loss. Everyone was just supposed to put it behind them, forget what had happened, and move on into a new future. What if you did mention Kennedy's death and expressed how upset you still were about it, and the response you received was disapproval for mentioning it? You were told to let go of it and move on. If you did not, you were labeled uncooperative or unpatriotic. It is difficult to imagine this set of events following his death. It sounds absurd, and certainly hard-hearted. This is not at all what really happened that week in communities all over the United States and many parts of the world. Instead, most public events such as concerts and college football games were cancelled, and people stayed home glued to their television sets watching hour after hour as the funeral rituals and the murder investigation unfolded. That week in America, we were all allowed to cry and grieve over our loss. We all attended the funeral.

In many organizations, however, major changes are announced, such as mergers or restructuring, and there is no funeral ever scheduled. People are not allowed to put an appropriate end to the story. In many cases, the message is sent around soon after the change occurs that to object or complain about the change will get you branded a troublemaker or poor team player. This is the organization's equivalent of being accused of being unpatriotic.

In one postmerger organization where I was going to give a speech to a large number of employees that included senior management and the CEO, I was warned repeatedly not to mention the name of the acquired company. The official stance in the company was that the acquired company no longer existed and was never to be mentioned again. This was more than a year after the merger, but the cultures of these two very different companies were still very much alive. They were not working toward blending the two cultures in any active way. There was no way they could do this because they were not allowed even to talk about the two cultures. When this order of silence surrounds a major change, the old ways do not just fade away. They simply go underground, and they often survive there for many years.

The purpose of a funeral is to officially mark the end of the old era and the beginning of a new one. If people are not allowed to carry out some form of ceremony or ritual that symbolizes letting go of the old, the resistance to the changes and to the new direction will be much stronger and last much longer. Funerals involve eulogies, burials, and the erecting of symbols that will be used to remember the best of the past. Funerals do not end the sorrow or the grieving for the people who attend, but they do act as a clear-cut event that marks the transition from the old to the new.

One nonprofit organization tells the story of a funeral of sorts that they had years ago. It involved large numbers of shoe boxes. These shoe boxes were filled with index cards that contained the names of all their subscribers. The organization was about to automate its mailing list, so they no longer needed the shoe boxes filled with names and addresses. Still, these shoe boxes were important to people who worked in the organization because they represented the successful growth of the organization. In addition to this, they had a strong commitment to ensure that their mailing list was never sold or given to any other group to use for advertising purposes. They had always guarded those shoe boxes carefully. So now what should they do with them?

It so happened that during the same time period, a new building was being constructed for their growing offices, so they arrived at the idea of using the new building as a tomb for the shoe boxes. At a ceremony to bury the boxes, they gathered to place the shoe boxes in the spot where the foundation was about to be poured and then watched as cement covered them. The shoe boxes were gone forever and were safely entombed where they could never be misused.

Every major change calls for a different kind of funeral. Given the permission to do so, any group of employees would be able to come up with some appropriate ceremony to mark the end of the old and the beginning of the new. If employees are allowed to participate in this type of cultural closure, they will be more willing to carry on into the future. They will still grieve, but they will resist less. The story was given a proper ending.

## Creating New Rituals and Ceremonies after the Change

After major changes in organizations, especially if they affect staffing patterns and job functions, new rituals will need to be established. One of the most important of these rituals is creating new settings for storytelling among employees at all levels. These are, in effect, the new tribal campfires. Right after a significant change, people may be uncertain about the key values, the goals, and the new rules of the game for how to behave successfully in the organization. This lack of certainty about the direction of the organization is usually very obvious after a change in the person in the top leadership position. If the new CEO or leader of a department comes from outside the company, this uncertainty can be quite intense. No one is sure what to expect. People hunt for stories about how the new leader operated in a previous job. If no stories are available, the anxiety rises even higher.

When a new CEO arrives, it is important to create opportunities both to tell stories and to listen to stories from the people in the organization as rapidly as possible. This can be difficult at first because that new leader is often overwhelmed with demands that absorb all the available time the person has. The problem is that the longer people in the organization have to wait to hear from the new leader and to tell their own stories, the higher the anxiety will climb. Feeling anxious and unsure about the future causes people to feel out of control of the events around them. This is a fast track to triggering hostility and resistance from employees.

Hostility and resistance are common human responses to feeling uninformed and left out of the opportunity to get to know and to be known by a new leader. When this happens, people are not in a receptive mood to be asked to put out the energy to make significant changes in their own behavior at work. The term *tribal campfires* is simply a metaphor for any setting where dialogue between people occurs, particularly if it becomes a ritual or regularly repeated activity. The routine of a ritual is an important part of its power. People count on that predictable pattern of events, and it helps to create order out of the confusion of change. Storytelling as a ritual gives employees an ongoing opportunity to have access to the leaders to share ideas. To maximize communications and minimize resistance and hostility, it would be better for a new leader to spend a few minutes with a group of people each week, rather than one longer period of time with no scheduled pattern for when the group will meet again. Daily, weekly, or monthly events that become rituals are an important part of the rhythm of life for any group of people.

One new manager of a department quickly established a pattern of a monthly lunch date with the people in her area. It was voluntary for whoever wanted to come, but it developed into a regular pattern for those who participated. The restaurants changed every month and picking out the next restaurant actually became one of the entertaining parts of the ritual. One of the informal "rules" that developed for these lunches was that no one ever discussed work. Families, books, movies, vacations, and other topics from people's personal lives were all a part of the conversations, but work was left back at the office. Even though work was never discussed, the fun, warmth, and friendly relationships that developed during these lunches carried over to the work setting and contributed to the ability of this group to work as a smoothly functioning team.

Even if the new leader is a person who is promoted from within, there is still a need for new rituals and the ongoing opportunity for dialogue and exchanging of stories. Even though it is the same person, it is a new role and that creates uncertainty and anxiety for the other people in the group. No matter what type of major change occurs in an organization, reducing resistance will only occur if people have an opportunity to listen, to talk, and to be heard. The storytelling must continue through the period of change and into the future.

# 18
# Using Storytelling for Creativity and Innovation

*This way is my way . . .*
*What is your way?*
The *way does not exist.*
FRIEDRICH NIETZSCHE[1]

## The Barometer Story

There was an exceptionally creative physics student who was given the following problem on a physics exam: "Show how it is possible to determine the height of a tall building with the aid of a barometer." The student did not want to give the standard solution that had been taught in the class, so he came up with a new answer: "Take the barometer to the top of the building, attach it to a long rope, lower the barometer to the street, and then bring it up, measuring the length of the rope. The length of the rope is the height of the building." The physics professor was not amused and gave him no credit for the answer.

   The student protested and another educator was brought in to arbitrate. The professor's protest was based on the fact that the student's answer did not demonstrate competency in the knowledge of physics. The student was given six minutes to come up with an answer that would demonstrate his knowledge in this field. The student then gave this answer: "Take the barometer to the top of the building and lean over the edge of the roof. Drop the barometer, timing its fall with a stopwatch. Then, using the formula $S = \frac{1}{2}at^2$, calculate the height of the building." The professor was satisfied with this answer and gave the student full credit. Just out of curiosity, the arbitrator asked the student if he had any other answers to the problem. The student responded, "Oh yes, there are many ways to measure the height of the building with a barometer." The student then proceeded to fire off the following alternatives:

- On a sunny day, measure the length of the shadows of the barometer and the building. Using simple proportions, you can calculate the height of the building.

- Climb the stairs of the building using the barometer length as a "tape measure." You would have the height of the building in "barometer" units.

- Take the barometer to the superintendent's office and offer to give it to him if he will tell you the height of the building.[2]

## How Does Storytelling Contribute to Creativity?

Storytelling is a mental process that draws on both logical, verbal thinking and visual, emotional thinking processes. As described earlier in this book, it is impossible to tell a story well if you are not visualizing the people and events of the story as you tell it. Without the "picture" being painted and the emotions being engaged, a story will fall flat. At the same time, if the teller does not also draw on logical, verbal skills as well, the story is likely to be jumbled and confused in the telling. The teller may be having a wonderful time telling the story, but the listeners probably have no idea what the teller is talking about.

### Logic-based Thinking versus Visual-based Thinking

The creative ability to generate large numbers of ideas about any topic, and particularly new ideas that have practical applications, is a mental process that is still something of a mystery. It is known that part of the answer for how this process works is through combining visual thinking with logical thinking in a way that produces better results than either one would if used alone. These two types of thinking are often referred to as left- and right-brain thinking because of a theory that these abilities are specialized skills "housed" in the two hemispheres of the brain. The two types of thinking seem to combine in a way that helps to generate new ideas. The following two columns are descriptions of the two types of thinking that combine to produce creative ideas that have some practical application:

| Logic-based Thinking (Left brain) | Visual-based Thinking (Right brain) |
|---|---|
| Factual | Intuitive |
| Analytical | Synthesizing |
| Reasoning | Spatial perception |
| Verbal | Gut-level feeling |
| Mathematical | Understanding analogies and metaphors[3] |

Because storytelling uses a similar process that is used in all types of creative thinking, drawing on both the logical and visual thought processes, it can help to trigger other types of creativity as well. A well-told story is an excellent tool to get a group of people thinking in new directions. It helps to trigger the listeners' own stories about similar experiences—or even contrasting, contradictory experiences. A well-told story stirs the mental juices on both sides of the brain. In the past few years, we have seen the publication of a number of very popular business books, such as *Zapp!* and *The Goal,* that use a storytelling format to get their message across. In these two books, readers are encouraged to look at the merits of the Total Quality Management approach for operating organizations. Usually this topic is addressed using an analytical approach, because it deals with factual data gathering, statistics, and analytical problem-solving tools. Reading about the quality techniques can, quite frankly, be very dry and boring. But with these two storytelling books, the whole concept comes alive and makes for interesting reading. *Zapp!* is a fantasy story complete with dragons, and *The Goal* is written like a novel, where even the home lives of the characters play a part in the story. These books manage to take a factual topic and present it in a way that taps into both left- and right-brain thinking through storytelling.

> *Storytelling taps into both the visual, emotional thinking, and the logical, verbal thinking of the human brain.*

There are several specific types of stories that are directly related to the creative process:

- Use of analogies and metaphors
- Use of stories to make the familiar seem strange
- Use of humor in stories
- Use of self-talk or stories you tell to yourself in your head

# Using Analogies and Metaphors to Trigger Creativity

*Analogies* and *metaphors* are figures of speech used to compare two things that are not necessarily similar in the literal sense. The two terms actually have very similar meanings and are often used interchangeably in general language references. These can be simple phrases such as "She is the flower of my life" (metaphor) or "She is as delicate as a flower" (analogy). Or they can be used in a much more elaborate form as a full-blown story that is intended to be used as a comparison to some other situation. One of the most famous uses of metaphors is the use of parables in *The Bible*. They are stories that are intended to teach or to make a person think about his or her behavior. The connection that is supposed to be made is the whole point of telling the story.

When using analogies for triggering creativity, you let an individual or a group of people make as many of their own connections as possible. For example, a simple analogy that usually triggers hilarious "right-brain" conversations in a work setting is to ask a group of employees to come up with answers to the question: *How is your organization like a circus?*

This is a question that is not really intended to be taken literally, but is used to generate comparisons and insights about how the organization functions. People almost always make connections, for example, about the presence of animal excrement in both settings. If you follow that general question with a second, more specific version, you can begin to see some of the ideas might have some practical implications: *How could you make your organization better by making it* more *like a circus?*

One group who used this question about the circus to look at their organization gave as one of their first answers: "We work on a high wire without a safety net." When asked the second question about how to make their organization better, they picked up on the safety net comment, noted that many circuses did use safety nets, and went on to have a lengthy conversation about what they could do in their organization to build a safety net under each other. There were many practical suggestions that came out of this discussion. The theory behind why analogies help to trigger creative thinking is because they confuse the logical, left brain just long enough to let the visual, intuitive right brain take off on a flight of fantasy—making strange and irrational connections. The logical thought processes come back into play when it is time to clean up the ideas and figure out how to turn them into practical applications.

Some uses of analogies are very down-to-earth and others are filled with fantasy and wildly illogical comparisons. For example, reading a biography can be a down-to-earth metaphor if people read it with the purpose of comparing the story to their own life. On the other hand, the contents of most fairy tales are filled with fantasy characters and events that could never happen in reality. The purpose, however, of telling about these fantasy events may be to help people make the comparison back to the real world and think about it from a different perspective. My first book, *Tribal Warfare in Organizations,* is really just one long metaphor. There are no "tribes" in the literal sense of the word living in organizations. The comparison is intended, however, to make people think about the similarities and to use that information to trigger new ideas about their own behavior in organizational settings. There are two main types of analogies that are used in creative thinking:

1. Real-life analogies
2. Symbolic analogies

## Real-Life Analogies

Any story that is told with the intent of comparison to the listeners' own lives or circumstances is an analogy. The teller is describing characters and plots from another setting or a past time and comparing it to the listeners' current situations. Most of the stories told in the Addendum at the end of this book are examples of story analogies that could be used in this way to make a point. They are, in effect, modern parables about well-known people that are used to make people think of new ideas about their own behavior or problem. Scientists and inventors often use analogies to help them develop new models. Alexander Graham Bell, for example, created the telephone by modeling it after the human ear:

> It struck me that bones of the human ear were very massive as compared with the delicate thin membrane that operated them. The thought occurred that if a membrane so delicate could move bones relatively so massive, why should not a thicker and stouter piece of membrane move my piece of steel.[4]

From that analogy came the telephone.

Role playing is one use of stories that are actually analogies.[5] In a role play, the people involved often pretend they are another person. The intent is usually to understand that other person's point of view or to see the situation from a different vantage point. Role plays can also help people experiment with new behaviors or skills in the imaginary situation in a safe setting. The intent is that the people participating in these activities will be able to make the comparison back to their real-life situations and apply their new ideas and skills in those settings. It is a simple form of acting that is used as an analogy for real life.

## Symbolic Analogies

Not all stories that use analogies or metaphors are based on comparing two different situations from real life. Many of the most powerful stories/analogies are about fantasy characters or symbols. Fairy tales and legends are classic examples of fantasy stories that are intended to have some comparison to the listener's current life.

The old story called *The Emperor's New Clothes* is a classic example of a fantasy tale that is easily applied to modern organizational settings. The message it carries is about the dangers of groupthink and how it can blind crowds to the fact that the emperor is walking down the street naked. It is not difficult to think of situations in many organizations that parallel this type of group blindness to the true facts.

There are many other folk tales that could be used in work settings to illustrate a point or remind people of an important characteristic. Many of these stories are hero stories that describe a person going up against incredible odds to defend what he/she believes in. One of these stories originated after the Civil War when the Chesapeake and Ohio Railroad Company was laying hundreds of miles of railroad track in West Virginia, right through the Allegheny Mountains. The story is about John Henry, the best steeldriver in the whole country, who was pitted against the steam drill and beat its speed for drilling nails by using both arms to hammer. This story started as a favorite hero story among southern black laborers, but eventually the songs and stories were recorded and played on radio, and John Henry became a well-known American folk hero. His motto, repeated frequently, was "A man ain't nothin' but a man. He's just got to do his best."

It does not really matter whether your preferences run toward Paul Bunyan, Johnny Appleseed, Pecos Bill, Robin Hood, or one of the other hundreds of legendary characters that have been passed down through the generations. There are enough characters, themes, and stories to fit almost any situation that you encounter in modern daily life, if you want to use a folk tale as a metaphor to compare to your current situation. These stories are intended to teach the listener some truth about living as well as to entertain. In addition to their pure teaching value, fantasy stories can also be useful to stimulate creativity in a group setting because people play off of each other's ideas.

Some symbolic analogies are even further removed from reality. William J. Gordon, founder of the creativity company, Synetics, and author of a book by the same title, has developed some of the most elaborate techniques for using symbolic analogies to help groups tap into their creativity. One problem that he uses as an example of the application of symbolic analogies is the development of a jacking mechanism that needed to be very small but able to extend out to a length of several feet and support up to 4 tons. The brainstorming of analogies included Indian rope tricks, steel tape measures, the hydraulics of the erection of a penis, and a bicycle chain that is both flexible and stiff.[6] Out of these comparisons, the group was able to look at jacks in new ways, and developed a new type of jack that solved the company's problem.

## When Analogies Stop Being Creative and Become Lying

One common use of stories is a leap beyond the truth that is not necessarily intended for any positive outcome such as generating creativity. The "flights of fantasy" are intended to trick the listener into thinking the story is the literal truth, instead of simply a comparison or analogy. This connotation of storytelling was brought home to me when I began writing this book. When I told people about the subject of the book, several people laughed and asked if the book was going to be about how to lie effectively in organizations. I found this both appalling and funny at the same time. It is frightening because it is an indication that many people perceive that stories have been used as a way to lie to them or trick them in the organizations where they work. This is another example of the negative use of a very powerful communication tool. I did find it funny, however, to think about the unlikely possibility that I would devote the time and energy to write a book on how to perfect one's lying skills in organizations.

In the movie *Housesitter*, Goldie Hawn played a funny version of an extremely talented storyteller. Her character's primary purpose in telling these wild stories, however, was to deceive everyone around her. There is no question that this type of storytelling is a form of creativity, but it is doubtful whether it has any positive use in real life. Storytelling as a form of lying was a great premise for a funny movie, but in real life this use of storytelling leads to a great deal of pain and heartache for the people who have to live or work around it.

## Using Humor in Stories

In my experience of working with groups of all sizes, it is clear to me that you can get a fairly accurate measure of the level of creativity that is occurring in the group by listening to the amount of laughter coming from the group. The more laughter, the more creative the group is probably being. Even if the subject matter itself is not funny, people who are using their right brains to generate visual, intuitive, metaphorical ideas usually find some way to make it funny.

Force fits, for example, tend to trigger weird ideas as well as serious ones. The group is looking at familiar ideas in strange ways and this often triggers laughter. Mark Twain was famous for his ability to word a familiar idea in a way that triggered laughter from his readers and audiences. One of his famous lines, for example, is "Man—a creature made at the end of the week's work when God was tired."[7] One of Abraham Lincoln's talents as a storyteller was his ability to use humor even when responding to the frequent verbal attacks that he endured during his presidency. Lincoln neutralized the impact of one particularly insulting speaker by stating that "the oratory of the gentleman completely suspends all action of his mind." He then went on to compare the speaker to a steamboat he had seen once during his days as a boatman. "It had a five-foot boiler and a seven-foot whistle, and every time it whistled the boat stopped."[8]

Will Rogers is another person who was famous for his use of humor to entertain and to make a point. American political observers, for example, love to use his quote about the political parties. Rogers is known to have quipped, "I do not belong to any organized party. I'm a Democrat." All these statements create mental pictures and cause the listener to make unusual combinations or interpretations of events around them. Not every story a person tells needs to be funny, but it will help to keep the creativity flowing if there is some humor mixed in along the way. This is particularly true if the message behind the story is a sensitive or controversial one. People can absorb touchy information better if they are allowed to laugh along with hearing the message.

## Constructive Use of Self-Talk: Stories You Tell to Yourself

Not all stories have to be told out loud to other people. Most people have a running story going on in their own heads all the time they are awake. Even when we are asleep, the stories continue during certain portions of sleep in the form of dreams. We are always telling stories to ourselves. The "self-talk" stories may, in fact, be the most important stories of all in shaping people's views of themselves and the world around them. It is highly unlikely that people who are outwardly cynical at work and at home tell upbeat, optimistic stories in their self-talk. The two probably go together in almost all cases. The only exception to this might be when a person is trying to hide his or her true thoughts or attitudes.

There is a term used by Peter Senge called the *left-hand column* to describe the difference between a person's thoughts and words when that individual is trying to hide his or her true thoughts.[9] Picture the verbal conversation between two people written out on paper as a script, much like a play. Then draw a line down the left side of the page to create an empty left-hand column. Now go back through the written script and write in the left-hand column what each of the two people are really thinking but not saying at each step of the conversation. The verbal script and the left-hand column script may not match at all. These are the cases where the self-talk or unspoken script is actually more significant than what is said out loud. It is more genuine and affects the person's opinions, feelings, and morale more than any politely spoken words ever will.

Self-talk has a particularly damaging effect if the topic of the self-talk is the person him- or herself. Many stress-reduction experts advise people to learn to monitor their own self-talk and to work on forming the habit of positive self-talk. One analogy that has been used is to suggest you stop talking to yourself like the prosecuting attorney and try switching your self-talk to sound more like the defense attorney.

If you want to inspire the best out of your own mind in terms of creativity, watch out for negative self-talk. People who are being picked on all the time do not have the time or energy to be creative. They are too busy defending themselves. Be sure that you are not in the habit of picking on yourself with negative storytelling to yourself and about yourself. My advice to people is to listen to your self-talk in your head. If the things you are hearing would make you angry if you heard them said to your best friend, then quit saying them to yourself. Most people would not tolerate someone verbally attacking their best friend with a tirade that starts with words like "How could you be such a stupid jerk . . . ?" So why put up with that verbal garbage inside your own head directed at you?

There has been a great deal of research in the past few years about the positive effects of a process called *visualization*. This is basically an elaborate form of positive self-talk done by an individual or even a group of people working together. Much of the research has been done with athletes in both individual and team sports to get them to visualize a story line of winning the game, hitting the ball perfectly, or swinging the club or racket with perfect form. Some of the research indicates that creating and repeating these positive mental images over and over in one's brain actually improves performance more than actual physical practice. Whether that turns out to be completely true or not, there is no question that getting yourself to form the habit of repeating positive verbal and visual messages to yourself is a helpful tool in improving your performance and your mental health.

## Creative Leadership as Catalyst and Storyteller

The commitment of the leader and all the individuals within an organization to never stop learning is one of the keys to sustained creativity and innovation. This ability to keep learning allows leaders to act as catalysts for change in an organization, continually reshaping their thinking to adjust to the changing environment around them. *Innovation* is usually defined as the actual application or use of a creative idea or invention. Without the application, the idea may have been creative, but it is also useless.

Leadership in an organization must play the role of catalyst to make sure that creativity and invention are translated into practical innovations. For example, the Wright brothers "invented" heavier-than-air flying in 1903 at Kitty Hawk, but it was more than 30 years before commercial aviation had grown to the point that it began serving the general public.[10] Engineers will often say that an invention does not qualify as an innovation until it can be replicated on a large scale at a reasonable cost.[11] It is the leaders' job to ensure that this transformation happens.

Because of this, the leadership version of creativity and innovative thinking is geared toward action and change. In their book *Corporate Culture and Performance,* Kotter and Heskett describe the leadership role in keeping an organization changing and adapting to new demands around it in the following ways:

- Leaders begin their jobs by trying to create an atmosphere of perceived "crisis."

- Leaders widely communicate data about this "crisis"-level need for change throughout the organization.

- Leaders develop and communicate a vision of what changes are needed.

- Leaders motivate and inspire people to overcome barriers to turn the new vision into a reality.[12]

It is difficult to imagine how leaders could conceive of these new ideas and visions, let alone communicate them effectively, without the use of stories. The use of storytelling as a tool for fostering innovation in an organization is essential to the ability to create both a visual picture of the new ideas and a rational understanding of what needs to be done. A well-told story with a carefully planned message will go further to communicate, inspire, and encourage creativity on the part of the listeners than any other leadership tool available. Abraham Lincoln made the following observations about himself as a storyteller. He said that although he has a reputation for being a storyteller, he did not consider himself to be one in the true sense of the word. Here is the reason that he gives for this opinion:

> It is not the story itself, but the purpose or effect, that interests me. I often avoid long and useless discussion by others or laborious explanations on my own part by a short story that illustrates my point. Storytelling is an emollient that saves me much friction and distress.[13]

This is the same motivation that seems to be what inspired Franklin Roosevelt's "Fireside Chats" almost one hundred years after Lincoln, during another economic and military crisis in the United States. When Roosevelt wanted to convince the American people to back the Lend-Lease Act that he was proposing for sending arms to England, he used a story to make his point. Here is what he said in that famous fireside chat:

> Now, what I am trying to do is to eliminate the dollar sign . . . the silly foolish old dollar sign. All Right!
> Well, let me give you an illustration: Suppose my neighbor's home catches fire . . . if he can take my garden hose and connect it up with his hydrant, I may help him to put out his fire. Now, what do I do? I don't say to him before that operation, "Neighbor, my garden hose cost me $15; you have got to pay me $15 for it."
> I don't want $15—I want my garden hose back after the fire is over . . . In other words, if you lend certain munitions and get the munitions back at the end of the war, . . . you are all right.[14]

During the great debate in Congress about whether or not to "lend" the munitions to England, Senator Taft responded to Roosevelt's story with a pithy one-liner of his own. He is quoted as having said, "Lending war equipment is a good deal like lending chewing gum. You don't want it back."[15]

When leadership is discussed in the context of change, it is important to be clear that the CEO is not the only leader in the organization. In fact, if the CEO is seen as the only leader, it will be almost impossible for the organization to be creative and innovative at the rapid pace that is required today. Whether a person is a leader of a work unit, a project, a department, an informal network of colleagues, or the entire organization, the role of catalyst is the same. These people cannot make things happen directly by themselves, but they are the guides and motivators who encourage large numbers of people to move together in common directions. Their creativity emerges through their ability to envision the future in a new way and then lead others down the path toward that future.

Not everyone in an organization is, or needs to be, a leader. If, however, there are only one or two people who identify themselves as leaders, that organization will not be able to muster the energy and momentum to develop creative ideas and turn them into practical innovations. If an organization wants innovation and change, leadership is not a term that should be reserved for the chosen few or the corporate elite. The term should be used instead with its old cultural connotation referring to the elders, who are the tribe's storytellers and guides.

# Conclusion

Stories play an important stabilizing role in our culture, according to Neil Postman, a New York University professor of communication arts and sciences. He uses this metaphor to describe the power of stories in all of our lives: "Without air our cells die. Without a story our selves die."[1] The collection of stories about our individual lives and our organizations' histories are the autobiographies that tell us who we are and where we fit within the communities around us.

Scherrie Forster, a professional storyteller and Ph.D. candidate in speech and communication at the University of Minnesota, contends that for most of us our formal education has "de-storied" us.[2] Modern education favors theories and numbers more than information shared in story, parable, or myth form. Because of this, many people do not see stories in their lives anymore. They see a string of events occurring around them and to them, but they do not necessarily translate these events into stories that carry important meanings and memories for them. This realization struck me in a particularly clear way recently when I was conducting a storytelling workshop with a group of professionals. I had asked them to tell some favorite stories from their personal histories. One woman in the workshop was frustrated because she could not think of any stories about her family. She explained to me that no one in her family talked about the past or told stories about their lives. We discussed her disappointment about this for a few minutes, and then all of a sudden she began to tell about some letters that she had found one time in the attic that had been written by her great-great-grandfather. In these letters, he was writing to relatives about the recent death of his wife from cholera. She went on to describe the letters and the stories he told about his life at that time. I turned to her and said, "And you are the person who just told me that you did not know any family stories!" We both laughed, and almost as though we had popped a cork from a bottle, she started telling one story after another about her child-hood and her family. There were all kinds of stories in her memory. She was simply not used to thinking of them in that way. To her, all this information in her memory was only a series of events that had happened to her, but she had never thought of them as or translated them into stories that told of her own personal heritage.

For many years, one of my favorite stories has been *A Thousand Clowns,* a play by Herb Gardner and later a movie about a character named Murray who knew that life was one long story. At one point in the story, he says the following lines to another character who seems to have forgotten this truth:

> You have got to own your days and name them, each one of them, every one of them, or else the years go right by and none of them belong to you.

That quote captures for me the inspiration behind the writing of this book. My life, your life, and every organization's life is a long chain of sto-ries worth telling. These stories are filled with wisdom and stupidity, suc-cesses and failures, hopes and disappointments. These are the stories about humanity in action. They are the clearest view of our past and a pathway to our future. My hope is that this book will inspire the readers to do more telling and listening to each other's stories.

# Addendum: Building Your Own Collection of Great Stories

## Retelling Classic Leadership Stories

There are many wonderful stories that have been told about leadership and organizational issues by many people over the years. Some of the stories are told about famous leaders, others are told by them, and still others are anonymous stories highlighting important characteristics of people that can be applied to life in organizations. These stories are repeated as a way of illustrating a point or describing a key value or characteristic. Many times, when leaders give speeches or are trying to explain an important issue, it is helpful to be able to draw on these classic stories to clarify the message. This addendum provides an anthology of a few of the great stories that have been told over the years. There are two purposes for retelling these stories here. One is to illustrate the power of these stories for communicating a message in a way that is inspiring and memorable. The second purpose is to describe a number of classic stories that the readers could use themselves in their own conversations or presentations. Retelling stories like these is often an excellent way to strengthen the message in your own efforts to communicate your message. There are many good sources of stories to draw on for your own use. Here are a few of my favorite sources:

> *Leadership,* a monthly publication similar to *Bits and Pieces,* which focuses specifically on leadership topics. The Economic Press, 12 Daniel Road, Fairfield, NJ 07004.

*Quotable Business,* Louis E. Boone. A book of short stories and quotes from well-known businesspeople. Random House, 1992.

*Speaker's Library of Business Stories, Anecdotes and Humor,* Joe Griffith. Another book of business stories and quotes. Prentice Hall, 1990.

Some of the stories told in this addendum are real-life "here's what happened" stories and others are metaphors with a message that can be used to make a point. A few are famous one-liners that create a quick visual picture in the listener's mind and represent a story in miniature. These one-liners could have been expanded into full-blown stories if the teller had chosen to do so, but the concentration of the message into one line creates a powerful and memorable image.

## Stories Told by Well-Known Leaders

The first collection of stories are ones that were told by well-known leaders. People love to hear stories that were told by famous people. Even if people have heard these stories before, they usually enjoy hearing them again.

**Taking Reasonable Risks.** Bill Gore, founder of W. L. Gore and Associates, the highly profitable maker of Gore-Tex and other synthetic-fiber products, used a metaphor to explain to his employees his expectations about taking reasonable risks. He used the term *waterline* to create a visual picture of when to take risks and when not to. He encouraged them to venture out and take risks, but cautioned that it was each employee's responsibility to learn where the "waterline" was. "If you make a mistake above the waterline, it will not sink the ship." A risk that was "below the waterline" was any action that, if it failed, would have a negative effect on the company in general. In these cases, everyone who might be affected by the risk taking should be consulted and included in the planning and decision making about whether or not to proceed.[1]

**Commitment to Quality.** Al Neuharth, who launched *Today,* the prototype for *USA Today,* in 1966, describes the way the employees prepared for the start-up of the company's production and distribution of their new newspaper. According to Neuharth, they "produced complete prototypes of the paper every day—printed them, put them on trucks, dropped them at delivery points to pinpoint timing." When they were finished with the day's dry run, they retraced their steps to pick up all the prototype newspapers and burn them at the local dump to keep them out of the hands of the competition before their kickoff day.[2]

**On Becoming a Leader.**  Johnnetta Cole, the first black woman to be president of Spelman College in Atlanta, Georgia, tells stories about the many roles that she has played in her life—including anthropologist, campus radical, professor, wife, mother, and so on. She then goes on to tell this story about her first days at Spelman when she was adjusting to the idea that she was now a college president:

> I have a ritual that I may cease to participate in, but I need that ritual right now. When I awaken in the morning, before I leave my bed, I tell myself again that I am the president of Spelman College. I need that ritual for several reasons. One is that I haven't spent a great deal of time imagining myself in this sort of a place, in a presidency, so that my image of myself really was not as a college president. My image of myself was to do things beyond being a professor, sure, but it didn't have much reality to it. Now I'm going through an imagining and being. So every morning I have to wake up and tell myself that I'm the president of Spelman College, and then I have to understand again what kind of institution this is.

She goes on to describe that at the same time she was learning to adjust to being a president, the experience of being at Spelman felt very "natural" to her. Spelman is an institution for black women and is "absolutely overflowing with history." She says, "You just can't be here without encountering what so much of black America is about."[3]

**Understanding the Customer Point of View.**  Jane Trahey, founder and president of a topflight advertising agency, had a trick she used when she needed to write a letter to a client she hoped to attract. She would write the letter, sign it, and mail it to herself.

Days later it would show up at her desk. It would be in the middle of all the regular mail and when she got to it she invariably read it in a totally new light. She would read it with as mean and cold an eye as she could. She would pretend she was the executive to whom the letter was directed.

"What does he think of me as he reads it?" she would ask herself. "Whom does he see? What have I said in the letter that makes him think I'm worth calling? What skills have I shown him? It's a revelation sometimes," she said, "not so much because of what you put in the letter, but what you've left out."[4]

**Fear in the Face of Downsizing.**  Robert Dilenschneider, public relations expert and author of the book, *A Briefing for Leaders,* tells a story about the time he was brought in by a national lumber company to help the plant manager prepare to announce the closing of the local mill. Jim, the plant manager, was scared to death about making the announcement.

Dilenschneider describes how he worked with Jim all day, practicing what he would say and anticipating the questions that the workers might have. They stressed the economic need for the shutdown, the generous benefits being offered the workers, and the retraining program that the company was offering. After many hours of work, Jim appeared to be ready for the presentation.

The meeting started at four o'clock in the afternoon, and about 300 men from the plant filed in to take their seats. Dilenschneider stood off to the side with his fingers crossed. Jim stood up, looked out at the audience staring at him, and said with his voice cracking, "My friends, . . . My friends, Mr. Dilenschneider has come here from New York today, and he has something to tell you . . ."

Dilenschneider describes his shock as "300 burly hulks—some with no teeth and at least five with 'Mother' tattooed on their arms" swung their chairs around to glare at him standing there in his three-piece suit. He says, "As I figured it, there was no way out. I took off my jacket, rolled up my sleeves, strode to the front of the room, and told them the plant was closing." It was a rough session with many groans and curses coming from the workers, but as Dilenschneider describes it, he survived, and "no one tried to saw me in half or break my arm."[5]

**Decisiveness.**   H. Ross Perot, founder of Electronic Data Systems, tells this story about the difference between EDS and General Motors after his stint as a board member at GM:

> The first EDSer to see a snake, kills it. At GM, the first thing you do when you see a snake is organize a committee on snakes. Then you bring in a consultant who knows a lot about snakes. Third thing you do is talk about it for a year.[6]

## Stories Told about Well-Known Leaders

This collection of stories are ones told *about* leaders. These stories are similar to the preceding ones. The only difference is in the point of view. They are told by friends or writers about the well-known people. Sometimes these are easier for people to use when they are first learning to tell stories because they do not have to take on the role of the person in the story. The storyteller can simply tell the story as a third-party observer.

**The Joy of Work.**  Julia Child was in the middle of one of her TV cooking programs when she lifted two lids from steaming pans and clanged them together exuberantly over her head, like cymbals. Condensed water from the lids showered down on her and all over the front of her blouse. She nonchalantly wiped her front with a towel and said laughingly, "I don't know why I did that. It was silly!" Ah, if only everyone could find such joy in their work![7]

**Commitment to Continuous Improvement.**   One of the stories repeated frequently by Boston Celtics' basketball fans concerns Larry Bird's never-ending commitment to practicing his playing skills. He was widely considered one of the best basketball players of all time, but even at the height of his career, he still would show up two hours early before each game to practice his shooting. "Good enough is good enough" was definitely not his motto. Even at the end of his career when he was in constant back pain, he continued to play each game with his old spirit, diving for every loose ball that came near him. He had earned the right to rest on his laurels, but he never did until the day he retired.

**Product Quality.**   There is a Procter and Gamble story told by a manufacturing manager about the time one of the district sales managers called him in the middle of the night. The problem he was calling about was a bar of soap.

"George, you've got a problem with a bar of soap down here. Do you think you could get down here by six-thirty this morning to check it out?"

This required a 300-mile drive in the middle of the night through the back roads of Tennessee for the manufacturing manager to check into the quality problem on a 34-cent bar of soap. George made the trip and fixed the problem. This story is told as a classic example of P&G's commitment to quality.[8]

**Modesty and Greatness.**   Eleanor Roosevelt is known all over the world as one of the great humanitarians of the twentieth century. Long after the death of her husband, Franklin D. Roosevelt, Mrs. Roosevelt continued in public life, working for the rights of oppressed and poor people in the United States and abroad. Her life accomplishments and status certainly gave her every opportunity to become arrogant, or at least very aware of her greatness in the eyes of other people. And yet, there are many stories told about her by friends and associates like the one described here.

"The thing is she was so modest. She never thought of herself as exceptional or extraordinary or important." Her friend went on to explain that whenever you traveled with Mrs. Roosevelt, she was always surprised at the reactions of people who met her. Once, when she was returning from a tour to promote the United Nations, she and the friend landed at an airport.

They looked out the window of the plane and saw that a red carpet had been laid out on the runway and children were waiting, holding flowers. There was a large welcoming party standing by the runway, obviously waiting for their plane to arrive. Eleanor turned to her friend and said, "Oh look! Somebody significant must be flying in."[9]

As a balance to this story, Eleanor Roosevelt is also quoted as saying, "No one can make you feel inferior without your consent."[10]

**Fun and Work.**     One of the legendary stories about Sam Walton, founder of Wal-Mart, is about the time he danced the hula on Wall Street. In 1984, Walton made a bet with the CEO of Wal-Mart, David Glass. Walton bet Glass that the company could not possibly produce more than an 8 percent pretax profit. He told Glass that if the company did, he would dance the hula on Wall Street!

The company hit the 8 percent profit goal, and in typical Wal-Mart tradition Sam had to keep his word and do his dance. In his autobiography he says, "I thought I would slip down there and dance, and David would videotape it so he could prove to everyone back at the Saturday morning meeting that I really did it." But that was not at all what his colleague had waiting for him.

When Walton arrived, wearing his grass skirt, he found a truckload of real hula dancers and ukulele players waiting for him. In addition to the dancers, Glass had notified the newspapers and TV networks who were all there to film the dance. Wearing a grass skirt, Hawaiian shirt, and leis over his suit, Sam danced what he describes as "a pretty fair hula." The picture of the crazy chairman of the board from Arkansas ran in newspapers and on television shows everywhere, and the people at Wal-Mart loved it.[11]

**Customer-Service Commitment.**     Jan Carlzon, chairman of the board and CEO of Scandinavian Airline System, told this story as an example of taking risks to produce high-quality customer service. "One time an important executive of Swedish business radioed ahead from his business jet as he was approaching Kennedy Airport to let SAS know that he would be a few minutes late for the flight to Stockholm." Carlzon says that the executive did not actually tell them to hold the plane, but that was certainly the unspoken message. One of the key customer-service commitments of employees at SAS is to run on-time airplanes. There were no standing instructions about how to handle a situation like this, but the employees sprung into action anyway.

When the business executive arrived at the airport, the plane had already departed as scheduled. An SAS official greeted the executive with a ticket on a KLM flight leaving in half an hour. It was the same type of aircraft, and the executive was assigned exactly the same seat that he would have had on the original flight. The business executive had no complaints, and SAS maintained its reputation for on-time travel.[12]

## Stories That Are Metaphors Applicable to the Workplace

This collection of stories contains metaphors that illustrate important leadership characteristics. These can be used to illustrate a key point or to draw attention to an important characteristic or value of people in the organization. Many times it is useful to give some type of explanation before or after these stories to ensure that the listeners understand your point. On the other hand, some storytellers purposely do not explain a metaphor, so that each person in the audience can draw his or her own meaning from the story. The choice is left to the storyteller to explain or to leave it open for a variety of interpretations.

**Teamwork and Interdependence.**   There is an old Sufi story about a blind man and a crippled man who stumble into each other in a forest. They are both lost. The two strike up a conversation, sharing their stories about wandering the forest for "as long as they both can remember." The blind man says, "I cannot see to find my way out." The crippled man nods and responds, "I cannot get up to walk out." As they sat there sadly talking, the crippled man cries out, "I've got it! You hoist me up onto your shoulders and I will tell you where to walk." Together, they found their way out of the forest.[13]

**Pacing of a Business.**   Titus, the emperor of Rome, had the symbol of a dolphin wound around an anchor inscribed on coins during his reign. The anchor represented delay and unchanging conviction. The dolphin represented speed and action.

Through the years, the dolphin and the anchor have been used as a family crest, with the explanatory motto *Festina lente*—"Hasten slowly." It expresses moderation between two opposing ideas. In business, it means the middle ground between acting too quickly and waiting too long.[14]

**Clarity of Direction.**   From *Alice in Wonderland:*

> One day Alice came to a fork in the road and spotted a Cheshire cat in a tree. "Which road do I take?" she asked. His response was a question: "Where do you want to go?" "I don't know," Alice answered. "Then," said the cat, "it doesn't matter."[15]

**Flexibility and Willingness to Change Course.** Late one night a sea captain saw the lights of another ship coming straight at his ship, so he had the signalman send a message to the other ship, "Change your course 10 degrees north."

Back came the response from the other ship, "You change course 10 south."

This annoyed the captain because it was not an appropriate response, so he signaled back again, "I am the captain of this ship, change course north."

Back came the response, "I'm a seaman first class. Change course south."

Now the captain was furious. This was an outrageous insult. He told the signalman to send back one more message to tell them, "I'm a battleship. Change course north."

And back came the response, "I'm a lighthouse. Change course south."

## Ministories in the Form of One-Liners

This last collection contains one-liners or quotes that stir up a visual picture and represent a type of ministory. Many times, when a person is speaking or trying to explain an important point, a pithy one-liner is the most effective type of story to use. Here are a few of my favorites.

**Dangers of Leadership Arrogance.** A quote by Mark Twain: "The official 'we' should be reserved for kings and people with tapeworms."[16]

**Small Beginnings Lead to Big Things.** A quote by Walt Disney: "Always remember that this whole thing was started by a mouse."[17]

**Leading Change.** Unless you are the lead dog, the scenery never changes.[18]

**Learning from Mistakes.** Babe Ruth not only set a home run record, he also set a strikeout record. A great batting average of .400 means the batter fails to get a hit more than half the time.[19]

**Importance of Lifelong Learning.** A quote from Harry Truman: "The only things worth learning are the things you learn after you know it all."

**The Value of Waiting for the Right Timing.** A quote from General Norman Schwarzkopf: "If the alternative to dying is sitting in the sun for another summer, then that's not a bad alternative. I'm not rushing into battle. I'm not General Custer."[20]

**Effective Communication.** A quote from Jack Welch, the CEO of General Electric: "Real communication takes countless hours of eyeball to eyeball, back and forth. It means more listening than talking."[21]

**Customer Service.** A quote from John Scully, CEO of Apple Computers: "Our customers are our number one sales force."[22]

**Winning.** "There is no finish line." Nike Corporation motto.

# References

## Introduction

1. Sam Keen and Anne Valley-Fox, *Your Mythic Journey, Finding Meaning in Your Life Through Writing and Storytelling,* Jeremy P. Tarcher, Los Angeles, 1973, p. 128.

## Chapter 1. Getting the Message . . . The Power Stories

1. Warren Buffett, *Berkshire Hathaway Annual Report,* 1991, p. 5.
2. Ibid., p. 16.
3. Ibid., p. 19.
4. Louis R. Pondy, Peter J. Frost, Garth Morgan, Thomas C. Dandridge, *Organizational Symbolism,* JAI Press, Greenwich, Conn., 1983, p. 103.
5. Ned Herrmann, *The Creative Brain,* Ned Herrmann Brain Books, 1989, p. 220.
6. Ibid., p. 221.
7. Pondy, p. 100.
8. Ibid., p. 100.
9. Robert Kriegel and Marilyn Harris Kriegel, *The C Zone Peak Performance Under Pressure,* Anchor Press, 1984, p. 84.

## Chapter 2. Is It a Positive or Negative Story?

1. Eugene Richards, *The Knife and Gun Club,* Atlantic Monthly Press, New York, 1989, p. 28.
2. Ibid., p. 165.
3. Ibid., p. 165.

## Chapter 3. Six Types of Positive Stories in Organizations

1. Joseph Campbell, *The Power of Myth*, Doubleday, New York, 1988, p. 123.
2. Ibid., p. 124.
3. Ibid., p. 144.
4. Rhonda Kerr, "His Style Doesn't Stop With Own Workers," *The Tennessean*, March 1, 1992, p. B2.
5. *The New York Times*, October 13, 1991, p. 25.
6. David Armstrong, *Managing by Storying Around: A New Method of Leadership*, Doubleday, 1992, p. 21.
7. Ibid., p. 22.
8. Joel Arthur Barker, *The Business of Paradigms: Discovering the Future*, Chart House, Burnsville, Minn., 1990, p. 19.


## Chapter 4. Retelling Your Organization's Stories

1. Warren Buffett, *Berkshire Hathaway Annual Report*, 1991, p. 16.
2. Louis R. Pondy, Peter J. Frost, Garth Morgan, Thomas C. Dandridge, *Organizational Symbolism*, JAI Press, Greenwich, Conn., 1983, p. 84.
3. Jan Carlzon, *Moments of Truth*, Ballinger Publishing Co., Cambridge, Mass., 1987, p. 23.
4. Ibid., p. 2.
5. Ibid., p. 2.
6. Pondy, p. 85.
7. Tom Peters and Nancy Austin, *A Passion for Excellence*, Random House, 1985, p. 181.
8. *Fortune*, September 7, 1992, p. 71.
9. Peters, p. 276.
10. Ellen Phillips, *The Tale-Teller Tells All*, Cricket Papers Press, Alexandria, Va., 1990, p. 1.
11. Donald T. Phillips, *Lincoln on Leadership*, Warner Books, New York, 1992, p. 139.
12. Ibid., p. 139.
13. Lucille Breneman and Bren Breneman, *Once Upon a Time: A Storytelling Handbook*, Nelson-Hall, Chicago, 1983, p. 18.
14. Ellen Phillips, p. 11.
15. Breneman, p. 67.

16. Ibid., p. 18.

17. Ibid., p. 21.

18. Ibid., p. 39.

19. Peters, p. 8.

20. Richard C. Whiteley, *The Customer-Driven Company*, Addison-Wesley Publishing Co., Reading, Mass., 1991, p. 117.

21. Ibid., p. 117.

22. Ibid., p. 118.

## Chapter 5. Your Corporate Heritage: Sacred Bundle Stories

1. Max DePree, *Leadership as an Art*, Dell, New York, 1989, p. 81.

2. Ibid., p. 82.

3. Ibid., p. 82.

4. Keith D. Wilcox, *The Corporate Tribe*, Wyer-Pearce Press, Excelsior, Minn., 1984, p. 145.

5. Ibid., p. 116.

6. Thomas Vannah, "The Joel and David Show," *New England Business Journal*, August 1990, p. 34.

7. *Fortune*, September 7, 1991, p. 105.

## Chapter 6. The Leader as Storyteller

1. Sam Keen and Anne Valley-Fox, *Your Mythic Journey, Finding Meaning in Your Life Through Writing and Storytelling*, Jeremy P. Tarcher, Los Angeles, 1973, p. xv.

2. Ibid., p. xi.

3. Ibid., p. xi.

4. Ibid., p. xvi.

5. Peter Senge, *The Fifth Discipline*, Doubleday, New York, 1990, p. 345.

6. Ibid., p. 345.

7. Ibid., p. 346.

8. Ibid., p. 346.

9. Robert K. Greenleaf, *Servant Leadership*, Paulist Press, New York, 1977, p. 7.

10. Senge, p. 351.

11. William C. Byham, *Zapp! The Lightning of Empowerment,* Harmony Books, New York, 1988, p. 78.

12. Senge, p. 240.

13. Ibid., p. 241.

14. Warren Bennis and Burt Namus, *Leaders, The Strategies for Taking Charge,* Harper and Row, 1985, p. 223.

15. Louis R. Pondy, Peter J. Frost, Garth Morgan, Thomas C. Dandridge, *Organizational Symbolism,* JAI Press, Greenwich, Conn., 1983, p. 86.

16. Donald T. Phillips, *Lincoln on Leadership,* Warner Books, New York, 1992, p. 17.

17. Ibid., p. 17.

# Chapter 7. Inspiring Stories or Corporate Propaganda?

1. Louis R. Pondy, Peter J. Frost, Garth Morgan, Thomas C. Dandridge, *Organizational Symbolism,* JAI Press, Greenwich, Conn., 1983, p. 95.

2. Ibid., p. 95.

3. Ibid., p. 94.

# Chapter 8. What Is Your Autobiography of Stories?

1. Mary Catherine Bateson, *Composing a Life,* Penguin Books, 1990, p. 34.

2. Sam Keen and Anne Valley-Fox, *Your Mythic Journey, Finding Meaning in Your Life Through Writing and Storytelling,* Jeremy P. Tarcher, Los Angeles, 1973, p. 69.

3. Ibid., p. 69.

4. Ibid., p. 32.

5. *Boston Globe,* June 28, 1992, p. 24.

6. Warren Bennis, *On Becoming a Leader,* Addison-Wesley Publishing Co., 1989, p. 65.

# Chapter 9. Who Are the Heroes in Your Organization?

1. Joseph Campbell, *The Power of Myth,* Doubleday, New York, 1988, p. 123.

2. Ibid., p. 123.

3. Ibid., p. 127.

4. Ibid., p. 131.

5. Ibid., p. 129.

6. Ibid., p. 161.

7. Charles Garfield, *Peak Performers, The New Heroes of American Business,* William Morrow Inc., New York, 1986, p. 141.

8. Ibid., p. 143.

9. Brian Dumaine, "Who Needs a Boss?," *Fortune,* May 7, 1990, p. 57.

10. Campbell, p. 163.

## Chapter 10. Storytelling and the New Employee

1. *Money,* July, 1992, p. 24.

2. Carl Sewell, Paul B. Brown, *Customers for Life: How to Turn That One-Time Buyer into a Lifetime Customer,* Simon and Schuster, New York, 1990, p. pxxi.

3. Ibid., p. pxix.

## Chapter 11. Storytelling and Relationships inside the Organization

1. Sam Keen and Anne Valley-Fox, *Your Mythic Journey, Finding Meaning in Your Life Through Writing and Storytelling,* Jeremy P. Tarcher, Los Angeles, 1973, p. xii.

2. Ibid., p. xv.

## Chapter 12. Protecting Employee Morale

1. *Fortune,* June 15, 1992, p. 71.

2. John P. Kotter and James L. Heskett, *Corporate Culture and Performance,* The Free Press, 1992, p. 58.

3. Ibid., p. 44.

4. Ibid., p. 44.

5. Ibid., p. 45.

6. Ibid., p. 142.

7. Warren Bennis, *On Becoming a Leader,* Addison-Wesley Publishing Co., 1989, p. 118.

8. Elisabeth Kubler-Ross, *On Death and Dying,* Macmillan Publishing Co., 1969, p. 38.

9. John P. Kotter and James L. Heskett, *Corporate Culture and Performance,* The Free Press, 1992, p. 84.

10. Ibid., p. 84.

11. Ibid., p. 85.

# Chapter 13. Storytelling and Relationships with Your Customers

1. Carl Sewell, Paul B. Brown, *Customers for Life: How to Turn That One-Time Buyer into a Lifetime Customer,* Simon and Schuster, New York, 1990, p. 11.

2. Ibid., p. 11.

3. Ibid., p. 169.

4. Ibid., p. 15.

5. Ibid., p. 97.

6. Ibid., p. 39.

7. Ibid., p. 41.

8. Ibid., p. 42.

9. William Manchester, *The Last Lion,* Little Brown and Co., 1983, p. 6.

10. Sewell, p. 46.

# Part 4. Storytelling as a Tool for Managing Change

1. Sam Keen and Anne Valley-Fox, *Your Mythic Journey, Finding Meaning in Your Life Through Writing and Storytelling,* Jeremy P. Tarcher, Los Angeles, 1973, p. 117.

# Chapter 14. The Folklore of Organizations Built for Change

1. Sam Walton and John Huey, *Sam Walton Made in America,* Doubleday, 1992, p. 27.

2. Ibid., p. 28.

3. Kilmann, p. 356.

4. Gifford Pinchot, *Intrapreneuring*, Harper and Row, 1985, p. 208.

5. John P. Kotter and James L. Heskett, *Corporate Culture and Performance*, The Free Press, 1992, p. 64.

6. Gifford Pinchot, *Intrapreneuring*, Harper and Row, 1985, p. 201.

7. Beverly Geber, "Can TQM Cure Health Care?," *Training*, August 1992, p. 28.

## Chapter 15. The Role of Storytelling in Creating an Adaptive Organization

1. Warren Bennis, *On Becoming a Leader*, Addison-Wesley Publishing Co., 1989, p. 143.

2. John P. Kotter and James L. Heskett, *Corporate Culture and Performance*, The Free Press, 1992, p. 40.

3. Ibid., p. 40.

4. Joe Griffith, *Speaker's Library of Business Stories, Anecdotes and Humor*, Prentice Hall, 1990, p. 122.

5. Peter Senge, *The Fifth Discipline*, Doubleday, New York, 1990, p. 206.

## Chapter 16. Using Stories to Communicate Effectively during a Change

1. Rosabeth Moss Kanter, *When Giants Learn to Dance*, Simon and Schuster, 1989, p. 86.

2. Ibid., p. 86.

## Chapter 17. Using Storytelling to Manage Resistance to Change

1. Michael LeBoeuf, *Imagineering, How To Profit From Your Creative Powers*, McGraw-Hill Book Co., 1980, p. 125.

2. Warren Bennis, *On Becoming a Leader*, Addison-Wesley Publishing Co., 1989, p. 97.

3. George S. Odiorne, *The Change Resisters*, Prentice-Hall, Inc., 1981, p. 29.

4. Bennis, p. 144.

5. Ibid., p. 144.

228                                                    References

## Chapter 18. Using Storytelling
## for Creativity and Innovation

1. Michael LeBoeuf, *Imagineering, How To Profit From Your Creative Powers,* McGraw-Hill Book Co., 1980, p. 22.

2. Ibid., p. 21.

3. Ibid., p. 11.

4. Ibid., p. 97.

5. Ibid., p. 98.

6. Ibid., p. 99.

7. Ibid., p. 97.

8. Donald T. Phillips, *Lincoln on Leadership,* Warner Books, New York, 1992, p. 72.

9. Peter Senge, *The Fifth Discipline,* Doubleday, New York, 1990, p. 196.

10. Ibid., p. 5.

11. Ibid., p. 10.

12. John P. Kotter and James L. Heskett, *Corporate Culture and Performance,* The Free Press, 1992, p. 98.

13. Phillips, p. 159.

14. Frank Freidel, *Roosevelt, A Rendezvous with Destiny,* Little Brown and Co., 1990, p. 360.

15. Ibid., p. 359.

## Conclusion

1. Ron Zemke, "Storytelling Back to Basics," *Training,* March 20, 1990, p. 44.

2. Ibid., p. 48.

## Addendum: Building Your Own
## Collection of Great Stories

1. Peter Senge, *The Fifth Discipline,* Doubleday, New York, 1990, p. 298.

2. Robert L. Dilenschneider, *A Briefing For Leaders,* Harper Business, 1992, p. 38.

3. Mary Catherine Bateson, *Composing A Life,* Penguin Books, 1990, p. 225.

4. *Leadership,* The Economic Press, September 1, 1992, p. 9.

5. Dilenschneider, p. 65.

6. Louis E. Boone, *Quotable Business,* Random House, New York, 1992, p. 95.

7. *Leadership,* The Economic Press, September 1, 1992, p. 1.

8. Tom Peters and Nancy Austin, *A Passion for Excellence,* Random House, 1985, p. 278.

9. Blanche Wiesen Cook, *Eleanor Roosevelt,* Viking Press, 1992, p. 2.

10. Abby Adams, *An Uncommon Scold,* Simon and Schuster, 1989, p. 250.

11. Sam Walton and John Huey, *Sam Walton Made in America,* Doubleday, 1992, p. 159.

12. Jan Carlzon, *Moments of Truth,* Ballinger Publishing Co., Cambridge, Mass., 1987, p. 84.

13. Senge, p. 176.

14. *Leadership,* The Economic Press, May 12, 1992, p. 24.

15. Boone, p. 81.

16. Senge, p. 214.

17. Boone, p. 4.

18. Warren Bennis, *On Becoming a Leader,* Addison-Wesley Publishing Co., 1989, p. 134.

19. Bennis, p. 117.

20. Boone, p. 31.

21. Dilenschneider, p. 23.

22. *Leadership,* The Economic Press, June 9, 1992, p. 22.

# Bibliography

Adams, Abby, *An Uncommon Scold,* Simon and Schuster, 1989.

Armstrong, David, *Managing by Storying Around: A New Method of Leadership,* Doubleday, 1992.

Barker, Joel Arthur, *The Business of Paradigms: Discovering the Future,* Chart House, Burnsville, Minn., 1990.

Bateson, Mary Catherine, *Composing A Life,* Penguin Books, 1990.

Bennis, Warren and Burt Namus, *Leaders, The Strategies for Taking Charge,* Harper and Row, 1985.

Bennis, Warren, *On Becoming a Leader,* Addison-Wesley Publishing Company, 1989.

Block, Peter, *The Empowered Manager,* Jossey-Bass Publishers, San Francisco, 1987.

Boone, Louis E., *Quotable Business,* Random House, 1992.

Breneman, Lucille and Bren Breneman, *Once Upon a Time: A Storytelling Handbook,* Nelson-Hall, Chicago, 1983.

Buffett, Warren, *Berkshire Hathaway Annual Report,* 1991.

Byham, William C., *Zapp! The Lightning of Empowerment,* Harmony Books, New York, 1988.

Campbell, Joseph, *The Power of Myth,* Doubleday, New York, 1988.

Carlzon, Jan, *Moments of Truth,* Ballinger Publishing Co., Cambridge, Mass., 1987.

Cook, Blanche Wiesen, *Eleanor Roosevelt,* Viking Press, 1992.

DePree, Max, *Leadership as an Art,* Dell, New York, 1989.

Deutsch, Claudia H., "The Parables of Corporate Culture," *The New York Times,* November 13, 1991.

Dilenschneider, Robert L., *A Briefing for Leaders,* Harper Business, 1992.

Dumaine, Brian, "Who Needs a Boss?," *Fortune,* May 7, 1990, pp. 52–60.

Freidel, Frank, *Roosevelt, A Rendezvous With Destiny,* Little Brown and Company, 1990.

Gardner, Herb, *One Thousand Clowns,* Random House, 1961.

Garfield, Charles, *Peak Performers, The New Heroes of American Business,* William Morrow Inc., New York, 1986.

Geber, Beverly, "Can TQM Cure Health Care?," *Training,* August 1992.

Greenleaf, Robert K., *Servant Leadership,* Paulist Press, New York, 1977.

Griffith, Joe, *Speaker's Library of Business Stories, Anecdotes and Humor,* Prentice-Hall, 1990.

Herrmann, Ned, *The Creative Brain,* Ned Herrmann Brain Books, 1989.

Kanter, Rosabeth Moss, *When Giants Learn to Dance,* Simon and Schuster, 1989.

Keen, Sam and Anne Valley-Fox, *Your Mythic Journey, Finding Meaning in Your Life Through Writing and Storytelling,* Jeremy P. Tarcher, Los Angeles, 1973.

Kerr, Rhonda, "His Style Doesn't Stop with Own Workers," *The Tennessean*, March 1, 1992.

Kotter, John P. and James L. Heskett, *Corporate Culture and Performance*, The Free Press, 1992.

Kriegel, Robert and Marilyn Harris Kriegel, *The C Zone Peak Performance Under Pressure*, Anchor Press, 1984.

Kubler-Ross, Elisabeth, *On Death and Dying*, Macmillan Publishing Company, 1969.

*Leadership*, The Economic Press, May 12, 1992.

*Leadership*, The Economic Press, June 9, 1992.

*Leadership*, The Economic Press, September 1, 1992.

LeBoeuf, Michael, *Imagineering, How To Profit From Your Creative Powers*, McGraw-Hill Book Company, 1980.

Manchester, William, *The Last Lion*, Little Brown and Company, 1983.

Odiorne, George S., *The Change Resisters*, Prentice-Hall, Inc., 1981.

Peters, Tom and Nancy Austin, *A Passion for Excellence*, Random House, 1985.

Phillips, Donald T., *Lincoln on Leadership*, Warner Books, New York, 1992.

Phillips, Ellen, *The Tale-Teller Tells All*, Cricket Papers Press, Alexandria, Va., 1990.

Pinchot, Gifford, *Intrapreneuring*, Harper and Row, 1985.

Pondy, Louis R., Peter J. Frost, Garth Morgan, Thomas C. Dandridge, *Organizational Symbolism*, JAI Press, Greenwich, Conn., 1983.

Ray, Michael and Rochelle Myers, *Creativity in Business*, Doubleday, 1986.

Richards, Eugene, *The Knife and Gun Club*, Atlantic Monthly Press, New York, 1989.

Saporito, Bill, "What Sam Walton Taught America," *Fortune*, May 4, 1992.

Senge, Peter, *The Fifth Discipline*, Doubleday, New York, 1990.

Sewell, Carl and Paul B. Brown, *Customers for Life: How to Turn That One-Time Buyer into a Lifetime Customer*, Simon and Schuster, New York, 1990.

Stern, Aimee, "Two Men and a Business," *Boston Magazine*, December 1990.

Vannah, Thomas, "The Joel and David Show," *New England Business Journal*, August 1990.

Walton, Sam and John Huey, *Sam Walton Made in America*, Doubleday, 1992.

Weber, Joseph, "A Big Company That Works," *Business Week*, May 4, 1992.

Whiteley, Richard C., *The Customer-Driven Company*, Addison-Wesley Publishing Co., Reading, Mass., 1991.

Wilcox, Keith D., *The Corporate Tribe*, Wyer-Pearce Press, Excelsior, Minn., 1984.

Zemke, Ron, "Storytelling Back to Basics," *Training*, March 1990.

# Index

Adaptive companies, 138, 139
  key values of, 142
  mind set of, 147
  need for change in, 140
  sacred bundles of, 143
  shared vision in, 154–157
  using futurists, 151–152
Armstrong, David, 23, 24
Arnold, Bill, 17–19

Barker, Joel, 25
Bell, Alexander Graham, 202
Bennis, Warren, 54, 184–185
Breneman, Bren and Lucille, 34
Buffett, Warren, 3, 4, 27

Campbell, Joseph, 16–17, 33, 79, 83
Career Shortening Gestures (CSGs), 64
Carlzon, Jan, 29, 216
Change
  communication and, 174–176
  importance of truth in, 172–174, 176–177
  managing resistance to, 184, 189
  role of gossip in, 179–180
Christ, Jesus, xiv, 79
Churchill, Winston, 35, 129–130
Continuous Quality Improvement (CQI),
  30, 78, 125–126
Credibility, 58–59
Customer
  -focused approach, 119
  stories, listening to, 123, 131
Cynicism, 7–9, 57, 61

Damage repair, 107–109
Dean, John, 19
DePree, Max, 41, 43
Dickens, Charles, xiv

Employees
  buddy system, 86

Employees (*Cont.*):
  in hero stories, 19
  involvement of, 30, 152–153, 156
  managing morale of, 84
  new, entering tribe, 42, 91, 93
  as storytellers, 145–146
  as team heroes, 80–81

Forster, Scherrie, 209
Fry, Art, 76–77, 143

Gardner, Herb, 210
Garfield, Charles, 79
Garrison, Jim, 19
Gault, Stanley, 32
Gordon, William J., 203
Greenleaf, Robert, 50
Grieving
  and morale, 115
  stages of, 110

Hero stories
  anti-, 78
  essence of, 17
  organizational, 76–78
  special uses of, 17
  *See also* Joseph Campbell
Hill, Anita, 19
Hitler, Adolf, xiv, 17

Jobs, Steve, 155

Kanter, Rosabeth Moss, 113
Keen, Sam, 49, 70, 94
Kierkegaard, 58
Kilmann, Ralph, 139, 147
King, Martin Luther, Jr., 17, 33, 79
Kubler-Ross, Elisabeth, 110

Leaders
  creativity of, 206

Leaders (*Cont.*):
  isolation of, 60–61
  responsibility of, 43, 50–53, 54
  well-known, stories by, 212–217
Lennon, John, 17, 74
Leonard, Stewart L., Jr., 19
Lincoln, Abraham, 33–35, 55, 130, 207
Listening, 36–37, 50, 64
  to customer stories, 123, 131

Marcus, Stanley, 116
Mission statement, 30
Moyers, Bill, 17
Mythology, 49
  *See also* Joseph Campbell

National Association for the Preservation
  and Perpetuation of Storytelling
  (NAPPS), 34
North, Oliver, 19
Not Invented Here (NIH), 188

Outcome definition, 14–15

Pathological optimism, 59
Perot, Ross, 45–46, 73, 101, 214
Peters, Tom, 36
Pollack, Sydney, 188–189
Postman, Neil, 209

Quixote, Don, 17

Rogers, Will, 205
Roosevelt, Eleanor, 215–216
Roosevelt, Franklin D., 142, 208

Sacred bundle stories, 41–48
  origin of, 42
  personal, 68–75
  protectors of, 49

Sells, Ray, 42, 54
Senge, Peter, 49–51, 155, 205
Sewell, Carl, 91, 116–118, 123, 131
Stories
  "Aren't we great," 22–23, 31
  grounding, 29–31
  instructive, 31–32
  "kick in the pants," 24–25
  mini-, 218–219
  negative, 11–12
  positive, 11–12
  sources of, 33–34, 211–212
  steam valve, 20–22
  survivor, 19–20
  "We know the ropes around here," 23–24
  *See also* Customer; Hero; Sacred bundle
Storytelling
  importance of, xiii–xiv
  opportunities for, 105–106
  skill, 34–37

Thinking
  how stories help, 5
  logic- vs. visual-based, 199–200
Thomas, Clarence, 19
Total Quality Management (TQM), 30, 78,
  146, 162, 167–168, 189, 200
Tribal campfires, 52–54, 104, 196
Trust
  how to increase, 103
  stories as barometer of, 102–103
Twain, Mark, 205, 218

Walton, Sam, 47–48, 84, 138, 216
Watson, Thomas J., 150
Welch, Jack, 31–32, 219
Whistle-blowers, 19
Whiteley, Richard, 37, 120–121

Zapping, 50–51, 53

## About the Author

Peg C. Neuhauser is founder and president of PCN Associates, a highly successful management consulting and training company. Trained in sociology and organizational psychology, she has brought a fresh perspective to solving problems for such clients as Du Pont, South Central Bell, and Prudential Securities. She also conducts a variety of seminars and is the author of the highly acclaimed *Tribal Warfare in Organizations.*